Praise for *Damn Yankees*

"I'm a fan of good writing, which is what we have with Rob Fleder's *Damn Yankees*."

—Jim Bouton, *New York Times Book Review*

"A real achievement, especially in regard to the Yankees, about whom so much has been written over the years. The key is the abiding focus on the personal, the understanding that what happens on the field is less important than how we render it our own. . . . That, for better or for worse, the teams we love make us who we are."

—*Los Angeles Times*

"A well-conceived exercise. . . . The Yankees are and will remain an institution. Love 'em or loathe 'em, this collection is a fine assessment of what that institution means."

—*BookPage*

"Editor Rob Fleder gathers twenty-four original, eclectic essays on the most loved and hated sports dynasty, the New York Yankees, and they all delight and often inspire. The collection shows that baseball continues to showcase the sensibilities and craft of some of our most acclaimed authors."

—*Cleveland Plain Dealer*

"The writing is alternately hilarious, nostalgic, heartbreaking, and touching. . . . *Damn Yankees* is a welcome and engaging addition to the tradition of marrying baseball and literature. For all baseball fans, regardless of team allegiance."

—*Library Journal* (starred review)

DAMN YANKEES

TWENTY-FOUR MAJOR LEAGUE
WRITERS ON THE WORLD'S
MOST LOVED (AND HATED) TEAM

◄‖Edited by ROB FLEDER‖►

An Imprint of HarperCollinsPublishers

A hardcover edition of this book was published in 2012 by Ecco, an imprint of HarperCollins Publishers.

FIRST ECCO PAPERBACK EDITION PUBLISHED 2013.

Library of Congress Cataloging-in-Publication Data has been applied for.

ISBN 978-0-06-205963-5

13 14 15 16 17   OV/RRD   10 9 8 7 6 5 4 3 2 1

For Marilyn, of course

CONTENTS

◄| SECOND |►

◄| THIRD |►

◄| HOME |►

◄| YANKEES BY THE NUMBERS |►

DAMN YANKEES

INTRODUCTION

Everyone has an opinion about the Yankees. More than an opinion in most cases, but an opinion at the very least. We are not talking here about the never-ending bar-stool chatter that sustains baseball fans, the daily sifting of heroes and bums, but the idea of the Yankees. This is a hot-button topic, though you can never be sure, when you press the button, what will go off.

I was reminded of this when I started to call prospective contributors for this book. In the matter of the Yankees, there is no neutral ground, no Switzerland. Extreme, even fanatical views are the norm. These views are not necessarily rooted in sports, because the Yankees, while certainly a great sports story, are also an institution, a myth, a symbol. And what they symbolize is everything good and strong and true about baseball and America and the human race in general. Either that, or pure evil, the bad guys, the black hats. Those predisposed to the latter view look for—and find—confirmation everywhere.

To wit: in September 2010, the front page of the *New York*

Times brought news of an important cultural trend: It seems that criminals, particularly those who inflict or threaten bodily harm, turn up more often than one might expect wearing Yankee gear. At arraignments, in mug shots, on surveillance videos, in victims' descriptions, the classic interlocking NY logo is a fixture. "A curious phenomenon has emerged at the intersection of fashion, sports and crime," the *Times* reported—and Yankeephobes will immediately recognize this intersection as the team's permanent home address—"dozens of men and women who have robbed, beaten, stabbed, and shot at their fellow New Yorkers have done so while wearing Yankee caps or clothing." When it comes time to pick headwear for a felony, only ski masks and silk stockings come close. (In the New York area, Yankee-clad criminals outnumber those showing Mets colors by a factor of roughly ten to one.)

This trend started in New York, but soon spread. Before you knew it, a man in suburban Chicago had stuck up a Chase bank wearing a Yankee cap; and a couple thousand miles farther west, in Seattle, a young man in a similar cap assaulted an eighty-one-year-old woman in her home. Many months later, when Muammar Gaddafi was finally killed, one of the insurgents who claimed credit for shooting the Libyan dictator in the head appeared in a widely circulated photograph brandishing Gaddafi's pistol and styling a flat-brimmed, slightly tilted Yankee cap.

Truth is, none of this came as a surprise to me. By the time the *Times* reported the correlation between crime and the Yankees, I had already talked with quite a few writers about the team. Naturally, there were those who believe the Yankees are exemplars of grace and the epitome of wealth and power—but, you know, in a *good* way. But what I heard with striking frequency was that they are and forever shall be the devil's spawn. *Of course* violent criminals wear Yankee caps. What better way to cover their horns?

Are we getting a little hysterical? Maybe. But consider what David Rakoff, the late comic writer whose lacerating wit was often turned on himself, had to say in an e-mail rant about the moral fabric of baseball and of the Yankees in particular, by way of declining an invitation to rant at greater length for this collection:

"I hate baseball because of the lachrymose false moral component of it all, because it wraps itself in the flag in precisely the way the Republicans do and takes credit for the opposite of what it really is. You know, the Mama Grizzly whose daughter gets knocked up and who quits her job but gets points as a sticktoitive protectress. Baseball—and by baseball I mean its codifying straight-guy interpreters, its bloated Docker-clad commentariat—traffics in that same false nostalgia, fancying itself some sublime iteration of American values, exceptionalism, and purity when, in fact, it's just a deeply corporate sham of over-funded competition . . ."

Rakoff went on to note that the team he loathed most of all was—who else?—the Yankees, "the apotheosis of Eminent Domain and rapacious capitalism." You don't have to be from Boston to hate the Yankees. Rakoff, though he lived in New York, was born in Canada. The passions stirred by the Yankees are international, if not quite universal.

◆

For all that, I believe that Yankee fans are much like other fans. I speak here from personal experience. Our devotion often begins, like that of fans everywhere, as an accident of geography. We are not evil because we formed an attachment to a particular baseball team (or, as some would suggest, formed that attachment to this particular team because we are evil). I grew up just north of New York City, not far beyond the Bronx, with the voices of Mel Allen and Red Barber in my ear and the Yankees in my heart; if my parents had lived fifty miles to the north, it would've been the Red Sox. It never felt like a choice. I was and always will be a Yankee fan. I was born that way.

Was I warped by my attachment to such a team? It's possible. After all, my god was Mickey Mantle, a carousing drunk with ungodly talent. And even as a little kid I could tell that the Yankees won far more often than was really fair. So it might be true that a kid growing up in the thrall of a supremely successful team can develop a skewed perspective on the world. It's not that we *expect* to win at all times and all things, but experience has taught us that it's at least worth a try.

And while I am not perverse enough to suggest that it was a handicap to grow up devoted to a juggernaut, I have noticed how often over the years I've felt compelled, after admitting my allegiance to the Yankees, to sheepishly apologize for it. I have been apologizing for the Yankees all my life. And yet, there they are, soft and fuzzy, at the center of all those cherished memories, the formative events that made me love baseball and my team forever: the first time my dad took me to the Stadium (a 7–0 drubbing by the White Sox); the moment I first laid eyes, from my seat behind a pillar, on the brilliant green of the field there; the undiminished thrill and the affirmation of hope whenever Mantle came through in the clutch, as he seemed always to do; the snapshots of each of my kids at their first Yankee game and the one of my oldest, much later, at that first fraught game in New York, post–9/11.

Listen to me: loyalty, devotion, allegiance, affirmation of hope, everlasting love . . . No wonder half the world hates the Yankees. All this mawkish sentiment is undignified. And for that, as well, I feel curiously compelled to apologize.

What requires no apology is what came forth from this extraordinary group of writers when their Yankee button was pushed. It's true I never knew exactly what I'd get when I mentioned the Yankees to them. All I knew for sure was that I'd get a rise.

And rise they did.

The contributors to this collection, from beginning (Roy Blount Jr., a son of the South, taking stock of his history with Yanks) to end (Steve Rushin, graveside but never grave, contemplating the mortality of Yankee immortals), tapped into reservoirs of knowledge and memory, passion and humor, to tell stories long in the making. This is not, as I say, the lightweight chitchat of baseball broadcasts and sports-talk radio. It's the voices of biographers with a fresh angle on their subjects (Jane Leavy on the Mick, Leigh Montville on the Babe); it's innovative experts (Bill James on the Yankees' catchers or James Surowiecki on their economics); it's esteemed memoirists (J. R. Moehringer, Dan Barry), young bucks (Will Leitch, Nathaniel Rich), and renaissance men (Frank Deford, Bruce McCall, Dan Okrent) with attitude and a bone to pick; it's celebrated novelists with hilarious and heartfelt stories to tell (Pete Dexter on Chuck Knoblauch and the meaning of life, Colum McCann on the baseball education of an Irish dad). Not to mention all the other heavy hitters who step up to take their cuts: Sally Jenkins, Charlie Pierce, Michael Paterniti, Richard Hoffer, Rick Telander, Roger Director, Tom Verducci, Steve Wulf, William Nack. My dream team.

Talk about a stacked lineup. It's a group well suited to take the measure of an epic subject, even as the legend continues, season by season, to grow. And yet the Yankee colossus draws from these writers what Colum McCann called, in another context, "sharply felt local intimacies"—the kind of memories and insights, highly personal yet communal, that can render colossal matters on a human scale. It's what good writers always do, what baseball can do on occasion. And what some of the best writers in the business have done here, under the spell of the game.

—*Rob Fleder, December 2011*

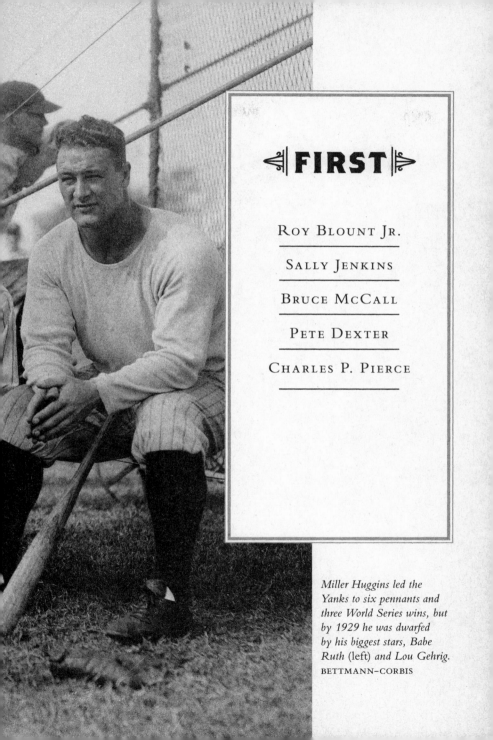

⊰ FIRST ⊱

ROY BLOUNT JR.

SALLY JENKINS

BRUCE McCALL

PETE DEXTER

CHARLES P. PIERCE

*Miller Huggins led the
Yanks to six pennants and
three World Series wins, but
by 1929 he was dwarfed
by his biggest stars, Babe
Ruth (left) and Lou Gehrig.*
BETTMANN–CORBIS

⊲ *one* ⊳

"I Have Feelings for the Yankees"

ROY BLOUNT JR.

Ben Affleck, the movie star, who I guess grew up rooting for the Red Sox, is quoted on the Web site Yankeeshater .com as saying, "I would rather utter the words, 'I worship you, Satan,' than 'My favorite baseball team is the New York Yankees.'" Okay, but is there no middle ground?

This so often happens: I am chatting with someone—a person who, quite correctly, roots for the underdog, or at least against vested interests—about an upcoming pennant race or playoffs or World Series, and he or she says, "Just as long as it isn't the Yankees. I hate the Yankees!"

And that person turns to me for confirmation of this all-but-universal American sentiment. (At least it is assumed to be all-but-universal by those whose hearts it fills.) And I hear myself saying, "Ah. Uh-huh. Mm."

Moral clarity is fine. But perhaps you are familiar with William Faulkner's novel *Absalom, Absalom!* In that novel, Quentin Compson, a Southerner in the North, cries out, in defiant semi-denial, "I *don't* hate the South! I *don't*!"

I *don't* love the Yankees! I *don't*!

But I do have feelings for them. And some of those feelings are positive.

Back in the 1970s I *played ball* in Yankee Stadium, twice. Once wearing an old uniform shirt of Whitey Ford's and pants formerly worn by Roger Maris—their names were embroidered in the lining. Somewhere I have a photograph (no big deal, it's not hanging on my wall or anything) of me in that uniform. I am posing with a chimpanzee. I don't remember why the chimpanzee was there, but it shows, I think—my posing with the chimpanzee shows— that just because a person is wearing pinstripes doesn't mean he is necessarily taking himself too seriously, or even seriously enough, considering that he is wearing Whitey Ford's shirt and Roger Maris's pants and is about to *play ball in Yankee Stadium.*

I was on a team made up of New York press people, opposing a Venezuelan media team, including the legendary broadcaster Juan Vene and also a man known as "the Bob Hope of Venezuela." ("Where is he?" said Maury Allen of the *New York Post,* who was one of our pitchers. "I want to trade quips with the Bob Hope of Venezuela!" Phil Pepe, of the *New York Daily News,* kept trying— jocularly, of course—to throw the game. "You *peetch*? *Peetch*?" one of the Venezuelans asked him. "You *dump*? *Dump*?" Pepe responded.) We also played, home and home, in Venezuela. And, yeah, I got a couple of hits. In pinstripes. And sure, it felt good. Also in pinstripes I made a couple of errors. So I know it can happen. Four errors, to be precise. All of them in one game. Three of them on one play. So I am saying that you can be dressed as a Yankee and still be human. Or worse. In Venezuela, when you make that many errors, people in the stands throw limes at you and holler, *"Burro!"*

They could have hollered, *"Yanqui go home!"* They didn't. Maybe because the way I carried myself made it clear that I wasn't trying to pass myself off as a real Yankee. No. Personality-wise, based on my acquaintance with a number of Yankees, I would say that I am not, how shall I say, *large* enough to be a Yankee, and also not worried enough about how I come off.

Ring Lardner once said he didn't like saying he was a humorist, because it was like saying, "I am a great third baseman." In Venezuela, I believe, I gave off a simple vibe: "I play, for better or worse, third base." Unlike A-Rod. A-Rod at third has a facial expression that says, "Okay, say I'm perceived as just, like, the prince, whereas the guy next to me is the king, which is okay, I mean, king is my natural position, I was king of my previous countries, and I was better at it than my friend the, uh, regent here, but, hey, I'm a bigger person than the kind of person who would insist on playing shortstop as long as it is so important to the person playing it to prove that it's his team."

Knowing my limitations, I have never even pretended to be a shortstop. Not that I wouldn't want to be Derek Jeter. In his prime. With a little more pop. And, sure, a better range factor. Who doesn't want to *look like* Jeter on the field? When Jeter retires as a player, he should be a body-language-and-facial-expression coach. Justin Bieber has a "swagger coach." Not that Jeter is to be compared with Justin Bieber on the best day Bieber ever had. Not that Jeter swaggers, either. Here is Jeter's look: taking things in his stride. Somebody said Arnold Palmer always looked like he just jumped down off the back of a truck. Jeter looks like he just came through swinging doors with a badge on his chest, and he also owns the saloon. Whereas A-Rod has this *frown*. Like he's going around *muttering* to himself. State of the Union speech, the faces behind Obama: Joe Biden has more of a Jeter look, John Boehner more of an A-Rod.

A sportswriter may have a favorite team. In baseball, I loved the Pirates of the Seventies—but I loved them because they provided such great copy. Something the Yankees were almost as good at. I wrote two long profiles, for *Sports Illustrated* and *Rolling Stone,* of Reggie Jackson, the only slugger I ever met who had a flair for metaphor. Here's how he stated the truism that a first baseman or third baseman has to be a hitter: "If you're going to hang out on the corner, you've got to lean on the pole." He showed me how to do sunflower seeds: crack one between your front teeth, and with the tip of the tongue lick up the nut and flick away both halves of the shell. I'm pretty good at this, when I have time to work on it, and I think if I were able to spend more time outdoors with nothing much to think about, I could almost get up to big-league speed at sunflower-seed-chewing, even at my age. Here, if you don't mind my quoting myself, is something I wrote about Reggie even before he was a Yankee: "He has the eagerly concerned, unsettled, open-eyed look of a man who will never be cynical, boring or fully aware (or unaware) of how he affects people."

For *SI* in 1984 I wrote a cover story about Yogi Berra that is enshrined (anyway, the cover photo by Walter Iooss is) in the Yogi Berra Hall of Fame, in Montclair, New Jersey. An anecdote from that story:

Yogi is about to appear on a radio talk show. The host says, "Yogi, we're going to play a game of free association. I'll throw out a name, and you just say the first thing that pops into your mind. Okay?"

"Okay," says Yogi.

They go on the air. "I'm here with Yogi Berra, and we're going to play a game of free association. I'll just throw out a name, and Yogi will say the first thing that pops into his mind. Ready, Yogi?"

"Okay."

"Mickey Mantle."

"What about him?" asks Yogi.

The first big-league game I ever saw was in Yankee Stadium in 1964. Yogi was playing left field. He caught a fly ball and fell over backward. But Yogi was a great player and a fine spirit. Once he attended a Little League father-son banquet and when he found out that there was a table of orphans who didn't get the souvenirs the kids with fathers got, Yogi went over to that table and ignored the rest of the banquet the rest of the night.

Getting back to the Faulkner reference: when I speak well of Yankees, it is not in order to prove that I don't hold the Civil War against them. The Union army did burn down my hometown, but I wasn't home at the time. And I have long eschewed any allegiance to the Confederacy. That's why I don't root for the Cubs. I played ball in a Cubs uniform, too, and against actual Cubs, that is to say veterans of the '69 Cubs, in the first fantasy camp ever held, back in 1983, to write a story for *SI*. So I have some feeling for the Cubs (that is to say, the '69 Cubs). But I am not about to be drawn into another Lost Cause.

When Catfish Hunter reported to his first spring training with the Yankees, I asked him whether, as a native North Carolinian, he had any misgivings about playing for a team called the Yankees. He gave me such a look. In my sportswriting days, other Yankees gave me looks that I shrugged off, because I knew they were over-interviewed and, in many cases, jerks. (I dare say Thurman Munson, mellowed with some years in heaven under his belt, will greet me there apologetically. And I will flip him off.) But that look from Catfish Hunter, I had that coming. My question was one that no transplanted Southerner would ask another one unless he was trying to provoke a dumb, stereotypical quote. Which is not to say that my ambivalence about the Yankees comes from my caring whether or not people might think, because of where I'm from, "Yeah, well, he *would* hate the Yankees. Probably hates Manhattan, the Bronx, and Staten Island, too."

I have too much class to worry about that. Joe DiMaggio, on the other hand, forbade Marilyn Monroe to include garlic in her cooking, because he didn't want to be stereotyped. And Joe defined Yankee class. Pete Sheehy, the longtime Yankee clubhouse attendant, once pointed to Joe DiMaggio's locker and said, "After the game he'd sit there. He had more class just sitting down than a lot of people have standing up."

The Yankee Clipper was, of course, a great player. I tried to talk to him once, for sportswriting purposes. He was sitting down, but he might not have been feeling as classy as usual, because he had taken a temporary job coaching for the Oakland A's. Instead of pinstripes, he was wearing a green-and-yellow uniform and huge white shoes. He wouldn't give me the time of day. And yet, when he died, the *New York Times* quoted, on the front page, something I had written: "He was the class of the Yankees in times when the Yankees outclassed everybody else." I know a little something about class, because I grew up rooting for the Atlanta Crackers.

People may find it amusing, today, that a team would go by that name, but the Crackers were the Yankees of the Southern Association. At one point they had won more pennants than any other minor league franchise. The Crackers' centerfield was even more spacious than the old Yankee Stadium's. And Cracker fans knew Cracker legends: Dick Donovan, a good-hitting pitcher (or it may have been Bob Montag, a small-time Babe), hit a home run all the way to Birmingham (or it may have been Chattanooga), because it landed in a freight train going by.

But the Crackers were local. The closest big-league team was the Washington Senators, who weren't good enough to be loved or hated. So my national rooting interests were eclectic. I focused on individuals. Eddie Mathews was a great third baseman who had been a Cracker phenom—hit a ball all the way over the magnolia tree in centerfield. Jackie Robinson and Willie Mays were from Paris, Georgia, and Mobile, Alabama, respectively, and there were *comic books* about Jackie. Bob Feller was from Iowa and had seen his best days as a pitcher, but I read his autobiography, so I bonded with him, until I met him forty years later. They were all too far away to see in person, but I could cut their pictures out of the *Atlanta Journal,* and they would pop up on television occasionally.

The Yankees were on TV all the time. Relatively speaking. In the 1950s you didn't have the plethora of televised ball we have today. There was the game of the week, and there was the World Series. When I started paying serious attention to baseball, I was eight years old. From then until I was twenty-three, the Yankees were in the World Series every year but two. Many people resented them for this. I took them in my stride. It wasn't as though they were standing in the way of the Crackers.

The Yankees' manager most of those years was Casey Stengel. Once I listened to the old Yankee outfielder Irv Noren talking about Casey as strategist. Casey sent him in to pinch-hit in a crucial situation, and when the count reached three and two, Casey called time from the bench and came hobbling over to take him aside. "If it's a ball, take it," Casey told him. "If it's a strike, hit it." And then he hobbled back. I met Casey at an All-Star game. "I'm here representing the foreign press," he said.

I still have the scorecard from an exhibition game I saw between the Yankees and the Crackers in the spring of '52, when I was ten and a half. The scorecard isn't dated, but after about three hours of flipping through *The Encyclopedia of Baseball* (remember that, the actual ink-on-paper book?), I have figured out the year from evidence in the Yankees' roster. The absence of DiMaggio, who retired after '51, doesn't prove anything, because Hank Bauer and Joe Collins, who were still Yankees, weren't listed, either—all three of them might have skipped the swing through Atlanta. Dating that scorecard for certain required getting down to the level of a pitcher named Bobby Hogue, who arrived from the St. Louis Browns in mid-'51 and went back to the Browns in mid-'52. In 1956 Al Hirshberg quoted someone's tribute to Hogue's slider: "The best I'd seen . . . But his was a natural slider, and he couldn't tell anyone how he threw it."

Another Yankee pitcher on the program that spring was Joe Ostrowski, who had won six, lost four for New York in '51, with a 3.49 ERA, and pitched two scoreless innings against the Giants in the World Series but would slump to 2–2, 5.63 in '52 and, after one last shot with the then–minor league Los Angeles Angels, would go back to teaching school, which he had done for three years after graduating from the University of Scranton. Just four years in the big leagues, but he had missed three seasons serving as a medic in Italy during World War II. In 1999 he would be quoted as saying that "Reaching that category of being a member of a team [the Yankees] I admired all my life was a dream come true." (I guess Ben Affleck would hate him for that.)

I'm looking, online, at a '52 Topps Joe Ostrowski card, autographed. Can it have been Ostrowski who, that day in Atlanta, signed my autograph book "Johnny Mize"? What did he think, that he was dealing with some kind of rube kid who didn't know what Johnny Mize, the Big Cat (from Demorest, Georgia), looked like? I'd rather think that Ostrowski or whoever it was didn't want to be the kind of Yankee who, when he signed a kid's autograph book, the kid would say, "Huh?"

On the same page of that book is the signature "Mickey Mantle." And it really was him. Thirty years later, Billy Martin mistook me for Mantle. I was writing a story about Martin when he was manager of the Twins. I called him at home. When he heard my voice, he got excited: "Mick? Is that you? Is that the old Mick?" When I told Martin who I was, we were both disappointed. In a way I liked him, but he's the only man about whom I ever thought, when I walked into a bar and saw him sitting there alone a couple of hours after I had interviewed him, "Should I go say hello? Naaah, better not." Ten years after that, I bumped into Mantle in a press box. I couldn't think of anything to say to somebody who hit a ball so far. Nobody else was such a great player while almost making a point of not living up to his potential. Remember a commercial he made, in which he said, "I was just a shuffling, grinning, head-ducking country boy"? When I said, "Nice to meet you, uh, Mickey," we both ducked our heads. He, because of who he was, and I, because of who he was.

During one of Martin's tenures as manager of the Yankees, I did another story, for *Life* magazine, about the relationship between him and George Steinbrenner. I'm sitting in Steinbrenner's office, and he's on the phone with somebody at the Hall of Fame. He's threatening not to have anything more to do with the Hall until they immortalize Phil Rizzuto. I liked Rizzuto, especially when he told me that he used to get Yogi to sleep, when they

were rooming together, by telling him bedtime stories, but Steinbrenner, to me, was not classy.

> The one, of course, for whom one feels
> The worst is George, who makes the deals.
> Or, anyway, approves of them.
> Now he knows he's been, ahem,
> Paying someone who's a screw-up.
> Okay, George, you'll back the truck up
> And fire a lot of folks for this.
> Be honest: is that not your bliss?

That's from a little booklet my wife, Joan Griswold, and I sent
out as a sort of Christmas card in 2001, verse by me, illustrations
by Joan. We had been caught up in the drama of the 2001 World
Series. The Bronx Bombers had another dynasty going, having
won four of the last five Series, and they had pulled this Series out
of the fire again and again. Destiny. When I tell you this, you may
hate me, but the truth is—maybe it's just the old Cracker-lover
coming out in me: I tend to root for destiny. Because it's such a
great story! But I know destiny is only what you make it. In the
ninth inning of the seventh game of that Series, you may recall,
the heretofore oozing-with-destiny Mariano Rivera blew . . .

Well, I don't want to say *blew* . . . The truth is, Rivera jammed
the hell out of Luis—I almost said Luis *Bleeping*—Gonzalez. By
all rights (here comes some sportswriting) the vibrations from
that bloody contact must have been ringing louder in Gonzalez's
fists than the cheers of the Diamondbacks' fans in his ears.

Jammed as he was, Gonzalez managed a weak little looper,
barely over the head of Jeter, who had screwed up earlier in the
inning by . . .

In Jeter's defense, he was playing on a bad foot.

I'm making excuses for the damn Yankees! Do the Yankees
need my help? No. Has there ever been anything I could do to

break the Yankees' hearts? No. So why should I have felt, when they blew that Series, that they had, let's say, dented my wife's and mine?

I'm not saying you can't detect a shred or two of you-bums-let-me-down in those holiday verses, but I'd say the Mrs. and I handled the whole thing pretty classy:

> *Though 'tis no season for sorrow or angst,*
> *Remember the needy: far from the Bronx*
> *They flew—to Phoenix, for goodness sakes—*
> *To find themselves surrounded by snakes.*

> *Tie game. Three on. And now Rivera*
> *Delivers. Or doesn't. Thus endeth an era.*
> *Lo, the shortstop limpeth—he*
> *And teammates need some sympathy.*

> *Although, Derek, you were hurtin',*
> *You stayed onstage until the curtain,*
> *Doing various balletic things.*
> *So take a load off. Have some wings.*

And Joan captured Jeter making one of his leaping throws from the hole, aided by angelic wings. Not that he needed them. Or would ever show in his face that he did.

◆

P. S., halfway through the 2011 season:

Different looks from Jeter now. Talk about range factor, he's beginning to encompass vulnerability. More than just a hint now and then of "Can it be that I am, after all, losing—*capable of losing*—it?"

Just my interpretation; I've never met Jeter myself. My friends Vereen Bell and Roy Gottfried, who teach English at Vanderbilt

University, are friends with a great Yankee fan named August Johnson, of that university's plant operations staff, who played for the New York Lincoln Giants in the last days of the Negro Leagues. A couple of years ago, the three of them went to Tampa for spring training. They got wind of Mom's Place, where Yankee players ate breakfast, so they went there hoping to get glimpses. Derek Jeter, himself, came in and sat down alone. August went over—natural thing for a Yankee lover to do—and joined Jeter, out of the blue. The two had a nice long chat.

"He's still getting his hits," manager Joe Girardi says of Jeter. But at a markedly—not yet *drastically*—slower pace than in previous years. Reggie Jackson in his last season said, "I don't want to go on wringing out the rag of ability."

And I don't want to become a Yankee *sympathizer*. But Jeter in summer is like my tomato plants: I check every morning to see how he's doing.

Street Heart

SALLY JENKINS

My hometown is in my skin—literally. The natural consequence of growing up in a jagged-edged bed of concrete, steel, and broken glass was a steady toll on the body, a semi-constant chipping away at my person, and my nicer side. There's a two-inch scar under my chin, the result of falling and splitting it open on an asphalt playground when I was a girl. For years afterward, tiny pieces of rock would work their way out of the scar tissue. To be reared in New York City is to be marked by it. So it's with a certain sadistic appreciation that I watch a jackhammer dig into a street. "That's right," I think, "take that you stony son of a bitch."

I would submit that New Yorkers love their hometown more complicatedly than a hometowner loves Kansas City or Detroit. For many of us, this love is complicatedly expressed in a grudging and complaining loyalty to the New York Yankees. For those of us who in the 1970s hunched over transistor radios in our wretched public parks with broken swings, and pulled for the Yankees with foul little mouths and hard vowels, the organization represents everything that the city ever was: a perennial world champion forged amid garbage piles and crime waves and cuttingly hard edges.

Their pinstripes didn't strike me then as representative of business attire, but rather of grids, the straight lines of the sidewalks on which we played from crack to crack. The desiccating tar grout made our base paths. Canopied entrances of high-rise buildings were our dugouts. Which was tricky. In order to catch a fly ball, you had to avoid a Hungarian lady with groceries, endure being screamed at in Polish by the doorman, and then field it off the awning. Once, trying to elude a tag, my brother hurtled headfirst into a metal door and opened a cut above his eye that took several stitches. A German woman told us that's what we got for being "hood-de-lumps."

We went to Rappaport's Sporting Goods and bought cheap orange mitts, and beat them mercilessly against the cement sidewalks to break them in. We rode stiff wooden skateboards down a steep block we named Suicide Hill, because of the pitch. We solved the problem of braking at the bottom by aiming for the bars of a large grate at the street corner. Hit the grate too fast, and the skateboard would stop dead, throwing you into a headfirst dive. But if you controlled it just right, you could vault neatly off and stick a flat-footed landing on the soles of your Converse All Stars. It was the scene of more stitches, this time for my other brother, in his scalp.

One afternoon I stood before my father, urchin-thin, hair stringy, grime-smeared, scabbed, and bruised. "Jesus Christ," he announced. "You look like a prizefighter."

New York then was a bullying attacker, as dangerously mean as the Yankees' rat-faced manager Billy Martin. Menace was everywhere, in the bushes and behind the rocks in Central Park, in alleyways and stairwells and subway tunnels. Rodents, molesters, muggers. An aunt of mine was once dining at a swank restaurant along the East River, renowned for its four-star cuisine and glimmering necklace–like views, when suddenly, in the midst of the elegant hush, a rat fell from the ceiling rafters onto an adjoining table. At night, my brothers and I planned guerrilla missions into the kitchen, armed with bug-swatters and cans of Raid. We would flick on the lights and fall upon cockroaches that scuttled across counters, fat and brown as cigar stubs.

By the time I turned thirteen years old in 1973, George Steinbrenner had bought the Yankees, and I had seen two corpses, one a shooting victim and the other a subway track jumper, whose bloody boots jutted from a body bag. I had experienced transit strikes, sanitation strikes, teacher strikes, and blackouts. I knew a couple of swear words in Puerto Rican, and I also understood the terms "stagflation" and "price controls" and "oil crisis." The city stunk, and it churned, and the rest of the country despised it, as we would discover in '75, when President Gerald Ford refused to give us a bailout. As the *Daily News* headline said: "Ford to City—Drop Dead."

But we were proud of where we lived, and knew the virtues of the place: it was a grit-encrusted survivalist camp, and yet a soaring spire, and to be from it meant we were savvy and resilient. No one personified this coal-lump-forged-into-diamond quality more than the Yankees, when they reached the World Series in '76 for the first time in a dozen years, and then won consecutive titles in '77 and '78. Could there have been a bigger thrusting of a middle finger to urban bankruptcy than to make Catfish Hunter the highest-paid pitcher in baseball? Or to sign Reggie Jackson for $3 million?

There was something insolently extravagant in those curling minks-tail mustaches worn by Hunter and Sparky Lyle, even as Steinbrenner insisted on cropped hair. Yet they were profoundly tough, too. We packed our mouths with extra Bazooka to try to look as firm-jawed as Graig Nettles. And when we went to the park to play ball, we skinned our knees proudly on the hardpan ground that glinted with mica, and asked ourselves, what other city had dirt that gleamed like silver-dust?

The Yankees' loyalty to each other in those years was querulous and fragile, yet it always ultimately won out, as did ours. Steinbrenner would fire the snarling Martin five times. Reggie bad-mouthed Thurman Munson; Martin turned on both Reggie *and* Steinbrenner, saying, "The two were meant for each other. One's a born liar, and the other's convicted." But then they'd take the field and shut themselves and everybody else up with epic performances: Reggie's skyscraper feat of three homers in a single game of the '77 World Series, the ball ascending in tiers along with the roars. The Boston massacre in September of '78, when the Yankees scored thirteen and fifteen runs at a time and Bucky F-ing Dent made the Beantowners cry with the crack of his bat, topped off by a twenty-second World Championship.

Eventually, the craziness of the "Bronx Zoo" years took its toll. There were too many arguments and off-with-their-heads trades and firings; Steinbrenner made twenty managerial changes in twenty-three seasons. My allegiance weakened somewhat, and I grew up and moved away for a while. But, like all New Yorkers, I would always come back.

Yankee Stadium was, of course, where we returned to when the city got bad again. It's said that September 11 happened to all Americans, and it did. But it happened to New Yorkers first and foremost.

Before, if there was a crack in the city, it was because we jack-hammered it there. Disaster was a crane falling. The danger was from within, not without. Then outsiders felled our two tallest buildings, twin towers that we had watched being built as kids. They had been completed in '73, the very year Steinbrenner bought the Yankees. On 9/11 they melted downward out of a perfect blue sky.

Every day the rescue and recovery workers labored to pry up the giant twisted pieces of steel, exposing the core of fire, and plumes of smoke would shoot into the air. New Yorkers felt the wreckage within their own hearts, a seemingly endless interior hemorrhage.

The posters of missing citizens fluttered from news kiosks and chain-link fences and concrete walls. Brothers, sisters, wives, husbands, cousins, friends. New Yorkers wept in taxis, their eyes watered on trains, or sometimes they just stood still in the middle of the street and cried. On September 23, more than twenty thousand mourners gathered in Yankee Stadium to pay tribute to the victims with a multidenominational service.

But New Yorkers also met the attack with defiance. "Watch," a union worker at Ground Zero said to me, just two days afterward. "We're going to build it back." The rebuilding seemed to start when the Yankees made it to the World Series against the Arizona Diamondbacks, and President George W. Bush came to throw out the first pitch for Game 3.

It was October 20, 2001, just seven weeks after the attack. The security lines outside the ballpark were endless. Helicopters hovered, and snipers peeked over rooftops. As the president, swathed in a New York Fire Department sweatshirt and a bulky bulletproof vest, warmed up in a tunnel, a Yankee came toward him. It was Derek Jeter. "You better not bounce it," he said. "Or they'll boo ya." The president threw a strike. Then, in Game 4, Tino Martinez hit that two-run homer in the bottom of the ninth with two outs, and Jeter walloped his own walk-off homer to tie the Series.

It didn't matter that the Yankees eventually went down in that Series, and, in fact, never even led. What mattered was that they restored New York's essential New Yorkness. They reminded us that scars can be badges of pride, and that the municipality is a phoenix continually rising from the ashes. The Yankees lost, but it was a good hurt. The kind the city itself has always inflicted on us, the people who choose to abide there, and who wear pieces of it.

◄| *three* |►

Take Me Out to the Oedipal Complex

BRUCE McCALL

It's the mid-fifties in the family manse in Windsor, Ontario. The modestly thin little book flops onto the coffee table in the living room where my old man customarily lounges with his after-work martini and Camels. The cover illustration shows a slimy black tide sliding down over a white field with vertical pinstripes, just about blotting out the iconic New York Yankees monogram in the center.

I had lovingly written, typed, illustrated, and hand-bound the book, the newest in a sporadic series, late at night in my bedroom. It was not some cheery Dad 'n' Lad project. Like its predecessors, it was a compact but vitriolic catalog of on- and off-field Yankee offenses, real and imagined—more like fantasized—complete with charts and graphs, planted for Dad to come upon all unawares, like the proverbial turd in the punch bowl. I was eighteen, and almost from the day in late puberty that I'd discovered baseball, I had found more joy in hating the New York Yankees than in loving any other baseball team.

My old man wasn't in the room. The terrorist prefers the premises to be empty when he plants his bomb.

Take me out to the Old Oedipal Conflict: my grandfather Walt, born in the 1880s, grew into baseball fanhood back in that sepia age when the only big league was the National. His son, my father, arrived in 1909, just eight years after the upstart Junior Circuit, the American League, had arisen to claim parity with the NL; by his teens the New York Highlanders had morphed into the Yankees and begun their decades of dominance.

My father didn't exactly worship his old man as a kid, so he hit on one sly and safe way for an otherwise powerless teenage son to stick it to him: he arrived at the dinner table burbling with enthusiasm for the American League and the Yankees.

We now segue into the next generation, only to find internecine warfare repeating itself. I didn't exactly worship my old man as an adolescent, either, so what better way of sticking it to him than to spin the tables all over again and not only declare my National League loyalty at every opportunity but, more pointedly, to publicly demonize his beloved goddamn Yankees?

That this was merely the recycling of an earlier father-son dynamic I didn't realize at the time. I thought it was my own unique form of intellectual patricide. This dragging of sports into service as a weapon in a paternal jihad was tasteless at best, but in my defense it certainly didn't originate in the McCall household, and most psychologists would agree that wherever it may erupt it's preferable to the Glock or the shotgun or—come to think—the baseball bats that have so often served as alternatives. Dad was too shrewd to respond directly to my provocation. That might precipitate debate, argument, perhaps fisticuffs—just what my seething soul was aching for. But open hostilities were never the Canadian way. All this and previous such efforts did was screw the silent tension between us a bit tighter.

◆

Underdog love, poor relation of the death wish, is widely under-rated as a fount of sports enthusiasm. First, the losers outnumber the winners in every sphere of life; to most of us, defeat is a more intimately familiar sensation than winning. Failure, when experi-enced often and deep enough, can feel almost comfortable. Sure, the undamaged among us naturally yearn to taste that vicarious thrill of victory by rooting for winning sports teams; but millions of us—those of us whose X-rayed brains would probably reveal strange black squiggles all over the happiness lobe—are driven in the opposite direction to vicariously suffer with the losers. I give you the Chicago Cubs, the Detroit Lions, the Toronto Maple Leafs, and their legions of diehard fans: for these sad-sack souls, winning would ruin everything. Second, it isn't enough to love losers. The necessary corollary is that you hate winners. Which is why there well may be as many Yankee-haters in the American population as Yankee fans.

Insofar as I deigned to recognize the American League, my sympathies were confined—of course—to its perennial bottom-feeders, the poverty-stricken Washington Senators (First in War, First in Peace, and Last in the American League) and the even lowlier St. Louis Browns, not just underdogs but dead ones. Even their colors marked the Browns as losers: musty brown amid the red, white, and blue spunkiness of sports heraldry bespoke de-suetude and debilitation and decay, fitting raiment for my kind of dream team. But the Brownies would win their only pennant in 1944, then revert to form the following year, acquiring the immortal mono-limbed outfielder Pete Gray. More ushers than patrons attended their games at Sportsman's Park. The Browns' enduring futility verged on the comic, even before three-foot-seven Eddie Gaedel came to the plate in 1951. The way they were so regularly fleeced by the Yankees in lopsided trades was poeti-cally fitting and, in a perverse way, only right.

A classic identification with the losing side underlay much of my Yankee hostility but not, I think, all of it. New York was then as now the nation's media capital, and New York and worship of success have always been intimately intertwined—to the enduring benefit of outfits like the Yankees. I squirmed through the endless flow of pro-Yankee media propaganda rolling out from New York across the nation. What a character, that Casey Stengel! What a genius, that GM George Weiss! What Greek gods, DiMaggio and Mantle! Meanwhile the fair-minded baseball nut had to scour the back pages of the St. Louis–based *Sporting News* every Friday for scraps about the Senators, the Browns, the Reds, the Pirates. Whatever staticky big-league broadcasts I could ever raise on the radio were, of course, Yankee games, relayed through a Buffalo station. How I hated that mellifluous homer Mel Allen. If I'd been a drinking boy, I'd have boycotted Ballantine beer.

But my anti-Yankee crusade wasn't entirely powered by loser paranoia. Mixed into the toxic brew somewhere was a genuine belief in Fair Play: I was precociously slow in coming to worldliness (e.g., refusing to take a sip of coffee until my late twenties, for God's sake). For example, everybody knew that even in the pre-Steinbrenner era the Yankees were uncommonly rich, in the classic idiom of the fat guy with a top hat and striped pants holding bags marked $$$ in both hands. Del Webb; Dan Topping; CBS; not canny skinflint owners like Connie Mack and Clark Griffith but Brilliantined millionaire "sportsmen." This, and all that winning and the media truckling must have infused the entire operation with arrogance and made the Yankees intolerable, I reasoned (if you could call such arrant speculation reasoning). And even if it didn't—and come now, what the hell would I know of the psychic state of the Yankee front office and clubhouse and dugout anyway?—well, it *should* have, so it probably did. Teenage boys enjoy license to take such wild lunges at logic and reality.

This had nothing to do with any provincial anti–New York bias. In fact, as a would-be cosmopolite stuck deep in the Canadian provinces, I worshipped the very idea of New York City and of course approved of the National League Giants, though they were neither all that good nor all that bad at the time and thus not interesting enough to win my heart. About the Dodgers I confess to ambivalence. Their myth-making machine ranked second in obnoxiousness only to the Yankees. Dem Bums seemed mired in phony Brooklyn folklore, a winning franchise closer to the Yankees than, say, the Browns, but forever cast in the adoring media as lovable ragamuffins. A publicity put-up job. Boo.

The Yankees presented themselves as a grim cohort that could have been nine robots. That monochrome uniform, as medicinal as a Smith Bros. cough-drop box, didn't help. Those home-uniform pinstripes added a banker's frosty touch. I later learned that the designer of the iconic NY Yankees logo was Tiffany & Co. Of course! Meanwhile, the St. Louis Cardinals wore a red cartoon bird perched on a yellow bat on their chests, with trim in gaudy red and blue. Now, that was a baseball uniform.

The Yankees never did anything to appease my hostility. On the contrary, their every move seemed to intensify it. Anybody with eyes could see that the Yankee roster of that era was a rogue's gallery: the ratlike Billy Martin, the thuggish Hank Bauer, the churlish Berra made lovable elf by his willing ghostwriters in the media, and the farmboy-turned-priapic-jerk Mickey Mantle. I even piled racial bigotry onto their list of sins. After all, just when major league baseball was finally discarding a century of Jim Crowism, the Yanks—backsliders, of course, in joining the progressive trend—traded away their only promising black player, Vic Power, to Kansas City before he could prove himself. And it seemed to be a ritual conducted late every August: the Yankees, already bloated with success, would use their millions and a jink in the rules to snap up a veteran from some cash-starved club in either league to bolster their pennant run. The Johnnys (Lindell and Sain and Hopp and Mize), Ewell (The Whip) Blackwell, Bob Kuzava, even the Cardinals' beloved Enos Slaughter, each whisked from the orphanage to the penthouse in the dark of night. It's how Louis XIV would have run a ball club.

We Yankee-haters, by God, knew who we were. We were

losers. We also knew that the devoted Yankee fan, wallowing in his smug prosperity, betrayed a contemptible character flaw. He was not only a front-runner but also a weakling and a sissy and a stranger to the humiliation and failure that toughens the spirit, readying you for more humiliation and failure.

◆

On the rational plane where I so seldom dwelled there was about all this a thick if hidden element of, well, idiocy. I was blithely unconcerned with, if not unaware of, the fact that the Yankee roster consisted of the exact same tobacco-chewing farmboy clods and California jocks and Pennsylvania coal-mine escapees as those on every other big-league team; that there was no New York Yankees finishing school somewhere in the Hamptons turning out an elegant and superior breed of ballplayer with manicured nails and nice manners. Indeed, a cursory look would show that any given Yankee lineup consisted of guys who were playing last year for the White Sox or Browns or Indians, and others who would be next year, because the Yankees traded ruthlessly and often, wrapping cash around has-beens and duds and head cases and palming them off on doormat clubs in exchange for their choicest chattels.

My baseball fever and the Yankee-hating that did so much to sustain it would ebb and fade over time, shunted aside by more important things like sex and career. But there would be no late-innings concord, no rapprochement with my father, who was—perhaps mercifully—gathered up by that great Will Harridge in the Sky before he would have had to witness the Yankees' mortifying loss to the lowly Pirates in the 1960 Series.

Bad timing for the born Yankee-baiter. Tragically bad timing. No sooner had I drifted away than true Yankee evil—an evil vile enough to repel even lifelong Yankee fans—was about to be served up on a platter. In the early seventies, a sulfurous miasma would descend and Yankee Stadium became the Kremlin. George M. Steinbrenner had arrived, an egomaniac wrapped in a bully inside an asshole, and ultimate confirmation that villainy and the New York Yankees would be synonymous for all time, every year a veritable feast for Yankee-haters for the next three decades. And I'd allowed my credentials to lapse.

So somebody please make sure my gravestone reads: "Here Lies Bruce McCall. Born Too Early."

◄| *four* |►

The Errors of Our Ways

PETE DEXTER

A sheltie is a medium-size breed of canine that walks around with a nest of shit in its pants. In his own circles this earthiness makes him fascinating company and kind of a celebrity at the off-leash park, although the same earthy quality is worrisome to families with toddlers who, being toddlers, hug dogs without caring which end they are hugging. Aroma-wise, there isn't much to choose from, one end or the other.

Shelties also bring to the playground a tradition of nipping. A sheltie is born to herd sheep, after all, a species nobody has accused of being too smart for its own good, and the herding of which amounts essentially to creating and then organizing panic, which means taking little bites of ankles and feet, and there are times, in spite of countless reminders, when old habits take over and a sheltie just has to have the feel of live flesh in his teeth. The sheltie himself is close to blameless. You are, after all, who you are. We should keep that in mind.

The sheltie who nipped the author last Christmas belongs to his daughter and answers—well, doesn't actually answer, but sometimes looks up—to the name Jonesy, and until the baby showed up no dog ever had it more his own way. In fact, until the baby showed up the dog himself had been the baby—doting parents, daily brushing, special food, a park next door, maintenance appointments to keep his nails clipped and the gunk off his teeth, endless toys—the salad days.

Naturally enough, the baby's arrival left the dog suffering from a lack of his normal attention and so, upset and confused, Jonesy went back to what works and bit the first stranger through the door. The resulting infection put the author in the hospital for ten weeks and very nearly finished him off. If the animal had sat on the author's foot after he'd nipped it, the author would not be here to tell the story.

Which probably would have been fine with Chuck Knoblauch.

But bygones are bygones, and things were not so easy for the dog, either. Once the baby showed up, barking in the night and herding humans, which had been baby-talk scolding offenses before, were suddenly federal cases, and in the way these things sometimes go, after his mistake—and it was a mistake, you could see the surprise on the animal's face as he sat on the floor with the author's ankle still in his maw along with the bitter mingle of human sweat and human blood, looking up and wondering how this could have happened—after that mistake, Jonesy was driven out one Saturday afternoon to the rural setting where he now resides, with afternoon naps under the porch and chickens to herd and no toddlers to clutch him from behind, and he is free to come and go as he likes and to bark in the night (the new owners are getting on in years and take out the hearing aids after the eleven o'clock news).

Which is as close as you get to a happy ending with dogs, but not so happy when you're talking about second basemen.

We have shifted now to the subject of Edward Charles Knoblauch who, like Jonesy, had a good thing going and then fucked the rooster. A colloquialism they use quite a bit out on the farm.

What the farmer and his missus are referring to when they say "fucked the rooster" is a class of mistakes that by their very nature are hard to forget. That happen in a moment of carelessness or bad luck and are as good as tattooed across your face for the duration of your life. That become so closely associated with your idiot self that later on when another idiot does exactly the same thing, your wife gets mad at *you* all over again.

The author speaks from experience here, having once made such a mistake—a miscalculation of the goodness of human nature in a not especially human precinct of Philadelphia—and the incident follows him to this day. Not just the memory of the night—which is kept in easy reach of the author's wife (who regular readers call "poor Mrs. Dexter"), handy as her purse any time the author, like Jonesy, feels his breeding and the undeniable itch to do what an author's got to do—but the myth of that night, which has a life of its own.

For example, about three years ago, twenty-five years after the fact, one of the weekly papers in Philadelphia heard a new version of the evening in question and flew a reporter to Seattle with the idea of going through the details with the author all over again.

The author was just finishing his seventh novel—we're talking about writing, not reading—and for unknown reasons concluded that the request for such an early interview was a signal that he had finally written a book that was exactly right, and he vividly remembers the feeling—dead bats dropping off the walls of his stomach into a river of bile—as he realized that what the reporter wanted to talk about wasn't the new book but a twenty-five-year-old street brawl the author had been trying to live down ever since it happened.

Which we suppose could be how the eventual subject of this essay, Chuck Knoblauch, feels when somebody comes poking around to ask about some night he, too, would prefer to forget. The difference being that Knoblauch has the good sense not to talk to any of them—or at least not talk to the author, who should have seen it coming, having gone through several hundred pages of material to write a sensitive appreciation of the psychological abnormality that affected him (known variously as Steve Blass Disease, Steve Sax Disease, and Chuck Knoblauch Syndrome, among other things)—and in all those pages found only one true-sounding, consequential remark by Knoblauch over the last dozen years: *Don't tell anybody where I live.*

So the author came to this exercise suspecting he was not in friendly territory and that there was an excellent chance Chuck Knoblauch didn't care if he appreciated his syndrome or not. That it was possible Knoblauch had been appreciated as much as he could stand.

Still, the author wanted to be part of this book and felt like he had something to contribute. Meaning that even if his insight into the game was a slim volume indeed, he did, as it happens, know quite a bit about fucking the rooster. So apologies to Mr. Knoblauch for the intrusion, but we are who we are and we do what we do. Ask Jonesy.

◆

The author first became aware of Edward Charles Knoblauch in the year 1998. He had just joined the Yankees, traded from the Minnesota Twins for four players and $3 million in cash (two of the players, Eric Milton and Christian Guzman, would go on to appear in All-Star games). In combination with the brilliant young shortstop Derek Jeter and first baseman Tino Martinez, Knoblauch was destined, according to the often brilliant young baseball writer Buster Olney, to become the greatest double-play combination in baseball history. Jeter to Knoblauch to Martinez.

Olney's column predicting that greatness appeared in the *New York Times,* and for several weeks afterward, having a certain reputation to maintain as a student of the game—a necessary part of the smugness that goes with being a Yankee fan—the author was not shy about expressing the opinion that the Yankees' new double-play combination was destined to become the greatest double-play combination in the history of baseball. Then, as will happen, somebody asked the author what he was talking about, and by now he'd forgotten what Buster Olney said and so explained that the story of the Yankees' new double-play combination was the story of America. Which is something he began using back at the University of South Dakota on essay tests when he had no idea what the question meant, much less the sound of an acceptable answer, and oddly enough it seemed to work— teachers were reluctant in those days to fail essays lauding the story of America—and still seems to work, if in a different way, which is to say people can be counted on to drift away when he starts with this stuff, wishing they hadn't asked.

So as we were saying, Jeter to Knoblauch to Martinez represented DNA from every continent on the earth except Antarctica, where it's too cold to mate, and you might also note the blue-collar, building-block sound of the name Knoblauch when it is fit in there between the other two. It was a name you could count on, like Kluszewski. Remember Ted Kluszewski? The author was a tyke—oh, fourteen or so, a bit of a late bloomer—but can still see those enormous arms and remembers being sure, even then, that you could turn Kluszewski loose with a bat in any city in America and he'd kill something for dinner.

Late blooming is also the author's excuse for not knowing who Chuck Knoblauch was before he showed up in New York. Knoblauch was already a highly decorated second baseman after all, Rookie of the Year in 1991, a four-time All-Star ('92, '94, '96, '97), and, in the year before he joined the Yankees, the winner of a Gold Glove, which, for those of you who are not students of the game, is an award you get for not throwing the baseball into the stands when you are supposed to throw it to first base.

And at the risk of ruining the suspense, we might as well get this part out of the way right now. There are no more Gold Gloves in this story.

◆

A second excuse for not having heard of Knoblauch is that the author climbed on the Yankee bandwagon late and under the tutelage of the previously mentioned Mrs. Dexter, she of the long memory, whose sporting instinct is rooted in slaughtering the underdog and who teaches that there are no real baseball players who aren't Yankees, at least not until George Steinbrenner buys them. Thus, technically, Chuck Knoblauch didn't exist until 1998.

Steinbrenner of course was the owner of the Yankees, one of those men whose death leaves the world feeling like a safer place. But more on George later. The deal he made that brought Knoblauch to New York was in many ways a typical Yankee negotiation. The Yankees got Knoblauch, who in one fell swoop fulfilled all their needs and desires, and in return gave up nothing they wanted to keep except the $3 million.

Knoblauch arrived in New York with a reputation as an excellent lead-off hitter, very smooth with the glove, a stealer of bases who had an exceptional eye at the plate—you have to get on base, after all, to steal bases—natural power to the opposite field, and a clean-cut (and the author might add shit-free) hairdo, a matter of no less importance to Steinbrenner and the Yankee tradition than to the parents of toddlers.

So. We are who we are and we do what we do, and a clean-cut, shit-free hairdo is vital to a good first impression.

And even though Knoblauch for a fact looked like one-half of the greatest double-play combination Buster Olney was ever going to see, and had both great talent and great promise, and filled all the Yankees' holes on offense and defense alike, and all for the relatively modest cost of $6 million a year (true Yankee fans quietly worry about the financial comfort of George and his family), what caught the author's eye first was the second baseman's intuitive and obvious understanding of what being a Yankee was all about. Knoblauch was a born irritant.

If the author may be permitted a short rumination:

As much as anything else, baseball is a game of manners. Good manners, bad manners, table manners, if constantly filling your mouth and spitting it out counts as table manners. In the bare essentials, it is also a game in which a visiting team is invited into your home ballpark, and two minutes after the players are in the door they are groping themselves and spitting sunflower seeds and tobacco juice, and picking their noses on camera in the dugout. And in baseball these familiar gesticulations signal good manners in the truest sense of the phrase, that is, making everyone feel right at home.

But it's not as simple as that, of course. A baseball game may begin with everybody feeling happy and right at home, but by the time it ends somebody isn't. And the worse the mood is on one side, the better it is over in the other dugout, and under the influence of euphoria, a player may stand half a second too long in the batter's box to watch his home run clear the fence, or steal a base with his team up 9–0 in the eighth inning, or cross the pitcher's mound after he's grounded out but before the end of the inning, and suddenly these attacks on civility are not just bad manners but declarations of war, beanballs and riots to follow. Why?

Because in spite of being a game in which the players—especially the Yankees—give lip service to the notion that they win as a team and lose as a team, etc., the true, unspoken principle of baseball etiquette, applicable to opponents and teammates alike, is: *Don't show me up.*

And at his best, Knoblauch's busy, hustling style of play did just that. Some days the effort alone was enough to make everybody else look lazy—everyone except Jeter, who, as Buster Olney predicted, did become one-half of the greatest double-play combination in baseball history, the only problem being that the other half, Joe Morgan, played for Cincinnati back in the 1970s.

Knoblauch would situate at the plate, a chesty little ball of muscle, and insist on strikes. He had the previously mentioned exceptional eye, and when crouched in his stance—half of his body leaning in over the plate, daring the pitcher to hit him—offered roughly an eight-inch strike zone, and could not be persuaded to swing at pitches outside it. As a rule, the pitcher would give in eventually and throw something over the plate, and Knoblauch, more often than not, fouled it off and made him do it again. Three, four, five, sometimes six pitches in a row. In the end, the pitcher would offer a fastball half an inch off the plate and Knoblauch would take it, ball four, and walk. Or the pitcher would throw something down the middle and Knoblauch would slap a single through the infield. And there he was, twelve pitches after he stepped to the plate, dancing off first base. The same place he'd be if you'd just thrown the first one inside and hit him on the kneecap.

Surprisingly enough, there is no official statistic in baseball, at least that the author can find, that reflects a player's overall irksomeness, nothing that accurately and thoroughly indicates the animus he generates in the enemy camp. Something that takes into consideration not only the number of pitches he fouls off during a season but the average number of pitches he sees per at-bat, or the number of times he backs out of the batter's box to twitch or to tighten up his batting glove or whack the dirt out of his spikes, or how aggravating he is on the base paths, or how often he is brushed back or thrown at and missed, as well as how often he is plunked—*plunk* being the laid-back, manly verb that fans, who often played a little ball themselves back in high school, use to indicate to their children that such happenings are small-time suffering, part of life.

If you want to talk real heroism, little man, try carpal tunnel syndrome from too much time in front of a computer.

It was an indication of Knoblauch's ability to annoy that he spent most of his twelve years in the major league with one-half of his body stamped black-and-blue from being intentionally hit with pitches. Or so I've read. As previously mentioned, Knoblauch was not responsive to repeated efforts to discuss either his bruises or his career as a metaphor for the meaning of life. Although in fairness we are making progress without him.

◆

It would be hard to argue that Knoblauch's first year in New York wasn't his best year in New York. Statistically and emotionally. Imagine for a moment being twenty-nine years old and playing baseball in New York City for $6 million a year. Imagine waking up knowing that of the tens of millions of humans in the metropolitan area and the five or six billion in the world, you are one of the two or three best at what you do. In this case, playing second base. Imagine life as a can't-miss proposition.

Imagine not having to imagine. For that first year Knoblauch had the world on a string. Hit well, fielded well, made pitchers throw strikes, drove everybody nuts on the base paths, and was instrumental in the winning of a then-record 114 games and the World Series. And by the time the World Series ended, Knoblauch, though not as beloved as Derek Jeter or Paul O'Neil or Bernie Williams, was at a place in life where absent a freak accident, he was a made man. The salad days, they're called, although the author has no idea why.

He does know that man cannot live on salad alone, that he also needs performance drugs and a sweetheart, and Knoblauch got himself some of one in the person of Stacey Victoria Stelmach and some of the other with occasional injections of the same juice Roger Clemens was using to maintain his high standards of fireballs and fair play, which would both come back later on to haunt them—Clemens and Knoblauch, but not so much Stacey Victoria—as most things that are any fun do.

For now, though, all he had to do was not fuck the rooster.

But, as Knoblauch was not the first to discover, the moment you realize that all you have to do is not fuck the rooster, you might as well buy it a nightie. It is a fact of life that when you want something not to happen badly enough, you have pretty much guaranteed that it will (except once in a while, it goes the other way; for instance, Tinkerbell and George Steinbrenner are both dead, so go figure).

◆

You could say that Knoblauch's problems got their toehold in 1999, his second year in New York. Strangely enough, to the author's eye, it showed up first at the plate. For eight years, Knoblauch's whole stay in the major leagues, he had come to the plate looking like an afternoon's work, and now, more and more, pitchers were through with him in three or four pitches. The swing itself had changed and he seemed to be thinking of home runs instead of slapping the ball through the infield, and Knoblauch as a power hitter was pretty ordinary stuff.

Not long afterward came the first real suggestion of what was in the offing. It began with softer, tentative throws to first base. Occasionally one bounced in, or pulled Tino Martinez off the bag to field it.

Knoblauch made twenty-six errors in 1999 and there were plenty more where those came from. Medical tests were conducted and showed inflammation in Knoblauch's elbow, but the elbow was treated and the inflammation went away and the wild throws didn't. The Yankees brought in a psychologist, whose Geiger counter must have revved off the plate when it passed Steinbrenner's office, but nothing helped Knoblauch.

Nothing helped. The medical explanation was that the wire from Knoblauch's brain to Knoblauch's arm had come unplugged. As those of you who are doctors already know, there are two halves to an electrical plug. There is the male half, which you will recognize by its prong, and the female half, which hangs around on the wall looking harmless. Ha! And Knoblauch's male half was saying, *Okay, Chucky baby, let it go,* and the female half was going, *Be careful, dear.*

And a little at a time, *be careful, dear* took over.

◆

If you are looking for a bottom, it probably came in June of 2000 when Knoblauch threw a ball to first base that hit the seventy-one-year-old mother of Keith Olbermann right between the eyes as she sat in the stands watching the Yankees play the Chicago White Sox. Knoblauch had just picked up a masse shot of a grounder stroked to the right side of the infield by a fellow named Greg Norton, who put his head down and dug for first base. Knoblauch threw the ball sidearm, about the way you skip rocks across water, and in fact skipped the old rock—an affectionate alternate term for the baseball—off the top of the Yankee dugout and into Box 47E, where Mrs. Olbermann had, until that moment, been watching Yankee games unmolested since 1934.

Knoblauch stared a moment, like watching a dog that's slipped its collar, and visibly sagged. Knoblauch, not the dog, who as you will remember is still out on the farm herding chickens. Knoblauch's head dropped and he seemed to be secretly checking himself for an open zipper, and he slowed to a modest jog, eerily reminiscent of a ballplayer rounding the bases after he has just parked one in the cheap seats. Which is still another affectionate term, this one for a long home run, the cheap seats being the farthest from home plate.

Mrs. Olbermann, you will notice, was not sitting in the cheap seats, which only goes to show that money can't buy happiness. Or maybe it can. The story of her plunking, along with her picture, appeared in newspapers all over America, making her an instant celebrity, and as her son Keith Olbermann, who, being a celebrity himself, knows what he is talking about, said, "She couldn't have been happier if they had let her pinch-hit."

Olbermann made this observation not at the time the incident occurred but as part of a remembrance on his television show a few days after his mother died. Her name was Marie.

This is not to say Knoblauch killed her. She hung on another nine years after the beaning, enough time to watch a few hundred more Yankees games and see her boy grow more famous and more contentious by the day. In one of many interviews, Mrs. Olbermann said she felt sorry for Knoblauch, and certainly held no hard feelings, which the author is pleased to announce brings us back to the meaning of life.

To recap: we are who we are; we do what we do; a clean-cut, shit-free hairdo is vital to a good first impression; never talk to anybody about the time you fucked the rooster; and if you want badly enough for something not to happen, it will. To that, you may now add this: you can't just bring Keith Olbermann into the world and not expect to pay for it somewhere down the line.

But if Mrs. Olbermann had empathy for Knoblauch, the Yankees did not, and pretty soon a decision came down that the ball rolled to the right side of the infield too often for Knoblauch to be the one trusted to pick it up. Knoblauch was moved to left field, where presumably he would be easier to hide. Now, however, with less to think about defensively and fewer chances to throw the ball away, Knoblauch's attention turned to hitting, instantly transforming him into a complete mediocrity at the plate.

Things then proceeded downhill.

Knoblauch spent his last game as a Yankee on the bench. As it happened, this was Game 7 of the 2001 World Series, and Knoblauch was hitting .056 for the first six. Enough said.

The Yankees lost the Series and moved Knoblauch again in the off-season, from left field to Missouri. Which is how you know you have fucked the rooster for good: they send you to rural America. Ask Jonesy.

◆

Myself, I have always thought Kansas City, Missouri, was an underrated town. A much more cultured place than, say, Kansas City, Kansas, or Sioux City, Iowa, except for North Sioux City, which is in South Dakota, and South Sioux City, which you will find in Nebraska. It turns out that the old saying that one stockyard is as good as another isn't true. In Kansas City, for instance, the aroma of butchery is not always in the air. And the streets are pretty clean and the people drive more politely than they do back East and many citizens are satisfied to drive their own vehicles without also trying to drive yours, and though they own horns (car horns, not cow horns), they don't necessarily blow them impulsively to herd rush-hour traffic, the way old Jonesy nips at chicken heels these days, pretending they are sheep. Thus Kansas City is quieter than New York, and its citizens walk more slowly, talk more slowly, and sleep better. It is a town that takes football more seriously than baseball, which all in all may not be such a bad thing for a baseball player trying to find his way out of a slump.

Yet even with calm days and sleep-filled nights Knoblauch could not find his way back. The things he used to do naturally now seemed beyond his reach, and where he had once confidently jogged out to second base as one of the two or three best second basemen in the world, he now jogged out to left field, not completely sure he was one of the two or three best left fielders in Kansas City.

And it was here in the heartland of America that Chuck Knoblauch played out his last, dismal season, appearing in only 80 games, hitting .210, and then was gone. He had hit .289 over a twelve-year career in the major leagues with almost 2,000 hits, 98 home runs, and more than 400 stolen bases. And yet he would be remembered exclusively for two incidents. The first occurred in the twelfth inning of the 1998 American League Championship

Series, New York against Cleveland, when, with the game tied 1–1, he ignored a baseball still in play and argued with an umpire while the Indians' runner, who had been on first base, scored what would become the game's winning run.

The other incident was the high hard one that caught Mrs. Olbermann between the eyes.

And now it was over, mercifully over.

Except it wasn't.

◆

The thing about fucking the rooster is, once you start, it's hard to stop. The world enjoys it, especially if you are a Yankee, and comes to expect it, meaning there is no chance that it will go unnoticed when you do it again. Thus three years ago Knoblauch reappeared in the sports pages, pleading guilty to misdemeanor assault after his common-law wife filed a complaint accusing him of punching her in the eye and choking her.

Now, the truth is, the author doesn't know much about spousal abuse. He witnessed a brutal example once but found himself lacking the courage to step in and stop it. His friend Fred's first wife—known as poor Mrs. McCurnin—hit Fred over the head with a skillet and all the author did was stand around hoping she didn't hit him, too. His pitiful excuse was—still is—that Fred's wife was bigger than he was. And armed, don't forget it. That happened in North Dakota, and the author was staying with Fred at the time, an extended visit. Now that the author thinks it over, his extended visit may have had something to do with why she hit Fred over the head in the first place. Be that as it may, the author stood frozen in fear, and the pan—or possibly Fred's head—made that *BONG* so familiar from the cartoon shows, followed by the lump that blows up and the bird that sings tweety-tweet from a little cloud over his head. Fred later reported that it sounded less like a tweeting than the slamming of a door.

And there is something else. In the interest of full disclosure, the author is compelled to mention that he himself was once accused of throwing a telephone at Mrs. Dexter, although she was not yet Mrs. Dexter. Which he knows is no excuse, not that he thinks he needs one. For one thing, if Chuck Knoblauch, a $6-million-a-year infielder, doesn't know where a baseball— which is a much handier size to throw—is going, how is the author supposed to know what will happen when he lets go of a telephone? For another thing, he didn't throw it *at* her but tossed it *to* her, as in *Here, call your mother and see if I care,* and the phone landed short of her foot, more or less where Knoblauch's throws to Tino Martinez were coming in, and the receiver bounced gently out of the cradle (these were the days when two-part telephones were connected by a cord) and rolled randomly, and the author cannot overemphasize *randomly,* into her foot, leaving not even a momentary discoloration, red, white, or blue, nothing, and fifteen years go by before she has occasion to visit a toe specialist on an unrelated matter, and the toe specialist inspects her feet and announces that he has found a bunion. He recommends surgery.

Mrs. Dexter has the surgery (did the author get thanked for buying his wife a new toe? I don't think so) and then, instead of turning into the grateful owner of a new $10,000 titanium toe, Mrs. Dexter gives the author a certain look that does not mean good things are a-comin' and says, "I hope you're proud of yourself now."

None of this is to say spousal abuse is not a serious matter. The author has nothing against shooting all the heroes who go home and beat up the wife and kids. But before we shoot them, or even stick them under the porch with Jonesy, we should be pretty sure that they are who they are and have done what they must do. Things, after all, are often not the way they look—in fact they are almost always not the way they look, especially in a police complaint or a court of law.

At any rate, Knoblauch pleaded guilty in Harris County, Texas, taking the misdemeanor assault charge instead of going to trial for choking a family member, which is a felony. And felonies and misdemeanors can be very different things in Texas. Other possible mitigating facts: (1) This is Texas, where they execute everybody, and (2) At the rate Knoblauch's hand-eye coordination was deteriorating, he might have been trying to choke Mr. Froggie. Which the author is pretty sure is a felony in Texas, too.

So Knoblauch pleaded guilty, got a year's probation, and told a reporter who had apparently tracked him down at his house in Houston that he just wanted to be left alone to raise his three-year-old son. What he didn't want was anything more to do with baseball. Of course, if Knoblauch were destined to get what he wanted, the balls he threw to first base would have gone to first base.

Then about this same time, largely due to his high profile as an error-prone former Yankee, Knoblauch fell under the scrutiny of the House Oversight and Government Reform Committee's investigation into performance-enhancing drugs in major league baseball, and was named as a user, along with eighty-some other players, in the now-famous Mitchell Report, named after its author, ex-senator George Mitchell, Democrat of Maine.

Regarding Knoblauch, the report found that during his stay with the Yankees he had injected himself with human-growth hormone approximately eight times.

Worse, Knoblauch hadn't responded immediately to the committee's invitation to be interviewed, and made himself scarce to the federal marshals who were sent to invite him. Then a subpoena was threatened, and he gave in, and with that, Chuck Knoblauch, who was once a made man, was turned into just another ex–baseball player with Congress sniffing up his skirt for needle tracks.

And here the story gets stranger. It turns out there is a law against lying to Congress. The author shits you not. On penalty of fines and incarceration. And even as the author sits, pen in hand, he must consider the spectacle of a pencil-necked, forty-six-year-old congressman from New York who has admitted sending pictures of himself and his pecker over the Internet to a much younger woman, who had not asked for the pictures, or had any reason to expect them. As the story developed, there were of course more pictures and more women. Six, he thought at some point (women, not pictures), meaning perhaps that the number would end up somewhere in the high seventies.

The congressman, Anthony Weiner, wept at a press conference, saying he had panicked and made a terrible mistake, letting down his wife and his constituents and all the people who believed in him, etc., etc., a confession that followed a week of resolute denials that he'd sent the pictures, and various suggestions that he was the victim of a joke or right-wing lunatics, or of technology itself gone wild in the wrong hands.

In the end, though, the congressman admitted before a national audience that he had sent the pictures and was now taking full responsibility for his *mistake,* which could only mean that Mr. Weiner didn't want to resign from Congress and go to work for a living. As the author awaited details of what kind of degenerate Weiner would turn out to be—and we all had to wonder what would happen when he found his testicles—he tried to imagine what Congress would look like if our elected representatives could go to prison for lying to the public.

But it may be best to set aside the whole subject of lying for the moment and focus instead on the bigger questions facing Congress. That is, can defending the national pastime against growth hormones make the citizenry forget $4-a-gallon gas, a housing market still in the toilet, and a national debt of $17 trillion? Can the Yankees buy somebody to save them from Boston?

Don't ask me. All I know is that we are who we are; we do what we do; a clean-cut, shit-free hairdo is vital to a good first impression; never talk about the time you fucked the rooster; and if you want badly enough for something not to happen, it will. Oh, you can't expect to bring a Keith Olbermann into the world and not pay for it somewhere down the road; and never send pictures of your pecker to women you don't know, because you'll end up hurting the very ones you love the most.

And that's it, everything we have learned from Chuck Knoblauch. Looking at it now it all seems a little unfair, what with George Steinbrenner dead and Knoblauch hiding out in disgrace somewhere in Houston and Roger Clemens waiting to hear if he'll go to trial again and maybe to jail for lying to our elected officials.

But then, nobody said it was a fair world, and for that Yankee fans everywhere—including the author and his pal Mrs. Dexter—can all breathe a sigh of relief.

◄| *five* |►

True North

CHARLES P. PIERCE

I grew up watching baseball with old men. Sometimes, I watched it on a little aquarium-size Motorola that was in the backroom of the barbershop where my father and I would go once a week to get our hair buzzed down to our scalps. Of course, that backroom was also where the barber used to keep all his copies of *Argosy* and the other "men's magazines," which, as the years went by, became vastly more interesting than the ball games were. One whiff of Wildroot today, and my mind is transported either to a waterlogged Fenway Park, where Jim Gosger is meandering toward the batter's box, or to some tropical island where a downed American pilot has happened upon a tribe of wild cannibal women who've discovered a technique for making skimpy lingerie out of palm fronds. Proust can have his doughnuts. I know which way I'm going.

Or I was at my grandfather's house. Charlie Gibbons was a sign-painting man after whom my parents named me. On Sundays, he would sit in a bilious-green leather recliner, accompanied by a box of unfiltered Camels and a quart bottle of Narragansett

Lager beer. And by me. I would sit next to him and try to figure out what about the game was making him so agitated. One memorable Sunday, a Red Sox third baseman named Frank Malzone booted an easy grounder. As I recall, the Red Sox were about 297 games behind the Yankees at this point, so I didn't know what all the commotion was about, but my grandfather exploded and called Malzone an ethnic slur and a profanity, which, in combination, rhymed with "plucking finny." My grandmother, showing impressive lateral movement for an old gal, hustled me out into the yard, where I threw a baseball against the side of the house and contemplated all I'd learned.

I guess you could say things were a little tribal back in the day.

◆

In every empirical sense, the great Yankee–Red Sox rivalry is a myth, and not merely because the historical box score is so dreadfully lopsided, the wonders of 2004 notwithstanding. I was too young to remember the battles of the late 1940s, when Williams came back, and the Red Sox bungled their way out of a couple of pennants. By the time I became aware of baseball—and of unfiltered Camels and Narragansett Lager—the Yankees were a dynasty and the Red Sox were a landfill. In 1967, the Red Sox turned the franchise around for good but, by then, the Yankees were in the middle of the long, slow slide that devalued the franchise to the point where it was easy pickings for that brigand shipbuilder from Cleveland. Then, for a while, both teams were pretty terrible. They had the great 1978 drama. That was true. Then, for a spell, the Yankees got better and the Red Sox got worse and then it happened in reverse to the point where, in 1986, the keepers of the myth were forced to dragoon the Mets into the legend despite the fact that replacing the Yankees with the Mets as the villain in a historical epic is like rewriting the *Iliad* so that Achilles chases Scrooge McDuck three times around the walls of Troy.

What I knew about the Red Sox and the Yankees was purely ethnic. Because of DiMaggio, the Italian kids I knew were Yankee fans, almost all of them. Their fathers and grandfathers had been Yankee fans, and they were Yankee fans. There was nothing wrong with this, of course, any more than it was wrong for my Irish friends to attach themselves to the University of Notre Dame, or for the African-American students at the school where my father taught to wear L.A. Dodgers caps because their fathers and grandfathers taught them about what Jackie Robinson had meant to them when he came up to that team in Brooklyn that didn't even play there anymore.

Years later, believing himself to be clever, that smug fathead Jerry Seinfeld made a big deal out of what he called "rooting for laundry," the basic conceit being that the rise of free-agency in sports and the fluidity of the modern roster had reduced fans to rooting for the team itself, no matter who played for it. That this is a modern concept is transparently ludicrous. So much of what baseball romantics claim is the sport's unique generational continuity is purely a function of rooting for laundry. The entire United States west of Pittsburgh and south of Chicago became fans of the laundry of the St. Louis Cardinals because KMOX threw the team's name across the landscape with 50,000 watts behind it. So much of what its most fervent acolytes claim as baseball's ineffable place in the American story depended on the simple fact that, reserve clause or no, players come and go, but that the team is the same, even when it packs up and moves to Los Angeles, because what it came to represent remains behind. That truth has managed to survive even the era of the gypsy owner, and expansion, and the fact that, for the third time, there is a fitful baseball team in Washington for everyone to ignore. For my Italian friends, growing up at half-past Mantle, for whom Joe DiMaggio was a spokesman for modern kitchen appliances, being a Yankee fan was more than just rooting for a winner, although it was that, damn their black souls. It was a way of speaking to the past in the modern syntax of the present. After all, Spike Lee

doesn't wear his Dodgers jersey because he's such a big fan of Andre Ethier. He wears it because of what that jersey came to represent at a moment of national moral crisis. It represented a claim
on the promise of the country—the redeeming of that unpaid
promissory note that Dr. King talked about on the Mall in 1963
before he wound into his big finish.

It took me a long time to realize what DiMaggio—and,
through him, the Yankees—had come to mean to all the grandfathers of all my Italian friends. Sometimes, it is important not to
lose your grip on those things that gave your family a purchase on
a place in the new country. It turned out that it was not as simple
as tribalism. It was something as real and solid as the immigra-
tion papers tucked away in a locked drawer, or the first time your
family's name appeared on a census form, or on the roll of eligible
voters. DiMaggio and LaGuardia meant to them what James Michael Curley and John L. Sullivan once meant to my family. That
the Yankees succeeded, wildly, down through the generations—
and that the old fellas found themselves grudgingly admitting that
the Mantle kid was pretty good, too—was the most unlikely historical bonus of all. It was about those parts of assimilation that
counted as triumph.

That's what all the old teams were, when they played in the old
ballparks tucked into the clamorous and narrow streets between
the tenements, with people's actual laundry hung out on the back
porches, and flapping in the summer breeze. It was a statement
of who you were, and where you'd come from, and where you
intended to make your stand. Rooting for laundry was your purchase on America.

◆

I grew up in a transplanted Europe. Instead of countries, we had
parishes. I was of the first generation born to the first generation
born to the last generation of the great migrations from Western
Europe. For more than seventy years, they came: Irish fleeing

the Famine, endless stillborn uprisings, and the gentle ministra-
tions of the British Empire; Germans and Hungarians fleeing the
sad rubble of their own aborted revolutions, and Italians fleeing
the political chaos that seemed to come upon that country by
the quarter hour, like radio traffic reports. ("Coming up next—
Garibaldi on the threes!") They came here and the first thing
they did was re-create the towns they'd left behind by building a
church and then building a neighborhood around it among themselves. In Worcester, where I was born, we identified the churches
by the nationalities of the people who worshipped there. There
was the "Swedish church" on Belmont hill; the "Polish church"
off Millbury Street, which was my grandfather's old beat when he
first came on the force; and there was a "Lithuanian church" not
far from it. There was no "Irish church" per se. Too many of us
had come in the first and second wave. Some of them organized
by county; St. Peter's, where my father was baptized and where I
went to elementary school, was a church full of Kerrymen, like
his father, the cop, and my grandmother, who came here because
she didn't want to be a shepherd all her life in the hills outside of
Listowel.

These were more than curious demographic phenomena, these
parishes. There were rules, hard and fast, and as unyielding as fish
on Friday was. I mean, yes, we were all Catholics and everything.
(Who made us? God made us.) But you would no more go to
Sunday mass at the "Polish church" than you would go up the
hill and sing with the Lutherans. In my mother's neighborhood,
on the other side of Worcester from where my father grew up,
there was a "French church" and there was the church in which
worshipped the lace-curtain Irish like my mother's family. You
literally could stand on the front steps of the French church and
hit my mother's church with a rock. I don't think she ever set foot
in the French church in her life.

The "Italian church," the biggest one anyway, was Our Lady
of Mount Carmel off Shrewsbury Street. It was huge and ornate
and it had a lovely view of downtown, at least until they built the

freeway about thirty yards in front of its main entrance. Shrewsbury Street was the Italian part of town, where you could shop
for the finest sausage, gorge yourself on the pizza, or finish off a
long evening with the antipast' at the Parkway Diner. If you were
thirsty, you could pick up a cold beer at the East Side Package
Store, which was owned by the family of my best friend in high
school, Angelo Iaconi. His family, or a part of it anyway, was in
the family business, as it were, and, once, it was my grandfather's
job to arrest the employees of Angelo's grandfather's various en-
trepreneurial enterprises in and around town. This all came to a
head when I was an usher at Angelo's wedding. I was standing at
the bar when, suddenly, I was surrounded by what appeared to be
Old-Timers' Day in the witness-protection program.

"You Sergeant Pierce's grandson?" one of the old gentlemen
asked.

"Why, yes," I replied, wondering what old grudge was being
exhumed here at the bar of the Wachusett Country Club. The old
gentleman smiled.

"He was a good man," the old gentleman said. "He would
come to the house."

In Worcester, as I was saying, we kept to ourselves, except everybody knew everybody else. How that worked, I never figured
out, but it was true. Within minutes, we were all laughing. By the
time the bride was dancing, we were all drinking Galliano, and
arguing about DiMaggio.

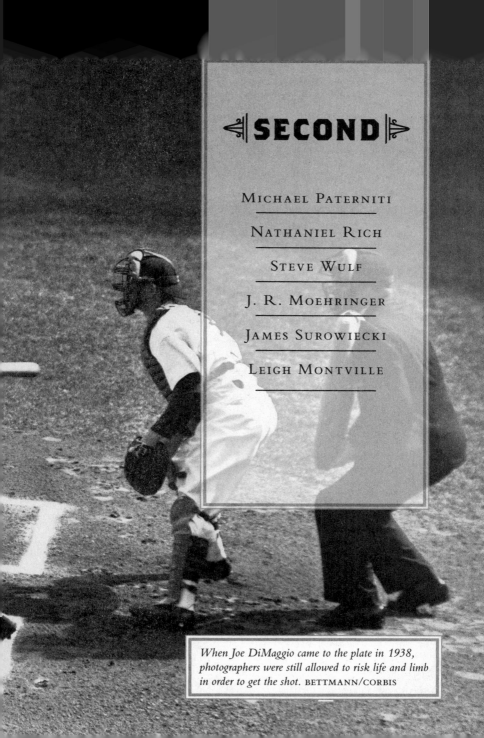

⊰ SECOND ⊱

Michael Paterniti

Nathaniel Rich

Steve Wulf

J. R. Moehringer

James Surowiecki

Leigh Montville

When Joe DiMaggio came to the plate in 1938, photographers were still allowed to risk life and limb in order to get the shot. BETTMANN/CORBIS

six

Gone Fishin'

MICHAEL PATERNITI

I'd say it ranks as one of my best nights as a magazine writer.
Easy. June of 1999, at the height of the big-bash era in baseball
(Mark McGwire, coming off his record-breaking 70 home
runs, was on his way to 65 more; Barry Bonds was two years away
from 73), and I was writing a story about Thurman Munson, the
Yankee catcher who died in a 1979 plane crash, the reporter-me
flying into Norfolk on a long, low arc, through ephemeral blue
sky, through heavy air and all that shattered ocean below, jumping in a rental car, the habitual riffling through radio stations until
it was dozens of voices blabbing in my compartment over country
roads to Hertford, North Carolina, to see Jim "Catfish" Hunter,
to talk to him about the old days, which, come to think of it, really weren't that old.

Going to see Catfish wasn't like going to see your normal interview subject: you know, chatting with Subject on the phone
ahead of time, getting directions, trailing down some lost country
highway, pulling into Subject's driveway, settling with Subject
for a while. A human shield had risen around the Hall of Fame

pitcher—he was fighting the mysterious ailments of amyotrophic lateral sclerosis, Lou Gehrig's disease, that just kept depriving his body of motion. His arms didn't work anymore, just hung there, occasionally swaying when he brought his body to a full stop after walking. So he couldn't talk on the phone. Couldn't hold it. And then didn't really want to talk on the phone anyway. The simple things we take for granted—opening the fridge for a look-see, walking up steps, hugging a wife or kid, pitching to a grandkid in the yard—had come to mock Catfish Hunter.

To actually get to Catfish you had to pass through one of his best buddies, Charles Woodard, owner of Woodard's Pharmacy, famous for its limeades and fifty-cent ice cream cones, and small-town, down-home friendliness. Charles said Mr. Jimmy liked lobster, and for each lobster over a dozen that I brought with me from the great state of Maine (where I live) I'd get another five minutes with Catfish. But there's only so much lobster one man can haul. And, as it turned out, Catfish wasn't having the best day. When I stopped at the pharmacy, Charles said if Catfish threw me off his farm a few minutes after my arrival, then that'd be it. That's just the way it was these days with Mr. Jimmy. Hit or miss. He hadn't given but a few interviews, and they weren't long ones at that.

"He won't be subtle, either," said Charles, then started giggling, in high-pitched, revving sounds. He was already imagining the choice string of abuse that would drive me out, the fight and pluck in Mr. Jimmy's voice, a sign that he wasn't all gone yet, that he still had some essential fiber of uppity strength, the dig-deep, ninth-inning kind he'd once used to out-finagle thousands of batters.

Catfish had been a rarity from the start, the youngest of eight kids, big and tough, a gifted athlete whether he was playing line-backer or shortstop. But it was his pitching—his speed and pin-point control—that brought the major league scouts trailing into tiny Hertford, like hounds on the scent, rolling down their car windows, asking, "Where's your ball field at?" And by the time high school was over—and despite a hunting accident in which he lost a toe—the blue-eyed country boy named Jimmy had been drafted by Charles O. Finley, the owner of the Kansas City A's. There were no college stops, or minor league appearances. Finley, one of the P. T. Barnums of baseball, asked the boy if he had a nickname, and when told no, Finley said: "You ran away from home when you were six to go fishing. You caught two catfish and were bringing in the third when they finally found you. That's your nickname. Now, repeat it back to me."

Down Route 7 a way, through heat and humidity that made the green trees seem greener and the smoke-fires seem smokier, came a brick house and a bunch of people standing around in the driveway who all looked like some version of Catfish—little Catfishes and stumpy, older Catfishes and young, lithe twenty-something Catfishes—and I turned in, stepped out with all those Catfishes giving me a little, suspicious, sideways look like I was an impostor leading off first, and I went around to the trunk and pulled out two boxes of lobster and said, "Lobster!" because I really couldn't think of anything else to say. A woman, Helen, Catfish's wife, smiled sympathetically and introduced me around to the family—a couple of Catfish's brothers, a son and daughter, a grandchild, and then more kin. She said, "Here's Mr. Jimmy." But Catfish didn't feel like looking me in the eye at first, just grunted. I didn't reach out my hand to shake his unusable one, because I knew it might make him think I was a fool, or that I was trying to make one of him. We just stood there for a while watching his grandson swat pitched Wiffle balls.

"C'mon, Taylor!" Mr. Jimmy yelled. "Ah wanna see yahr Mahk Ma-Gwyyyr!"

At some point, his older brothers made to leave, just nodded and said, "See you tomorrow," as if the reminder of another day might help pull Jimmy through another night. If the disease worked by subtraction, they were trying to add it all back, in clusters around the man. They drove off in pickups, beneath banners of thick Spanish moss. After they left, Catfish grunted again and led me to a bench under an oak with a view over the tobacco fields of his little farm.

Here was a legend—especially to me, the boy who grew up on those seventies Yankee teams—who'd won five World Series rings, a Cy Young Award, and eight All-Star berths in a fifteen-year career. He'd thrown a perfect game, thirty complete games in one season, and became the highest-paid player in baseball when George Steinbrenner shelled out $3.2 million for his services over five years, prompting Bob Dylan to write a song about him ("Catfish, million dollar man / Nobody can throw the ball like Catfish can," went the chorus). What Catfish Hunter had come to embody, all in one person, was the old-school, mythic ballplayer with a direct line back to the great pitchers—Cy Young, Pudd Galvin, Old Hoss Radbourn—the ones who'd never had the luxury of "relief" but bull-headed their way to the end of games as a point of pride. And then Catfish was poised at the leading edge of a new era, one of arbitration and free-agency, of vagabond stars moving from team to team for big money.

When he made the jump from Oakland (where Finley had moved his A's) to the New York Yankees in 1975, he told me now, he did everything to make sure that money didn't enter into relations with his new teammates. At a spring training pool party, everyone pelted each other with tomatoes, a sudden free-for-all like the Tomatina de Buñol—Catfish pulped from head to toe—and a young pitcher was made to do shots and spun around on a high stool until he barfed. Then, Catfish was the first one on his hands and knees to pick up the mess.

"See, I was a fahm boy," he said, a mischievous glitter in his eye. "I knew a little about tomatoes and slop."

He told stories about Sal Bando, and that famous A's team, how the bunch of them went drinking together after games, and grew their mustaches for the $300 bonus Finley had offered if they did. He told stories about Thurman Munson, and how much he loved the man, though the pressure of New York could make anyone crazy, and one night he remembered Thurman firing a gun in the parking lot at the Stadium, and Catfish turned to him and said, "Geez-ass, Thurman, now why'd yah go an' do that?" And he remembered that when each season came to an end, all he wanted was the first plane back home, to this farm, to his friends in Hertsford. He couldn't wait to hunt and fish—and ride the tractor.

As we sat there, the white light let out of the sky until everything turned ripe and tangerine-colored, the fields rolling to wherever. It was dinner time, and two big tables were set on the lawn for about twenty. The family began gathering in a big circle to pray, and I figured this was probably my cue, time to find a motel somewhere, see if I might catch a ball game on the tube. But as we ambled back, Mr. Jimmy grunted one last time, chucked his head for me to follow, made a place next to him in the circle, and then, when everyone took up each other's hands, I reached down and found his without thinking, the huge paw of his right hand, the one that had delivered the Yankees the impossible 1978 World Series championship with the clinching victory in Game 6, soft now from disuse. What did it feel like to hold that hand? It felt as if some powerful electricity was being transmitted through that circuit of people and shot through to Mr. Jimmy. Holding his hand made me their momentary conduit. It felt overwhelming. Then, we bowed our heads.

After the amen, everyone looked to sit. There was a chair open next to Catfish, to the other side of Helen, who was instantly cracking lobster and feeding it to him from her fingers. But I sat at the second table, and I'd like to think that he took this as proof that I wasn't there to crowd him or to itemize his physical demise, bite by dribble. Ten minutes passed . . . and then another ten . . . and another, and I still hadn't been kicked out, until I forgot about the passage of time altogether, and was just made to feel part of things. At some point, I put away my notebook and pen, and laughed as people laughed genuine laughs and Mr. Jimmy started telling stories—fishing stories, appropriately enough—and we all turned to him. It was dark now, and his face was lit gold by candles set on the table to keep the bugs away, as that great walrus mustache moved to chew and talk. ". . . An I nevah did see such a looka shock when he reeled up dat rubber tie-ah!"

Sometime after my visit Mr. Jimmy lost his balance and fell from the front steps at his house, the same ones he stood at the top of as I pulled out later that night—after pie and then a bucket-load of crabs that were brought late by Mr. Jimmy's son-in-law, brought to please Mr. Jimmy, and after his son kissed him good-night, gently atop his head (" 'Night, Daddy," he said), and his daughter did the same. And then Catfish invited me inside to chew the fat, to shoot the shit, to sit in adjoining La-Z-Boys for a while and just let a little bit of living, a little bit of the past settle in. To make this one moment last by filling it with all the other moments of a good life.

A few months later, when he was rushed to the hospital, when he wavered in a coma, when an AP photographer stole onto his floor and tried to take a picture of Mr. Jimmy with one eye shut and the other half-open, struggling to regain consciousness, language fell away. There was no more *good life*. It was just the filling and emptying of lungs, the cardiogram's peaks and valleys. Finally, he muttered his wish to go home, for that's where he wanted to die. The same fields where his daddy before him did.

There were tributes, of course, about how Mr. Jimmy remained down-to-earth all his life, about the things he did as Catfish on the mound, about all he gave back to his hometown and family. "If you don't like Catfish, you don't like people," a former teammate had said about him, and that seemed a fitting epitaph. But what comes to me now is that candlelight. Catfish, Mr. Jimmy, Daddy—all of him in that light. That comical bushy mustache and his mouth moving beneath it, gritty voice growling and reeling and pitching story after story. Gales of laughter; fits of pleasure. In that light, there was something clean and pure and artful about him, and something mischievous and lovable and absolutely, undeniably authentic. He looked like a boy, and he looked fifty-three, his real age. And though more than half of him was already gone, well, wherever he was going next, that's exactly where you wanted to be.

◄‖ *seven* ‖►

The Queens Speech

NATHANIEL RICH

I submit for your consideration two men.

The first has bad posture, prematurely graying hair, a tremulous smile, and the pale, somewhat ashen skin of a person who has spent excessive time bathed by the glare of a computer screen, analyzing statistics. Poor guy, his back is hunched. There is a bitterness in his laughter. His eyes squint. Sometimes in conversation his voice abruptly cracks and he gazes off into the distance; an interminable silence follows, and despite your efforts to rouse him, he is catatonic. At last he comes to with a sad little smile. "I'm sorry," he sighs. "It just came back to me . . . a memory. A horrible memory." Though he will refuse to discuss this memory, it is likely one of the following: an ace pitcher allowing seven first-inning runs in the final game of a season that hangs in the balance; a second baseman dropping a routine pop-up with two outs in the bottom of the ninth, while the winning run races around third; a batter, frozen in terror, watching a curveball slice through the strike zone for the final out of the playoffs.

Now meet the second man. He does not consort with the likes

of the first man. This gentleman is robust, with a healthy paunch and a clear gaze. His smile is as crisp as a new hundred-dollar bill. He has a hearty handshake and a loud voice. He slaps your back; he makes boisterous, off-color jokes and winks slyly. He'll pay for your drink—hell, he'll pay for your girlfriend's drink, too. He has season tickets, but he's usually too busy to use them. But on those rare nights—usually when important clients are visiting and ask to see a game—he grabs a crisp navy baseball hat from his office closet, calls the car service, and tries to arrive in the Bronx no later than the fourth inning. Upon being shown to his seats, he can be overheard asking the usher, "Did I miss any home runs?"

With which of these two men do you identify? Since you are reading this book, the answer is likely the second man—the Yankees fan. If you empathize with the first man, that means you are a Mets fan so full of self-loathing that you actually purchased an anthology about the Yankees for the sole purpose of tormenting yourself. That is so like you, Mets fan, you sad, sad person.*

◆

As a Mets fanatic, I am often asked why Mets fans hate the Yankees. I don't think that "hate" is the right word. Do Jainists hate Christians? Do the Stoics hate the Epicurians? Do masochists hate sadists? There is not an animosity between Mets and Yankees fans so much as a profound philosophical abyss. (I'm speaking of real fans here: not dilettantes who will vanish the second Derek Jeter retires and/or the team has a losing season.) No, really, some of my best friends are Yankees fans. They are a particular type of Yankees fan, a microscopic minority of Yankees Nation—perhaps fewer than 5 percent of the fan base—but they exist. They are

---

* Let's get one thing out of the way: there is no such thing as a person who is a fan of both the Yankees and the Mets. Anyone who identifies himself in this way is, in actuality, a fan of neither team. I hope, Yankees fan, that we can agree on this point if nothing else.

fans of long standing: obsessive, passionate, and, most astonishing to me, they live in constant fear. No matter how much success their team has, they still expect the worst.

Yet even they embrace the Yankee Doctrine, which, like that of any authoritarian regime, can be reduced to a single credo: Win At All Costs (WAAC). At first glance, WAAC would seem unassailable. The object of a baseball game is to win; the object of any season is to win the championship. Everyone knows that this is true, or at least knows that it's important for fans to believe that this is true. Players, especially those who sign with the Yankees as free agents, go so far as to insist that the reason they chose to take a higher contract offer—and not a lower one from a poorer, worse team—is to give themselves a better chance at winning a championship.

The Yankees fan's undying belief in WAAC has been upheld by his team's history. The team has won frequently enough—twenty-seven championships in the past eighty-eight seasons, or nearly once every three years—that there has not been any time to question whether WAAC might have certain flaws as a governing theory. The Yankees fan has been hardened by success, and goaded by the pronouncements of George Steinbrenner ("Winning is the most important thing in my life, after breathing") and, more recently, by his slightly less eloquent son Hank ("We just have to fucking win"). But on some late nights, perhaps in the off-season, does the Yankees fan ever hear a small voice in his head ask whether winning is, in fact, the most important thing in the life of a baseball fan?

This is the point in the Mets-Yankees dialectic where a Yankees fan begins to suspect the Mets fan of sour grapes. *You pathetic Mets fan,* he thinks, *you wish you could win one-tenth as many titles as we have.* I concede this—2.7 titles would be an improvement of .7 on what the Mets have won. And accusations of title-envy would be an appropriate retort to naysayers from fans of the other twenty-eight baseball franchises. But consider this: Mets fans, unlike, say, Padres or Pirates or Astros fans, were not forced by the rigid imperative of geography to support a losing team. At some point we had a choice in the matter. We are New Yorkers, after all—we could have rooted for the Yankees with impunity. And you cannot argue that we unthinkingly inherited our love of the Mets from our parents—familial loyalty represents a smaller fraction of our fan base than most teams, because the franchise has only been in existence since 1962. Consider that there was a moment, likely at a very young and impressionable age, when, presented with the two alternatives, the young baseball fan turned his back on the perpetual champions. He chose, instead, to cast his lot with a laughingstock franchise that promises its supporters nothing more than broken hearts, delivered punctually every September. Do you, Yankees fan, ever wonder why a person would do such a thing?

This brings us to a better question: Why do Yankees fans hate the Mets? (For they assuredly do—if you require proof, try wearing a Mets hat to a Mets-Yankees game at Yankee Stadium.) The Yankees fan is unlike the New York Giants fan, who is generally indifferent to the plight of the sad-sack Jets, or the Knicks fan to whom the Nets are no more significant an opponent than the Charlotte Bobcats. Why does the gluttonous Yankees fan root against the Mets? Isn't it enough that his team has dominated the sport for nearly a century? Why does he call WFAN radio talk shows and mock the Mets and their fans? Why does the Yankees fan descend from his baseball Olympus to criticize Jose Reyes or Oliver Perez? I'm not wounded by the attention—I appreciate it, the way a younger brother is grateful for the attention of his older brother, even if it comes in the form of sucker punches to the kidneys.

I ask you, Yankees fan: Is it possible that the persistent existence of the Mets fan forces you, like a Bible literalist reading *The Origin of Species* for the first time, to question the very bedrock on which your entire fandom rests? Does the very existence of an avid Mets fan base UNDERMINE THE BELIEFS YOU HOLD MOST DEAR?

Roll your eyes all you want, but consider the following thesis: *Mets fans are better baseball fans than Yankees fans.*

To clarify: I limit "better" to meaning "more knowledgeable, devoted, and soulful." And I don't claim that every Mets fan is a better fan than every Yankees fan. There are plenty of cretins who wear the orange and blue, as there are certain vintages of Yankees fans who deserve the respect of every Mets fan. (See chart, p. 76.)

WAAC has turned the Yankees into the baseball version of a multinational bank—the UBS of MLB—whose employees are forced to adhere to strict clothing and facial-hair codes, speak in bland platitudes, and smile crisply. The new Yankee Stadium is a convention center with some dirt and grass in the middle. But forget about the franchise itself—consider how WAAC has demoralized the Yankees' fan base. When all that matters is the final result of a game, why bother to show up to the Stadium in time for the first pitch? And once the outcome is no longer in doubt—even if it is only the sixth inning—then why stay through the ninth? (Only Los Angeles Dodgers fans rank lower than Yankees fans in average number of innings observed.) With such lofty expectations, the highs can never be high. A championship restores the team to its rightful place in the universe; never will it be, as it was in 2004 for the Red Sox, a euphoric, mind-exploding, once-in-a-lifetime glory. Will a Yankees fan ever tell his grandchildren about the World Championship of, say, 1999? Excessive winning, like too many tabs of ecstasy, mutilates the brain's pleasure receptors. It makes committed Yankees fans crabby, impossible to impress, bored. Any fan who expresses rabid excitement at a big win against the Red Sox in May will be exposed as an amateur. There are only three possible outcomes to a Yankees season: embarrassment (2004), disappointment (2005–2008, 2010), and satisfaction (2009). Euphoria doesn't enter into it.

This is sad for the Yankees fan. When all that matters is wins and losses, you lose something: namely, the joy of the game. The sublime crack of a hard line drive, even one that ends up landing in a fielder's glove. The rigorous strategic analysis that underpins every pitch, no matter what the score. And the bizarre things that occur at the ballpark every day: the fly ball that hits the pigeon above the centerfield wall and drops back into play, covered with blood and bird bone; the bunted ball that lands directly on the third base line and freezes there, as if Velcroed to the ground; the first baseman who, trailing a foul pop-up behind home plate, falls headfirst into the front row of the stands and comes up without the ball but with a hot dog clutched between his teeth.

The joys of baseball—its whimsy and beauty and its unique mixture of simplicity (hit ball with bat) and complexity (2–2 count in a tie ball game, second time through the order, speedy runner on third, one out, cleanup hitter on deck, batter is having trouble seeing breaking pitches but hit one for a double in his previous at-bat, etc., do you throw the slider or the cut fastball or the curve?)—are lost on fans who follow the Yankees because they want to root for a winner. The WAAC sensibility grants about as much appreciation for these simple joys as the Visigoths had for the Circus Maximus or the Baths of Caracalla when they ransacked Rome. Yet such joys are the consolation of fans of middling teams around the league.

This brings us back to the Mets, who, over the last quarter century, have not, strictly speaking, been a middling team. If only they were middling—if only they were hopelessly bad. How much easier it would be for their fans. The genius of the Mets is to convince their fans, *every single year,* that they are a genuine contender, only to self-destruct by the end of the season in some shocking fashion. Nearly every winter the Mets spend a fortune on free agents, they make dramatic trades, they hire a new pitching guru. Every spring they play credibly; they often occupy first place. The Mets fan, highly skeptical of his team's success up to this point, begins to wonder: Can this possibly be our year? At the trading deadline, a young prospect is jettisoned for a proven, if aging, former All-Star. Some years they build up a commanding division lead into September; occasionally they advance to the playoffs. The skepticism falls away, replaced by a childish sense of wonder. I won't—can't—dwell on the details. Suffice to say, by September, it has all fallen apart, and spectacularly.* They are the cruelest franchise. Any Mets fan will recognize this as a wild understatement.

For a glimpse of what it's like to live through the stunning emotional swings of being a Mets fan, I present a sample of text messages I received during September 2008—the second of the Mets' two recent late-season collapses:

> **9/7:** Looks like the Mets decided they had fun last year and wanted to do it again.
>
> **9/24:** Oh Lord help us
>
> **9/24:** Misery
>
> **9/24:** My heart cant take it anymore. I still have faith, though
>
> **9/25:** I said I had faith last night, but as of now the Mets are done. You have no idea how furious I am.
>
> **9/26:** In my darkest hour . . . They're alive, and I was wrong.
>
> **9/26:** It's definitely praying time.
>
> **9/27:** Tomorrow is the big day!
>
> **9/28:** I have a bad feeling now.
>
> **9/28:** Hard to believe

---

* Fine, if you really want a partial litany of the Mets' disgraces: They rally at the end of July from last place and take the division, miraculously win the pennant, and make it to Game 7 of the World Series—only to fall short (1973). They lose the National League Championship series to a team they've beaten ten out of eleven times during the regular season (1988). They blow a seven-game lead with seventeen days left in the season—the worst collapse in history (2007). They repeat the feat the very next year. In just the last two seasons they have dropped several routine pop-ups in high-pressure situations (Ryan Church, Daniel Murphy, and Luis Castillo come to mind), lined into game-ending triple plays (Jeff Francoeur), had their closer (Francisco Rodriguez) tear a ligament by punching his father-in-law in the face; lost a game because an outfielder (Church again), while racing home to score the winning run in extra innings, neglected to step on third base.

9/28: I'm gonna blow my head off

9/28: You knew this was going to happen

9/28: Why died I not from the womb? Why did I not give
up the ghost when I came out of the belly?

9/29: Sorry for your loss. Hockey season soon!

That last one was from a Yankees fan.

The Mets often bring their fans into contact with the higher questions. I don't mean, How did this team blow it again? The questions that arise during a Mets fan's darkest moments are existential, even vaguely spiritual. Why do I continue to hitch my personal fortunes to those of this team? The players don't root for *me,* after all. They don't even know I exist. Why do I care about sports? What kind of success might I have in life if I devoted to more constructive pursuits the roughly one thousand hours a year (a cumulative forty-two days) that I spend on Mets-related activities? Who needs a heart anyway?

Like true masochists, Mets fans have made a tradition of celebrating our various humiliations. There is substantial indignity in being a Mets fan, and not just because our mascot is an imbecile with a giant baseball for his head. Since 1962, Mets fans, like any group of marginalized losers, have taken refuge in freakdom. We celebrate with a pathetic devotion the misfits and oddballs who have populated this team over the decades. Whereas the Yankees have a pantheon of players like Babe Ruth, Lou Gehrig, and Joe DiMaggio, the Mets have Jimmie Pearsall, who ran backward around the bases after hitting a home run; Bobby Valentine, who, after being ejected from a game, snuck back into the dugout wearing a fake mustache and sunglasses (earning a two-game suspension); and, most recently, the folk hero R. A. Dickey, a literary scholar from Tennessee who developed an unhittable knuckleball in his late thirties. He is, as of this writing, the Mets' best pitcher. This is a franchise that, in its founding year, made the strategic decision not to spend its resources on the best players they could find, but rather on the players with the silliest names:

Choo Choo Coleman, Marvin Eugene Throneberry ("M.E.T."), Vinegar Bend Mizell. Was it really any surprise that the current ownership invested the team's funds with Bernie Madoff? Not to Mets fans, it wasn't.

Finally there is the shame of the Mets Curse, which allows Mets players to succeed only once they've been traded or released. This is especially true when a Met joins the Yankees. No one in a Mets uniform has ever pitched a no-hitter, but two former Mets, Dwight Gooden and David Cone, pitched them for the Yankees. As a player with the Mets in the mid-seventies, Joe Torre was best remembered for hitting into four double plays in a single game. That was enough to convince the team's management to hire him as a player-manager. His managerial record with the Mets from 1977–1981 was 286 wins against 420 losses. His teams never finished better than fourth place. With the Yankees he was 1,173 and 767. He made the playoffs all twelve seasons.*

I refuse to talk about the walk-off walk in Game 6 of the 1999 NLCS, the 2000 World Series, or the game I attended on May 20, 2006, when Billy Wagner blew a four-run lead in the ninth to the Yankees. Nor will I discuss the atrocity I witnessed at Yankee Stadium on June 12, 2009, when Luis Castillo dropped a routine pop-up with two outs in the bottom of the ninth, allowing the tying and game-winning runs to score, while Yankees fans around me pounded me on the back and screamed into my face. How much trauma do you expect a person to take?

It didn't have to be this way.

When I was a child I visited my grandparents every March in Florida. My grandfather took me to games at Municipal Stadium in West Palm Beach, the spring training home of the Atlanta

---

* The inverse of the Curse holds as well. Players who played their worst seasons after putting on the Mets uniform include: Gil Hodges, Willie Mays, Duke Snider, Yogi Berra, Warren Spahn, Richie Ashburn, Ken Boyer, George Foster, Rusty Staub, Vince Coleman, Roberto Alomar, Tom Glavine, Pedro Martinez, and Jason Bay.

Braves and Montreal Expos. We arrived several hours before each game and stayed after they ended. I asked anyone who walked in or out of the players' entrances to sign a baseball my grandfather had bought me for that purpose. Because I didn't know much about archival ink at the time, most of the autographs have now faded, but I can still make out Andres Galarraga, Tim Wallach, and Otis Nixon.

The highlight every spring—for me and for the large population of New Yorkers residing in southern Florida—was when the New York teams would visit for games. The Mets were only a couple of years from their spectacular run of the 1980s, but the Yankees, in the midst of their longest playoff drought in franchise history, were the bigger draw. They were the only team for which the stadium security staff had to rope off the ten yards between the players' entrance and the team bus.

After one Yankees/Expos game in the spring of 1991, I left early to take my position behind the yellow rope. Middle-aged men soon pressed all around me, holding bats and posters, Sharpies tucked behind their ears. Every time a player emerged from the clubhouse door, the crowd pushed forward, barely restrained by the outstretched arms of the overwhelmed Municipal Stadium security guards. When the slender, storklike figure of Don Mattingly peeked out from behind the door, the autograph collectors burst into a state of frenzy. The yellow rope was stretched to breaking and the security guards began to panic. Mattingly warily eyed the distance between the clubhouse door and the team bus, and seemed to calculate that he'd be unable to make it safely, at least not without having his clothing torn off along the way. He raised one hand in a pleading gesture.

"All right!" he said.

The crowd hushed, stunned that Donnie Baseball had addressed them as equals.

"Now I'm only going to do one," he said. "One for the kid."

He walked directly over to my position in line, pushed several men out of the way, bent over about four feet, and signed my baseball. Before the crowd could protest, he had disappeared into the tour bus.

I did not need that experience to convince me that Mattingly is the most sympathetic Yankee of all time. His career occupied the fourteen consecutive years (1982–1995) that the Yankees failed to make the World Series. He was a legendary player marooned in the Yankees' worst era. He was hard-nosed, blue-collar, dignified. If anything should have made me a Yankees fan, it was the kindness he showed my eleven-year-old self.

But it was too late for me to be saved. By that point, I'd already been a Mets fan for five years. If you do the math, you will see that I became a fan in 1986, the year the Mets won their last championship.

That's right: I was a fair-weather fan. I happened to have been born during the Yankees' lost decade, the only time in history that the Mets were the city's most popular team, and the most dominant team in baseball. If I had been born at any other point in the century, I would have been a Yankees fan. But, damn it, I started following the sport in 1986. Sure, I was six years old at the time, but I knew even then that it was not a decision to be taken lightly. I've kept my allegiance ever since.

Not a day goes by that I don't regret it.

Earning Your Stripes

YEAR IN WHICH YOU BECAME A FAN	DO YOU HAVE TRUE YANKEE PRIDE™?	EXPLANATION
1903	YES	You've been there from the beginning—heck, you were a Highlanders fan! Also, you're 108 years old. Aww. You're sweet.
1904-1961	YES	You've been a Yankees fan for half a century or more. You've earned your stripes.
1962-1964	NO	You chose to follow a team that had appeared in the World Series five consecutive years and 22 of the last 29 seasons, winning 16. There has never been a fair-weather fan who has enjoyed such fair weather in the history of American sports. I bet your favorite basketball team is the Harlem Globetrotters.
1965	NO	The same as above, only you were unlucky, since this was the first Yankee team in four decades to finish below .500.
1966-1975	YES	You stood by Mickey Mantle at the end of his career, and stayed with the team during the doldrums, when the only exciting baseball in town was being played by the Mets. I tip my orange-and-blue cap to you.
1976-1981	NO	You only began to root for the Yankees once a shipbuilding

Earning Your Stripes

YEAR IN WHICH YOU BECAME A FAN	DO YOU HAVE TRUE YANKEE PRIDE™?	EXPLANATION
		magnate from Cleveland took over management and decided that the best way to win was to throw money at stars from other franchises. Your single-minded pursuit of winning by any means necessary—including ruining the sport by ushering in an era of abject, mercenary greed—disturbs me.
1982–1995	YES	The Mattingly years. You stuck by the team at its worst. You earned what happened next.
1996–Present	NO	You named your dog Jeter. You named your son Derek. You named your daughter Giambina. You rub Derek Jeter Driven Deodorant stick under your arms. You don't buy all this talk about Roger Clemens injecting steroids. Your favorite players after Jeter are "Mo," "Robby," "A-Rod," "CC," "Tex," Jorge (pronounced "George"), and "Swishalicious." You don't know the names of any other players. You're a grown man/woman. How can you look at yourself in the mirror?

eight

The Latin King

STEVE WULF

There comes this sacred moment in the ritual of batting practice at the cathedral in the Bronx. When certain left-handed hitters step into the cage to take their cuts, conversation softens to a whisper, heads tilt toward the batter, ears register the sounds of perfect contact, and eyes follow the arc of the ball as it lands in the right-field seats. It happened with Ruth and Gehrig and Mantle and Maris and Jackson and Mattingly—hitters whose beautiful strokes fit Yankee Stadium as naturally as pinstripes.

And now it happens with Robinson Cano. The Stadium is new, but the BP tradition lives on. He steps in before an early-season game against the Orioles, and the players and coaches, the members of the media and early-arriving fans momentarily stop what they're doing to pay attention and homage to him. When the balls begin flying out, the congregants smile at each other as if to say, "Did you see what I just saw?" And when one of the balls ricochets off the seats in the upper deck above the UTZ potato chip sign in left, Cano himself laughs in delight.

◆

Estadio Tetelo Vargas is the Yankee Stadium of the Dominican Republic. Located in the center of San Pedro de Macoris, it defines baseball history in the D.R. So many great and good players have come from San Pedro, and all of them have spent quality time at the stadium, first as kids hanging around outside and in, then as prospects in the summer leagues, ultimately as returning heroes for Estrellas Orientales in the winter league. "We could see the lights of Tetelo Vargas from my house," Cano recalls with a twinkle in his eye.

What little—*muy poco*—I know firsthand about Dominican baseball I learned in a couple of trips down there for *Sports Illustrated* some twenty-five years ago. The first was to profile Cardinal pitcher Joaquin Andujar, who lived in San Pedro during the off-season and was a trip unto himself. The second was in 1987 to round up all the Dominicans who were starting shortstops in the majors. There were six of them at the time: Tony Fernandez (Blue Jays), Mariano Duncan (Dodgers), Julio Franco (Indians), Alfredo Griffin (A's), Jose Uribe (Giants), and Rafael Santana (Mets). They were spread out all over the Dominican Republic, but finding them wasn't all that hard, because we had the benefit of a unique GPS system—pull into town, find a street game, and ask the kids to take us to the house of the *shorly,* the shortstop.

There's a palpable magic to *beisbol* in the D.R. We could see it in the children fielding stuffed socks with cut-up milk cartons, and the teenagers throwing 90-mph fastballs at the academies that were springing up around San Pedro, and the adults at Tetelo Vargas recounting players and feats like ancient balladeers.

Those starting shortstops had agreed to meet for a photo shoot in the San Pedro town plaza, and then convene for lunch at a restaurant called *El Piano*. Sitting at opposite ends of a long table were Fernandez, better known as "Cabeza," and Duncan, and during lunch, baseballs were passed and juggled around so that they could autograph them to mark the occasion. At one point,

Duncan said, "Watch this," and flung a ball the length of the table. Cabeza, head-down, right hand occupied by a fork, caught the ball cleanly at his left ear with his glove hand. The looks on people's faces all said the same thing: Did you see what I just saw?

◆

At the time of that all-shortstop lunch, Robinson Cano was four years old. He was named for Jackie Robinson by his father, Jose Cano, a minor league pitcher who would eventually get a cup of coffee with the Houston Astros. The Yankees had originally signed Jose, but they released him after only three games in the low minors. But what did the Yankees know? At the time, their knowledge of Latin ballplayers was very limited.

Back then, the franchise did not exactly embrace diversity—it was as if they thought the YANKEE GO HOME signs in Latin American countries were meant for them. For the entire length of Roberto Clemente's career—1955 to 1972—the Bombers had only eight Latin ballplayers of any significance, and no more than two at a time. Even as late as '86, as the Hispanic population in New York City was exploding, the Yankees had no Latinos in the regular lineup and only one (Alfonso Pulido) on the pitching staff.

But the mind-set was changing in the scouting department. "We knew we had to go international," says longtime Yankee scout Gordon Blakeley, "and George [Steinbrenner] backed us up. It wasn't about appealing to the Latin community, although that would be a benefit. It was about putting the best possible team on the field."

Bernie Williams, a Puerto Rican, arrived on the scene in 1991, and his success paved the way for other Latino Yankees: Panamanian Mariano Rivera in '96, Puerto Rican Jorge Posada and Cuban El Duque in '98, and Dominican Alfonso Soriano in 2002.

In the meantime, Robinson Cano was growing up in San Pedro and hanging around Tetelo Vargas Stadium, where his father sometimes pitched. Players like Pedro Guerrero, Rafael Ramirez, and Andujar lived in his neighborhood. As a seventh grader, Robinson was moved to Newark with his mother while his father pitched in Taiwan. The relocation did nothing for his baseball talents—he took up basketball—and he fell in with a tough crowd. So his father made him an offer: "Do you want to play baseball every day in the Dominican Republic, or do you want to go to school up here?" Robinson chose the baseball option, and the rest is starting to look like history.

The Newark years weren't totally lost, though. Robinson became a Yankee fan. "Bernie Williams was my favorite player," he says. And according to legend, one day in 1996 he announced to his Newark cousin, "I'm going to be turning double plays with that guy someday." "That guy" was the rookie shortstop Derek Jeter.

Blakeley first saw Robinson play at the Yankees' academy outside of Santo Domingo. "He couldn't run very well," Blakeley recalls. "He played shortstop, and although he could catch it, I didn't see anything special. But when he took BP—the bat was lightning in his hands. I also noticed that his father was a big man, which I took to mean that he would one day have power."

The problem was that Jose Cano put too high a price on his son's talents, so other scouts backed away, including his next-door neighbor, who was an Astros scout. When Blakeley and Yankee scout Vic Mata got the price down to $125,000 in 2001, they signed him. "Then and only then did I really know I would be a major-leaguer," says Cano.

Major-leaguer, yes. But as Blakeley says, "Nobody had any idea that he would be a superstar."

◆

A nice old man is sitting in the press dining room at Yankee Stadium, exchanging pleasantries with a host of baseball people. Tom Giordano, now a special assistant for the Texas Rangers, has been in the game for sixty-three years, playing or working at one time or another for the Pirates, (Kansas City) Athletics, Reds, Indians, Orioles, even the Seattle Pilots. The name "Robinson Cano" comes up in conversation. "Best damn player on the Yankees," he says. "Best damn second baseman they've ever had. Here's the scary thing: he's getting better."

The really scary thing is that few people saw this coming. After Cano was signed, the Yankees tried him at third and short before moving him to second base. His progress through the minors was steady but not exactly eye-catching: he didn't hit .300 until 2004 in Double-A. Before that season, he was one of five prospects offered to the Texas Rangers in exchange for Alex Rodriguez; the Rangers chose infielder Joaquin Arias instead. He was part of a proposed deal with the Royals for Carlos Beltran that fell through, and he was also offered to—and rejected by—the Diamondbacks for Randy Johnson. "He wasn't putting up big numbers," says Blakeley, "because we were willing to stretch him a little, put him at a higher classification than we might normally do."

And at every step, he became stronger and faster. On May 3, 2005, he was called up to replace veteran Tony Womack at second—and promptly went 2 for his first 23. Manager Joe Torre called him into his office and told him not to worry. The next game, he got two hits, and a few weeks later, he was over .300. By the end of the season, Torre was comparing him to Hall of Famer Rod Carew.

But Torre, too, was wrong about him. Yes, he hit a Carew-like .342 in 2006, but he also had much more power. And while Carew had to move from second to first base, the Yankees had no such plans for Cano. "Great range," said Giordano, "and the strongest arm of any second baseman in the game." If anything, the Yankees might have moved Cano counterclockwise. "He could be a fine shortstop," said Blakeley.

Over the next two seasons, Cano regressed some, hitting .306 and .271. When new manager Joe Girardi benched him in '08 for failing to hustle after a ground ball, casual observers thought Cano might be getting too comfortable for his own good—he had signed a six-year contract extension for $55 million before the season. Blakeley thought just the opposite: "He's always had a tremendous work ethic, and I think he was putting too much pressure on himself. The more comfortable he became, the better he became."

Cano was back on track in 2009, with 25 homers and a .320 average, and the year after that, he became a superstar to rival Jeter and A-Rod: 29 HRs, 109 RBIs, a .319 average with a slugging percentage of .534 and an outrageous OPS of .914. He won both the Gold Glove and Silver Slugger awards for second base, and he finished third in the AL MVP voting. (As for 2011, well, those who saw the Home Run Derby won't soon forget the scene of the winner, Robinson, embracing his batting practice pitcher and father, Jose.)

Felix DeJesus, who covers the Yankees for both *Listin Diario* and MLB Espanol, sees a newfound maturity in Cano to go along with his ascension. "He has come into his own," says DeJesus. "He and Melky Cabrera were inseparable, so I think after Melky was traded, Robinson was better able to establish his own identity. And he's learned a lot from Jeter about how to conduct himself. I do know that he's much more active in the community, both in New York and the Dominican."

Together with Yankee coach Tony Pena, Cano has raised money to buy ambulances for his region. "So far we have been able to buy four," says Cano. "It's a great need in the Dominican, and I am happy to help."

◆

Giving Back is also part of the magic of Dominican baseball. That hasn't changed in the twenty-four years since I was down there— major-leaguers were and are beyond generous to the children in their country—and neither has the grinding poverty that's leavened by *beisbol*.

I've saved this dispatch from my own son, John, who went down to the D.R. to play a series of games with a team of New

York City collegians a year ago. In the Cano family tradition, I'll
let him take over:

*We were in a town in Altagracia, at the eastern tip of the island.
We drove up a large hill in our van to get to the field, and there
were these great, tall peaks behind first base. The field itself looked
unplayable, an uneven dirt infield with no real bases, and the infield
was littered with rocks and pieces of broken glass. To be honest,
though, I can't remember any bad hops—I guess the gods of baseball
were with us that day.*

*Here's something I remember from before the game started. As
we were getting settled, I looked into the outfield and watched as a
little boy played with his sock baseball. He must have been four or
five, and he would throw the ball as high as he could and chase it
down like an outfielder. He was barefoot and wearing hand-me-
down shorts with an old tank top, but he had a huge smile on his
face and was having the time of his life. I remember thinking this is
what Pedro Martinez or Jose Reyes must have looked like.*

*At the end of the game—I struck out the last batter with a curve-
ball that made us both laugh—every single kid from the town came
rushing toward us. Over the course of the week, I had given out a
few pieces of equipment, but every time I did so, a coach or teammate would tell me that I should wait until the last game. They were
right. The local kids surrounded six of us, and we gave out balls and
T-shirts. I gave the player I struck out my black Akadema glove.*

*On the way to the van, I found myself walking alongside a little
boy the same age as the one I had seen playing in the outfield. I
remember motioning with my hands that I didn't have anything left
to give him. At that point, though, I remembered the metal cleats
on my feet. I stopped, untied them, and handed my size 11 shoes to
a four-year-old boy. His smile was as big as the kid's with the sock
baseball—not a bad trade.*

WAIT FOR IT. Just as the Yankees were slow to embrace Latin America, so, too, have Yankee fans been slow to embrace Cano. You'd think 24—Jackie Robinson's number backward—would be a hot-selling Yankee jersey, but it trails 2 (Jeter), 13 (A-Rod), 25 (Teixeira), 42 (Rivera), and Posada (20) in sales figures.

That's not the fault of the organization. Thankfully, the Yankees are no longer just vanilla. There were sixteen foreign-born players on their 2011 Opening Day roster, the most in the majors. The Yankees are second in the majors in money spent for international free agents. They hold regular press conferences and luncheons for the Hispanic media. Their ticket prices don't exactly encourage the Dominicans in Washington Heights to cross the Harlem River, but then again, they don't encourage anybody without a lot of disposable income. "Believe it or not," says DeJesus, "Washington Heights is still Red Sox territory, what with Manny Ramirez coming from the neighborhood, and the popularity of Pedro Martinez. You can still find people arguing that Dustin Pedroia is a better second baseman than Cano. But that's changing."

If you can't actually go to the D.R., the next best thing is to take the 1 train to 191st Street and St. Nicholas Avenue. As you walk up the stairs on the uptown side, you'll see a beautiful mosaic by Raul Colon that depicts a meringue-dancing couple, a little girl skipping rope, and a little boy playing baseball.

On the street, every man seems to be wearing some team's colors—hey, there's a Cano jersey. Members of a girls' softball team wait for the light to change. On the southeast corner sits El Nuevo Caridad, officially billed as "Un Cuadrangular en Sabor" (A Home Run of Taste) and unofficially known as the best baseball restaurant in New York City. Where else can you find specials named after Juan Marichal, Manny Acta, Carlos Silva, and (Yankee equipment manager) Lou Cucuza? And, oh yes, Robinson Cano: *bistec, arroz, habichuelas, limonada, y* cheesecake for $19.

As the sun sets, the Mets wrap up a doubleheader sweep on the TVs and give way to the Yankees-Orioles game. Phil Hughes struggles, and so does the Yankee lineup against Jake Arrieta. But then in the bottom of the fifth, with the Yankees trailing 5–0, A-Rod leads off with a double. Heads turn and the conversation softens: Cano is up. He rips a double to deep left-center. *Tu viste lo que yo vie?* Did you see what I saw?

The Yankees go on to win 6–5. And we get to see what Cano goes on to do.

nine

The Oldest Living Yankee

J. R. MOEHRINGER

He had plenty of money but dressed like a bum. He had a keen mind and a prodigious vocabulary, but often went hours, even days, without speaking. He took early retirement from his job selling insurance and devoted his golden years to doing nothing. By which I mean nothing. On a typical morning, before lying down for his morning nap, which was only slightly shorter than his afternoon nap, he'd stroll a few times around his ramshackle house in Manhasset, Long Island, gazing blankly at the trees, the grass, the dog. Sloth was his habit, his hobby, the thing that made him Grandpa.

And then, some days, without warning or explanation, he'd be full of pep. Telling stories, joking, laughing. Sometimes he'd grab a mitt and play catch with me in the backyard, throwing better-than-average fastballs and dewdrop curves. Or else, just as unexpectedly, his random bursts of energy and extroversion might take a darker turn. He might thunder, rant, curse, heap abuse on the first person to cross his path, usually my poor grandmother.

I spent many hours of my childhood watching my grandfather,

studying him, wondering about his erratic behavior. After all that watching and studying and wondering, and even after writing about him in a memoir, I never really solved him, nor truly befriended him. He died fourteen years ago, at the start of spring training, and though I love him and miss him and think about him all the time, in my mind's eye he remains aloof, always just beyond my reach. I see him in his Yankees cap, standing on the front lawn, staring at the sky, and I wish I'd gone running up to him once and said—what? I don't know. Something. Anything that might have soothed him or pried him open or brought us closer.

Of course there were no such magic words. There never are. "The thing I might have said," the commonest of human regrets, is almost always illusory. But logical or not, whenever I think of my grandfather, that feeling is there. That sense of missed opportunity wavers at the edge of every memory, especially one, which involves the earliest years of the New York Yankees.

◆

The only consistent fact about my grandfather, the only thing that never changed throughout his life, was his love of baseball. He loved baseball with a purity and ardor I've never encountered in anyone else, and I've spent much of my life in stadiums, as a fan, and in locker rooms, as a journalist.

His failure to play in the big leagues, after starring in the semi-pros, was a permanent teaspoon of acid in the pit of his stomach. Shattered dreams of baseball glory caused his mood swings, or exacerbated them—and yet baseball still had hold of his heart. Baseball was the thing that got him out of bed in the morning, and it was the reason he rose from his naps. He followed the pennant races with religious fervor, pored over every box score, devoured every local sports page, watched every game, start to finish, Yankees and Mets, from his favorite chair, a lumpy old La-Z-Boy carefully positioned six feet from the living-room Zenith.

I loved baseball, too, because Grandpa did. If he'd loved demolition derby, I'd have ridden my Schwinn again and again into the side of the garage. If he'd been a duck hunter, I'd have painted decoys and practiced quacking. Dadless, lonely, I mimicked most men in my general vicinity, and I was frequently in the general vicinity of my mother's mercurial old man. When my mother and I couldn't afford our own apartment, we lived under Grandpa's roof. Even when we managed to be on our own, I spent half my time at Grandpa's. Before school I'd wait there for the bus. After school I'd wait there for my mother to finish work.

I was seven when I began lying at Grandpa's feet while he watched baseball on TV. But it wasn't enough to just be near him, to adopt his love of the game. I aped his rituals, kept to his schedule. Immediately after a Yankees game, Grandpa liked to watch WPIX Action News, with Jerry Girard on Sports. So I watched, too. Sometimes he'd watch the rerun of *The Odd Couple* that always followed the news. So I watched, too. When he couldn't sleep, Grandpa would gaze at an old episode of *The Honeymooners*. By the time I was ten, I could do a pretty fair Jackie Gleason.

I also absorbed his peculiar rooting argot.

"I'll be a son of a bitch!" he'd say when Bobby Murcer or Felipe Alou booted a ball.

"Son of a bitch," I'd say under my breath.

"He's a goddamn hitting fool!" Grandpa would say about any player—usually Thurman Munson—riding a hot streak.

"Goddamn hitting fool," I'd whisper to myself, practicing the phrase, as though learning a new language, which I was. Grandpa-ese was guttural, heavily accented, and sounded more warlike than Medieval German.

My grandfather's signature expression, which he'd roll out whenever the announcers made an observation with which he agreed, was: "Bet your ass."

Phil Rizzuto: *The Yankees look kind of sluggish tonight.*
Grandpa: *Bet your ass.*

When Grandpa deemed the observation especially trenchant, he'd spice up the phrase thusly:

Frank Messer: *If he walks one more batter, Virdon's going to pull him for the righty.*
Grandpa: *Bet your sweet ass.*

Often he'd use this phrase to put off, or put down, anyone who tried to interfere with his baseball rituals—again, usually my poor grandmother.

Grandma: *I was hoping to run the vacuum in here, are you going to be watching baseball all day?*
Grandpa: *Bet your sweet ass.*

I'll never forget the first time I tried to drop this phrase into casual conversation with my mother. She was not amused.

Once or twice a summer Grandpa would come downstairs and make an announcement. He was heading into "the city," twenty miles away, to take in a game. He said it with considerable self-regard, hands on his hips, the way Marco Polo must have announced his trips. After a nine-months-pregnant pause, he'd look down and ask if I wanted to come along. Talk about your rhetorical questions.

As with watching games on TV, there were strict rituals when journeying to Shea or the Bronx. We'd always drive Grandpa's dark blue Ford Pinto. We'd stash the Pinto a half mile from the ballpark, to avoid paying for parking. We'd walk at a brisk pace through sketchy neighborhoods, dodging junkies and drunks, often as the National Anthem began to play in the distance. We'd always buy the cheapest possible seats and stay in them until the final out. And we'd never buy a souvenir. No cap, no pennant, no T-shirt. Grandpa didn't believe in such frivolities.

He did, however, accept that growing boys need to eat. As the hot-dog man or soda man drew near, he'd say reluctantly, "Want anything?" My stomach would answer with a crowd-like roar before I did. No matter how sharp my hunger, I'd never independently ask for food. That kind of impertinence would have been unthinkable. I'd have sooner run onto the field and tackled the batter.

The most thrilling part of every baseball outing with my grandfather was the conversation. A ballpark brought out the best in him. The smells and sounds of a game gentled his spirit, made him almost engaging. This wasn't the manic, one-sided affability he sometimes exhibited at home; this was solid, give-and-take conversation, or something like it. For a worshipful grandson, therefore, live baseball came to equal live connection—all the more precious because it was so fleeting.

After the game Grandpa and I would walk back to the Pinto, through the same sketchy streets, now pitch-dark and much sketchier. Excited, wired, sure that we were about to get mugged, I'd talk and talk about nothing, and Grandpa wouldn't answer. He'd be reverting to his default mode, the brooding, Byronic figure. Hands clasped behind his back, eyes on the pavement, he seemed to be replaying the game in his mind, or else replaying his life, imagining what it might have been like if he'd been a Yankee or a Met.

Despite all the great players we saw, all the baseball history we witnessed, those many games I attended with Grandpa have run together in my mind, forming a vast, watery baseball Monet. Only a few stand apart, in particular a meaningless contest between the Yankees and the Milwaukee Brewers, which grows more meaningful the older I get.

It was 1976. I was eleven. Our seats were a little worse than usual, in the *upper* nosebleeds. My grandfather was on my left, and on his left was a man who looked like he'd escaped from a Grimm fairy tale. He wasn't merely old, but Paleolithic, and fragile as a twig. Despite having fewer teeth than hairs, he was loudly working his way through a bag of peanuts, which made me hungry. He was also talking nonstop to Grandpa, which made me furious. I expected Grandpa to be equally annoyed, to repel this decrepit intruder. Instead Grandpa was charmed. In the second or third inning I saw Grandpa sit up straighter, turn slowly to the man, and declare: "I'll be a son of a bitch! You played—*for the Yankees*?"

"I did," the man said. "In fact, I'm the oldest *living* Yankee."

The man mentioned the name of a Yankee who'd recently passed, bequeathing to him the Oldest Living title. All at once Grandpa forgot about the game taking place several miles below us. He forgot about the Yankees, the Brewers, and me. He turned to face the man and began bombarding him with questions, rattling off the names of long-dead Yankees, hoping the man might have known them, played with them. Indeed, the man knew each name Grandpa threw out, and he had a story to go with it.

I thought my grandfather might hyperventilate. This man had lived his fondest dream. This man had worn the hallowed pinstripes. This man had sped around the bases of Yankee Stadium, had dug his cleats into the same sacred batter's box that once held Babe Ruth, and now fate had seated this man on my grandfather's left. Though he was seventy that day, Grandpa's face was pure boy. His cheeks were pink, and his eyes—I never saw them so clear. At one point, as the Oldest Living Yankee paused to brush peanut shells from his lap, Grandpa turned and clapped a hand on my shoulder. "Say! This is my grandson. He loves baseball, too, although I think he's more a Mets fan."

"No one's perfect," the Oldest Living Yankee said.

Grandpa turned to me. "Do you know that we are in the presence of greatness? This gentleman is the Oldest Living Yankee!"

I smiled vaguely and gave the man's hand a weak shake, then turned back to the game, cursing his existence. Because of this man I was starving. Hot-dog men and soda men were passing by, a Macy's Parade of food, and Grandpa, bewitched by his new friend, was failing to notice. Worse, because of this man I was being robbed of my semiannual conversation with my grandfather. I was so disappointed, so irked, I snubbed the Oldest Living Yankee, forgot his name the second I heard it.

And now it's gone, always just beyond my reach.

I know a few things about him. He was probably in his late eighties that day, meaning he was probably born in the late 1880s. He couldn't have been born later than 1895: the first Yankee team took the field, as the Yankees, in 1913, and if he was with them that day he must have been at least eighteen. No matter what year he was born, he almost certainly played for the Yankees during that cusp era, that somnolent Dark Age before the Dawn of Ruth.

Still, that era wasn't as sleepy as people think. Back when fans were "bugs" and fastballs were "hoppers," the Yankees were replete with outsize characters, and the Oldest Living Yankee must have known them all. He must have known Wally Pipp—born February 17, 1893—who in 1916 became the first Yankee to lead the American League in homers. (It was the dead-ball era, so his winning total was a whopping 12.) Most fans know Pipp as the unluckiest man on the face of the earth; he complained of a headache on June 2, 1925, and was replaced in the lineup by Lou Gehrig. Few know that Pipp discovered young Gehrig when he was a stud at Columbia, and pushed the Yankees to sign him. Even fewer know that Pipp, after retiring, became one of the first writers for a brand-new magazine, *Sports Illustrated*.

The Oldest Living Yankee might have had a wealth of stories about Pipp, or about Muddy Ruel—born February 20, 1896— one of the most interesting catchers in Yankees history. After playing for New York from 1917 to 1920, Ruel went to Boston, then Washington, where he helped jump-start the career of his boyhood idol, fireballer Walter Johnson. The two became great friends, and when Johnson died in 1946, Ruel was one of the pallbearers. In his free hours and off-seasons Ruel attended law school and became the first professional baseball player admitted to practice before the U.S. Supreme Court. But that wasn't his strongest claim on history. Not by a long shot. It was Ruel behind the plate that dreadful day in August 1920, when Carl Mays came up and in, beaning Ray Chapman, who died the next day. The only major leaguer ever killed by a pitch.

Speaking of Chapman, when the Indians made him their starting shortstop, they shipped steady, reliable Roger Peckinpaugh to the Yankees. The Oldest Living Yankee might have known Peckinpaugh, might have ached for him when he moved on to the Senators and committed eight errors in the 1925 World Series, giving Pittsburgh the championship. Hell, the Oldest Living Yankee might have *been* Peckinpaugh, who died in 1977.

The Oldest Living Yankee might have gotten in a few hands of gin rummy on the Pullman to Cleveland with King Cole—born April 15, 1886—who was reportedly the model for Ring Lardner's fictional scamp, Alibi Ike. He undoubtedly knew Ping Bodie—born October 8, 1887—the presumed model for Lardner's other classic hero, Jack Keefe, from the comic novel *You Know Me Al*. Bodie, whose nickname referred to the musical sound his massive bat made when it struck the ball sweetly, was also called "the Wonderful Bop," the best baseball nickname I've yet come across. Straddling two eras, Bodie hung on with the Yankees long enough to become Ruth's first roommate. Easy gig, since Ruth never met a curfew he didn't ignore. "I room," Bodie said, "with his suitcase."

On those rare occasions when Ruth was present, he and Bodie must have talked a lot about food. Bodie could eat. In 1919, in Florida, he took part in a surreal spaghetti-eating contest. His opponent: a gluttonous ostrich named Percy. Bodie won when Percy's goggle eyes rolled up into his head during his eleventh plate of pasta, and he fell onto his knobby knees, beak smacking the canvas.

I wonder if the Oldest Living Yankee told that story to Grandpa. I did hear them, at one point, laughing it up.

After the game, as we left the Stadium, I said nothing. I was hungry, my feelings were hurt, so I gave Grandpa a dose of his own medicine. Silence. He, on the other hand, wouldn't shut up. It was Oldest Living Yankee this, Oldest Living Yankee that. I didn't listen. I couldn't. I blocked out the name of the Oldest Living Yankee, along with all his stories, and now in my sub-conscious he's melded with my grandfather, a mirror image, an equally unsolvable riddle. I'll never know the true identity of the Oldest Living Yankee, just as I'll never know the true identity of my grandfather. On that day at Yankee Stadium I see two mystery men seated to my left. I know less, will always know less, about either of them than I know about Pipp and Ruel and Bodie, et al.

I suppose I could find out. I could spend a few hours on Baseballreference.com, look up every Yankee, see which ones were born after 1895, which ones were alive in 1976, whittle the list to a logical few, a likely one or two. And someday I might do that.

But for now I don't really want to know.

Knowledge is power, yes, except when it isn't, except when knowing something would spoil a few soothing illusions. I say my grandfather was dark and moody because of his bitterness about never playing pro ball. Maybe. That's one theory. It's my theory. I'd rather think that shattered dreams were the cause of Grandpa's moods. I'd rather think there was some romantic gran-deur at his core, not merely coldness, eccentricity, a chemical imbalance, or some mix of the three. So long as I don't know definitively who the Oldest Living Yankee was, he might have been anybody, he might have played against anybody, alongside anybody, might have known any legendary figure I care to name from the 1910s or 1920s or 1930s. The possibilities are limitless, so long as I don't think too hard, dig too deep, and the same goes for my grandfather. Had he been able to hit a curve, had he been swifter on the base paths, had his arm been a bit livelier, it would have been him telling those stories to some man from Long Is-land, him reminiscing about all those old-timers, him annoying some sourpuss kid.

Baseball, which feeds our desire for numbers and facts and

statistical minutiae, also indulges our need to mythologize. As spring arrives, as Opening Day nears, it's a time for promise and hope. Let autumn worry about reality; let winter have the truth. My grandfather didn't become the man he wanted to be, and he may not have always been the grandfather I needed him to be. But when I remember that summer day in 1976, does he always remain the man I choose him to be?

Bet your sweet ass.

◀ *ten* ▶

Billion-Dollar Baby

JAMES SUROWIECKI

When you think about the New York Yankees today, two things come immediately to mind: winning and money. And that's the way it's been for most of the team's history—back in 1950, the great L.A. sportswriter Jim Murray wrote an article for *Life* magazine lamenting the Yankees' already-long-standing hegemony over the game and explaining it in terms that sound very familiar: "The Yankees traditionally dominate baseball by sheer economic might." But while that history makes it easy to take the Yankees' current success for granted (that is, the Yankees are supposedly rich and successful because they've always been rich and successful), the curious reality is that forty years ago, when a George Steinbrenner–led consortium bought the Yankees from CBS, the team was neither winning nor making money. In fact, it looked like a dog of a franchise.

In 1973, the Yankees hadn't been to the World Series since 1964. They'd had four losing seasons in the previous eight years. Attendance had fallen to less than half of what it had been in the late 1940s. And William Paley, the boss of CBS, was so weary of putting money into the team that he sold it for less than he'd paid for it nine years earlier, letting Steinbrenner snap up the franchise for a mere $10 million. Looking at the Yankees then, it was hard to see much economic might. Yet by the time Steinbrenner died in 2010, the team alone (not even including the enormously valuable YES Network) was worth well over $1.5 billion. In other words, over the last four decades, the value of the Yankees has risen better than a hundredfold. Steinbrenner was a notoriously fickle, erratic, and seemingly shortsighted boss. Yet during his tenure, the Yankees not only reclaimed their familiar position at the top of the league but also became arguably the most valuable franchise in American sports.

So how did this happen? The team had, of course, enormous built-in advantages. The Yankees play in the country's biggest media market, in an industry that carefully restricts competition and therefore protects teams' profits. (Consider that in 2010–2011, there were five London teams in the Premier League, while for the last fifty years, there have only been two New York teams in the majors.) Baseball has no salary cap and only limited revenue-sharing, which makes it easier for teams with bigger budgets to use their money to greater effect. And Steinbrenner had great timing, too. Not long before he bought the team, New York City had invested $100 million in rejuvenating Yankee Stadium. The advent of free-agency meant that it was possible to rebuild teams quickly, if you were willing to spend the money. And most important, Steinbrenner bought the Yankees just in time to cash in on an enormous explosion in the revenue generated by professional sports, thanks largely to television. While baseball may no longer have the cultural dominance it once did, its national and local television contracts and its Internet arm (which now generates close to half a billion dollars a year) have made it a far more lucrative business than it once was. The pie, to put it simply, has gotten much bigger.

As the travails of the Mets and the Dodgers demonstrate, though, being a big-market team can't guarantee success on its own. More important, to call the Yankees "successful" doesn't really capture how well the franchise has done in the last fifteen years—what had been a moribund company when Steinbrenner took it over is now, according to *Forbes*'s rough estimates, worth almost 90 percent more than any other team in baseball. And while there's no gainsaying how flaky and irrational Steinbrenner could be (Bill Madden's biography of Steinbrenner is worth reading just for the descriptions of the Boss's myriad mystifying decisions and self-parodic rages), it's a mistake to think that the Yankees' financial success happened in spite of Steinbrenner. The truth is that for all his flaws, he was a singularly effective owner, and he helped drive one of the most effective turnarounds in American business history.

Of course, Steinbrenner's effectiveness had nothing to do with the part of the game that he was obsessed with—personnel decisions. In that area, he probably subtracted value from the team. Instead, Steinbrenner's real knack was for marketing, and the key to the Yankees' financial success during his tenure was that the team did an extraordinary job of reviving and then extracting as much value as possible from the Yankee brand. That process began, consciously or unconsciously, with Steinbrenner himself. In the early years in particular, his over-the-top spending on free agents was important not just because of the players it put on the field, but also because it helped transform the image of the franchise by demonstrating that the team would do whatever was necessary to win. These days, it seems implausible that the Yankees would have to demonstrate this. As Will Leitch writes in his book *Are We Winning?*, "The Yankees must dominate. That is the brand. If the Yankees aren't world conquerors, lording their financial and cultural superiority over the penny-pinching peons that make up the rest of baseball, then who are they? That's the New York way." But while this is a perfect description of the Yankees today, and would have been a perfect description of the Yankees between 1921 and the 1950s, it was not the way anyone would have written about the Yankees in the early 1970s. The familiar aura of dominance had been replaced by an aura of overpowering mediocrity and boredom— that's why it was called the Horace Clarke Era. And because CBS didn't really seem to care much about the Yankees, there seemed to be little prospect of that changing. What Steinbrenner's seemingly reckless spending did was alter this equation. Similarly, his endless histrionics, disruptive as they were to the team, guaranteed a steady flow of front-page headlines and helped make the Yankees news again. It's no coincidence that Yankee attendance nearly doubled between 1971 and 1976, even before the team went to the World Series for the first time in twelve years.

Still, the all-publicity-is-good-publicity approach could only have gone so far—and indeed, in the 1980s, Steinbrenner's antics on the personnel front did more harm to the franchise than good. Yet even as Steinbrenner was decimating the team on the field, he made a number of key moves off the field that helped transform the team's finances. In 1988, Steinbrenner decided to move the broadcasts of Yankee games from WPIX to the fledgling MSG network. This was hardly an obvious decision, since MSG was still struggling for viewers. But Steinbrenner recognized that MSG was desperate for summer programming, and that the Yankees would provide the network with instant legitimacy, and he used that leverage to sign a deal worth almost $500 million over twelve years. These days, that doesn't sound all that big, but at the time it was an immense amount of money, and really reshaped the economics of the regional-sports-network business (while also inflating the Yankees' coffers).

In 1998, Steinbrenner again broke new marketing ground when the Yankees signed a licensing deal with adidas for $95 million. This was the first-ever team-specific licensing deal—prior to it, major league baseball controlled the trademarks and licensing for all the teams. Steinbrenner simply ignored this arrangement, and when MLB tried to stop him, he sued it and every team in baseball. He got his way. And while the total amount of money was relatively small, it was a revenue stream that had previously not existed. (Not surprisingly, when the deal with adidas expired, the Yankees dumped adidas for Nike, in what one presumes was an even more lucrative arrangement.)

Aside from the actual dollars, the licensing deal was also important because it testified to the power of the Yankee brand. And a few years after that deal, Steinbrenner made a much more dramatic and lucrative move to exploit the Yankee name, leaving MSG and starting an entire cable network devoted primarily to the team. The YES Network, which debuted in 2002, is now the most valuable regional sports network in the country, which makes starting it seem like an obvious thing to have done. But at the time, the notion of starting a network from scratch (even in partnership with the New Jersey Nets and Goldman Sachs) seemed to many a risky and hubristic endeavor. Instead, it significantly increased the Yankees' television revenue and provided the team with a near-nonstop marketing platform. And while the Yankees technically don't own the network (a holding company instead owns the baseball team and YES), the close connection between the two meant that the success of one increased the value of the other.

Finally, of course, the Yankees built a new stadium, which brought with it a host of new ways to milk fans out of their money. And while the team, unlike many others, did end up paying for the stadium largely on its own, it did so with subsidized money, since the bonds it issued to pay for the stadium were guaranteed by the state, significantly holding down costs. This, too, one could argue, represented a kind of leveraging of the Yankee brand—by 2000, it would have been a brave New York politician who could have contemplated allowing the Yankees to leave the Bronx (even if that was an utterly implausible scenario). More to the point, the stadium itself, with its $2,000 box seats and $11 beers, was evidence of how the Yankees had been able to turn success on the field into profit off it. The team had raised ticket prices steadily over the years, which was a reasonable response to rising demand—in 2007 and 2008, the team drew more than 4 million fans. The new stadium was a logical, if extreme, extension of that process. In that 1950 article for *Life,* Jim Murray said the Yankees' biggest advantage was that they "had more fans paying more money than any other club in the history of the game." That was still true in 2010. The only difference was that the fans were shelling out far more money than Murray could ever have imagined.

Steinbrenner's genius (which longtime fans who've been priced out of the stadium might well call his evil genius) was, in other words, that he recognized the potential value of the Yankee brand and then set about turning that potential into reality. The best analogy to what he did for the Yankees, in fact, is probably what Michael Eisner did when he took over Disney in the 1980s. Hard as it may be to remember now, Disney at the time seemed like a dinosaur. It felt culturally irrelevant, its animation studio was struggling, and it was barely profitable. Eisner resurrected the animation division, which he saw as central to the brand. He invested heavily in theme parks and in marketing, both starting the Disney Channel and opening Disney stores. And he raised prices. The basic insight he and Steinbrenner shared was that for the right product, people were willing to spend more. You just had to ask for it.

Of course, that strategy only works if you're actually putting out a product that people want to see. But Steinbrenner's off-the-field innovations made it rational for the Yankees to spend enormous amounts of money to put the best possible team on the field, because the Yankees now had myriad ways to profit from its players, and from its success. If you own your own network, control your licensing rights, and can easily raise ticket prices, then going to the playoffs and World Series becomes much more lucrative. So, too, does the impact of superstar players—think, for instance, of how much extra money the Yankees made from Derek Jeter's pursuit of 3,000 hits. Playoff appearances typically generate tens of millions of dollars in revenue, keep attendance high, and are essential for keeping season ticket holders around—one of the reasons why people are willing to shell out tens of thousands of dollars for season tickets is so that they'll be guaranteed playoff seats. And that, in turn, makes it more rational to spend heavily even on players who might only get you an extra one or two wins, since the economic difference between winning, say, 94 games and winning 96 games could well be immense (unlike the difference between winning 80 games and 82 games, which is negligible). This doesn't mean that the Yankees haven't wasted huge sums of money over the last twenty years on players like Carl Pavano. But the evidence suggests that the team didn't overspend systematically—since the value of the franchise has continued to rise, that must mean that the Yankees have received more value from their players than they've paid out.

You might think that winning, or going to the playoffs, would be less important economically to the Yankees than to other franchises precisely because the Yankees win so much. But as industry analyst Vince Gennaro has shown, the striking thing about New York fans is that they punish failure, but they also reward success. They don't get bored with it or used to it. That means the Yankees have to keep winning, but it also means that if they do, they should continue to reap the benefits, with more success translating into more money, which, in turn, makes it easier to keep being successful. This is the virtuous circle that the Yankees have taken advantage of for most of their history.

Perpetuating that virtuous circle depends, of course, on winning. But it also depends on the willingness of the team's owners to take the long view, and to be willing to put up lots of money today in the hope of getting much more back down the line. And over the course of their history, one of the Yankees' great strengths has been that they've had owners who were willing and able to do just that. It's no surprise that the Yankees have regularly been among the most profitable teams in baseball. But what's striking is that the vast majority of those profits were poured right back into the team. This was true in the 1920s—during that decade, the Yankees were tremendously profitable, and yet their owners didn't take a penny in dividends—and it was true during the Steinbrenner Era. In fact, this is really the great paradox of the Yankees' rise to dominance over the past twenty years: Steinbrenner was often shortsighted and willful, and yet he ultimately was focused on the long run, recognizing that the way to make real money in sports is not by maximizing short-term profits but rather by investing in the long-term value of the franchise. The recipe for a billion-dollar franchise, in the end, isn't "Win, make money, win some more." It's "Win, make money, spend money, and win again." The Yankees have done just that for most of the past ninety years. And there's no obvious reason why they can't do it for the next ninety.

eleven

Media Babe

LEIGH MONTVILLE

The pictures would be on TMZ; that annoying host, whatever his name is, would ask his crew of annoying teenage gossip reporters what they had found in the field and, sure enough, one of them would present another report about Babe Ruth.

The video would be shaky, of course, taken by assorted cellphone cameras, but the leading man would be easy to recognize. Yes, there he was, the Babe, the Bambino, the Sultan of Swat. Yes, of course. He would be shown in all of his late-night glory at the site of yet another car crash, his newly banged-up exotic roadster pulled over to the side of, say, Riverside Drive, as police lights flashed in the background and papers were examined and maybe a request was made, you know, to recite the alphabet backward. Maybe a woman, name unknown, very pretty, dressed for the evening, would hide her face from the camera. Maybe the woman would not be his wife.

"Who's the babe, Babe?" the first late-arriving paparazzi would ask.

"Having a little trouble with that backward alphabet?" the second would ask. "The next letter is 'W.'"

"Where were you heading, this late at night, Babe?" the third would inquire. "Aren't you playing against the Indians tomorrow afternoon at the Stadium?"

The drumbeat of celebrity would never stop for the most famous athlete in the world if he were caught in this modern social media machine. Just the thought of George Herman Ruth unleashed today, on the up-to-the-moment, ever-present now—photographers and bloggers on his perpetual case, everything snapped, snipped, ATTACHED, laid out for public discussion, bemusement, and faux outrage. It is staggering. He would be on every night.

Bill O'Reilly: *You made more money than the president, Babe. What do you think about that?*
Bambino: *I had a better year than he did.*

BABE BLASTS BARACK

◆

More than sixty years have passed since the famed slugger of all sluggers died on August 16, 1948 (he actually made that comment about President Herbert Hoover in 1929), but the random daily events of his oversize life still could be stretched easily across any week's headlines in the supermarket tabloids, streamed across the bottom of the morning ESPN feed, recorded on YouTube, derided and defended on Twitter and Facebook. No man ever was more ahead of his celebrity time than the Babe was.

Before there was Tiger Woods' secret love life exposed, there was the Babe. Before there was LeBron James, using enormous physical talent as a bargaining chip with ownership, there was the Babe. Before there was Ben Roethlisberger, making a fool of himself . . . Before there was A-Rod . . . Before there was T.O. . . . Before there was Mike Tyson . . . Before there was Manny Being

Manny . . . Hell, before there was Lady Gaga and Lindsay Lohan and Charlie Sheen and, sure, Sarah Palin and the entire Kennedy family . . . Yes, there was the Babe. He was the model for whispers, shouts, and public hoo-ha. He was the full celebrity package.

Maybe baseball wasn't even broadcast on the radio when he started playing in 1914. Maybe television was mostly a rumor when he finished in 1935. He still set the standard. He was larger than ordinary life. He hit baseballs to places never before seen. (When he hit his record 54 home runs in 1920, his first year as a New York Yankee, that was more home runs than fourteen of the other fifteen *teams* hit.) He smoked cigars. Drank scotch. Drank anything! Wore raccoon coats and spats and those goofy little caps. Laughed. Danced. Sang with the band. Crashed cars. Kissed babies and strange women. Stayed in a different hotel from the rest of the team. Made twenty, thirty times the money most of his teammates did. Lived a different, celebrity-filled public life. Endorsed anything. Made headlines. Always made headlines.

The pieces fit. He was in New York, New York, the home base of all media. Perfect! He was a winner, a talent, plus he was a truly outrageous personality. Perfect! His face and body, though not beautiful, were distinctive, recognizable, a photographer's dream. His comments, though not deep, were eminently quotable. His activity was constant and borderline scandalous. He was a story possibility every time he stepped outside his front door, ready for fun, unafraid of consequences. He seemed to live his life in a constant jam.

Would he have fit onto the modern stage? Oh, yes, he would. He would have commanded that stage. Or at least the back pages of the *New York Post* and the *Daily News*.

"Here's a story from Florida," Brian Williams says from the set of the NBC Nightly News. "In the midst of hard economic times, raging unemployment, skyrocketing gas prices, one financial constant remains: Mr. George Herman Ruth announced today that he will require an ungodly amount of money for his services on the baseball diamond in the coming year . . ."

A fine indication of the man's pop-culture stature came in a poll conducted in March 1933, toward the end of his career. The Depression had hit, had hit hard by now, and the Babe was in the news as he went through the last of many protracted salary battles with Colonel Jake Ruppert and the management of the New York Yankees. Salaries were being sliced everywhere—the salary of Judge Kenesaw Mountain Landis, the commissioner of baseball, had been dropped $10,000 to $40,000; the salary of Yankees teammate Lou Gehrig, coming off a season in which he hit .349, with 34 homers and 151 RBIs, from $27,500 to $22,500—and there was agreement everywhere that Ruth's salary also should be sliced. The question was: By how much?

Adjutant Andrew Laurie decided to take a poll at the Gold Dust Lodge, a shelter run by the Salvation Army in Manhattan, which housed and fed more than two thousand homeless, jobless, destitute men. The Babe was fighting a major reduction in his previous salary of $75,000. Laurie asked his clients how much the star of stars' new salary should be.

More than half of the men responded, 1,171 votes tallied. The Babe's salary, the men decided, should be $43,999, but the votes varied wildly. One man said the Babe should work for free. Another said he should be paid the unimaginable sum of a million dollars per year to play baseball.

Two years earlier, Ruth's salary had been $80,000, the highest figure he would ever make. The poll asked if *anyone* should make $80,000 per year. This vote was close: 599 men said no, 572 said yes. Auld then asked the 572 men who said yes who that man making $80,000 should be. This was the most interesting vote of all.

The winner was any president of the United States, with 185 votes. Second was the Babe with 140 votes. President Franklin Roosevelt was third with 135 votes, and then the list dropped all the way to former New York governor Al Smith at 12 votes. Albert Einstein, William Randolph Hearst, Gene Tunney, Tom Mix, Enrico Caruso, Thomas Edison, Walter Winchell, John D.

Rockefeller, and Lou Gehrig were relegated to a group that received 2 votes or 1. No woman received a single vote.

The average pre-Depression salary of the 1,171 voters had been $49 per week. The cost for keeping each man in the shelter, two meals per day, was $1 per week. The Babe signed his contract for $52,000 for the 1933 season two days after the poll was announced. This was a $23,000 pay cut, but still a grand figure considering the times.

Seventeen days earlier, President Roosevelt had declared a bank holiday, simply to save the remaining banks in the country.

"If you weren't around in those times, I don't think you could appreciate what a figure the Babe was," Richards Vidmer, baseball writer for the *New York Times,* once said. "He was bigger than the president. One time, coming north, we stopped at a little town in Illinois, a whistle-stop. It was about ten o'clock at night, raining like hell. The train stopped to get water or something. It couldn't have been a town of more than five thousand people, and by God, there were four thousand of them down there standing in the rain, just wanting to see the Babe.

"Babe and I and two other guys were playing bridge. Babe was sitting next to the window. A woman with a little baby in her arms came up and started peering at the Babe. She was rather good-looking. Babe looked at her and kept on playing bridge. Then he looked at her again and finally he leaned out and said, 'Better get away from here, lady. I'll put one on the other arm.'"

That was our boy.

Whoopi Goldberg: *What do you think about this Babe Ruth?*
Barbara Walters: *A troubled soul.*
Elizabeth Hasselback: *Somebody should have given him a good spanking a long time ago.*

He was fallible. That was what the public liked about him. He was overpowering on the field, a colossus, an amazement, but he was human off the field. Human? He was hyper-human, a caricature of what human should be, lows and highs and all intermediate sensations multiplied, forever the kid from the orphanage in Baltimore let loose in a fast and exciting world. He traveled from jackpot to jackpot, always apologizing in the end for his mistakes.

An example. His season in 1925 was a low point. The fast life seemed to lay him low. His statistics took a sudden dip—a .290 average, 25 homers, 66 runs batted in—as he piled up a string of embarrassments. He became sick in spring training, said it was a touch of the flu, but his teammates thought the problem was venereal disease. None of them would shower with him. None would touch his towel.

He came back to the lineup, let a bloop to right field drop, had a fight with starting pitcher Waite Hoyt in the clubhouse. The Yankees, worried about his conduct on the road, hired a private detective to trail him. The private detective reported that in one night in Chicago the Babe had been with six different women. He was suspended. He fought with the baseball commissioner. He fought with manager Miller Huggins. He said he was sorry. The press staked out his home and the home of his mistress. He hit 10 home runs in the final 29 games of the season. Just for spite.

"Babe Ruth has the mind of a fifteen-year-old," American League president Ban Johnson said in the midst of it all.

BABE RUTH MAD, DENIES ORGIES, a headline in the *Chicago Tribune* read.

Good stuff.

"I have been a Babe and a Boob," he told Joe Whitworth, a writer from *Collier's* magazine, as he laid out his plans for a return to baseball glory after the season ended. "And I am through—through with the pests and the good-time guys. Between them and a few crooks I have thrown away over a quarter million dollars."

He estimated he had roared through $500,000 in gambling, bad business deals, and high living. He said he once had worn twenty-two new shirts during three hot days in St. Louis, then left them for the maid. He was going to make amends now. He had hired a personal trainer, Artie McGovern. Artie also trained Wall Street executives, playwrights, and John Phillip Sousa. More good stuff.

The *Daily News,* which began operation in 1920, the year Ruth was traded to New York, was so in love with his many deeds and misdeeds that it assigned a special reporter to cover the man during the entire season and much of the off-season. The reporter, Marshall Hunt, a Tacoma, Washington, native, back from World War I, wound up following his man through paternity suits, bowling alleys, great numbers of speakeasies, assorted whorehouses, Hollywood movie sets, the mysterious death of a first wife, the marriage to a showgirl second wife, golf courses, and, oh, yes, a number of baseball games.

The pace was hard. Hunt's career at the *News* ended before Ruth's career with the Yankees. Hunt was an alcoholic.

"We'd play golf every morning," the reporter said about the times he'd go to Hot Springs, Arkansas, to cover the Babe's preparations for spring training. "Then we'd tire of the food at the hotel and I'd hire a car and then we'd go out in the country looking for farmhouses that said 'Chicken Dinners.' What the Babe really wanted was a good chicken-dinner-and-daughter combination and it worked out that way more often than you would think."

The possibilities for stories never stopped. One rival reporter said he saw Ruth drain a bottle filled with whiskey in one gulp. Another reporter said he saw him order eighteen hot dogs from the porter on a train. Ruth offered the dogs to his teammates, but everyone else seemed to be full. Ruth ate all eighteen by himself. Waite Hoyt, the Yankees' pitcher, later a broadcaster, said that Ruth routinely made bets on horse races from the clubhouse. He called bookies on the clubhouse phone.

He once spent a day in jail for speeding, yes, on Riverside Drive. He was driving at a heedless twenty-six miles per hour in a twelve-cylinder that sounded like a fuel-burning calliope when it went down the street. He sat down to size up the electric chair when the Yankees went to Sing Sing prison for a day. He asked Tony Lazzeri "who the wops were voting for" at a rally for Al Smith. Tony said the wops were voting for Al.

There were fistfights with teammates. (The one with Hoyt was not unusual.) There were fistfights with opposing players. There were fistfights with fans. There was a called shot in Chicago. There was an embarrassing end to a World Series in 1926, last out of the last game, Ruth thrown out attempting to steal second base. There was always something.

"Nobody with the Yankee club seems to know much about Babe's unofficial activities," sportswriter Westbrook Pegler wrote. "He runs alone and where he runs or what he does are matters of no interest whatsoever so long as he shows up at the yard no later than 1:30 P.M.—and hits home runs."

This might have been another first—the first definition of a superstar in American sport.

@baberuth
Torpedo of Truth tour continues tonight! Listen to me sing! Hear me talk! Hang around, share a libation! See the man who's in the news!

He was everywhere. That was another factor in his popularity. Not content with his salary from the Yankees, he doubled and tripled his income off the field. He was a businessman. He was a self-promoter.

He and Gehrig or some other Bronx Bomber took off on assorted barnstorming tours as soon as the regular season ended, went up and down the Northeast states, across the entire country more than once. Ruth probably played against more town teams, batted against more local hotshots and half-ass politicians than any professional baseball player who ever lived. He played against black teams, white teams, played in Cuba, played in Japan, tried cricket in England. He was in vaudeville shows during assorted winters, said his lines, sang a little, strummed a ukulele. He was in movies when they were silent, was in them again when they had speaking parts.

He had a business manager named Christy Walsh, now pretty much considered the first sports agent, the inventor of that position. Walsh won the job when he went to New York in 1921, posed as a beer deliveryman to gain access to the Babe's apartment at the Ansonia Hotel, and convinced him of the need for representation. Walsh's first business deal set up a nationally syndicated newspaper column for his client, ghostwritten, of course, and the partnership expanded from there.

In a letter to Ed Hughes of the *New York Telegram and Sun,* Walsh detailed a tour that Ruth took with outfielder Bob Meusel at the end of the 1924 season. The tour began on October 11, the day after the completion of the World Series Ruth "covered" between the Washington Senators and the New York Giants, and ended on December 6, when he returned to New York from Los Angeles. These were the highlights as reported by Walsh:

The Babe covered 8,500 miles on the trip.

He played in 15 cities in 6 states.

He got 17 home runs in 15 games.

He drew 125,000 people. The games were under the auspices of a leading newspaper in each city, with the backing of one of the following organizations—Elks, Knights of Columbus, or American Legion.

He made 22 speeches at breakfasts, luncheons, dinners, and banquets given in his honor. Seven were given from Pullman platforms.

He rode 250 miles on a locomotive through Montana.

He autographed nearly 5,000 baseballs. He autographed 1,800 baseballs for the San Francisco Examiner *alone—all of which were sold for charity.*

He headed 4 parades, accompanied by mayors and city officials.

He wore his dinner coat 19 times and complained of so few opportu-

nities. Two years ago he considered dinner coats things to be avoided. He wore a silk hat once. (Under protest.) Someone told him he looked good in it, so then he bought it.

He refereed a four-round bout in Hollywood, California. And was presented with a wristwatch by the American Legion. He appreciated the watch, but feared other players would make unkind remarks.

He batted 1,000 autographed baseballs to 10,000 Los Angeles schoolboys and later nearly fell off the roof of the grandstand.

He beat Douglas Fairbanks in a game of "Doug." (Similar to tennis.) Fairbanks had previously beaten (Bill) Tilden.

The railroads refused to take his money for food. The hotels gave him rooms for nothing.

He was Jack Dempsey's guest in Los Angeles.

He drove a golf ball 353 yards, breaking the course record at Rancho Golf Club, Los Angeles.

He visited 18 hospitals and orphan asylums.

He posed for nearly 250 photos in every city. Total, 3,750.

He struck out twice with three men on base.

He failed to get a home run at Tacoma, Kansas City, Stockton, Los Angeles, or San Diego.

But he got 17 home runs at Altoona, Minneapolis, Spokane, Seattle, Portland, Dunsmuir (California), San Francisco, Santa Barbara, Oakland, and Fullerton.

He and Bob Meusel always played on opposite teams. His team won 15 games. Meusel's won none.

He ate 4 steaks at one meal.

He talked over the radio at San Francisco for 12 minutes before he knew he was being "framed."

He refused to wear a nightgown or pajamas at any time on the trip—despite continued protests of Walsh and Meusel. He later was presented with a big red flannel nightgown at a public luncheon at the Biltmore, Los Angeles.

He established distance records for batted balls at 5 ballparks. He was the first left-hander to drive a ball over the left-field fence at San

Francisco. He was the first player who ever drove a ball over the wall at Kansas City. He drove a ball to the top of a fir tree at Dunsmuir (California), a distance of 604 feet and 5 inches (measured by a surveyor).

He was made a life member of the Lions Club at Dunsmuir and started a Christmas fund, which has since reached $900. (Dunsmuir is a few miles from Mount Shasta. Population less than 5,000.)

The last game was in the smallest city—Brea, near Fuller-ton, California. This is Walter Johnson's boyhood home. Johnson pitched. Ruth also pitched—his first full nine-inning game in seven years. Ruth beat Johnson, 9 to 1. Ruth got 2 home runs. Johnson's team got but 4 hits and no runs until the ninth inning. Other batters against Ruth's pitching were Ken Williams, Ernie Johnson, Jimmy Austin, and Meusel and Walter Johnson. Population, 3,500; at-tendance, 15,000.

After the final game, October 31, Ruth played at a Los Angeles theater.

He is about 10 pounds overweight, but otherwise in fine condi-tion.

Stop the presses.

TONIGHT'S TV HIGHLIGHT—Will the Babe survive on Dancing with the Stars? Watch as the Bambino, the Big Bam, the Caliph of Clout goes head to head with Cloris Leachman, Kirstie Alley, Ralph Macchio, Hines Ward, Sugar Ray Leonard, Lance Bass, Kristi Yamaguchi, Donny Osmond, Bristol Palin, Joey Mc-Intyre, Warren Sapp, Hélio Castroneves, Apolo Anton Ohno, Drew Lachey, Belinda Carlisle, Penn Jillette, Li'l Kim . . .

So when somebody famous does something stupid or outra-geous late at night in public . . .

So when somebody else is both a SportsCenter highlight and a SportsCenter lowlight in the same day . . .

So when you get on that familiar rant about how the athletes of today are overpaid, overloved, overindulged, flat-out over-the-top . . .

Remember the Babe. Remember well.

He was there first.

Mickey Mantle had prodigious power from both sides of the plate, but he launched his most memorable tape-measure homers from the left.
ART RICKERBY/SPORTS ILLUSTRATED/GETTY IMAGES

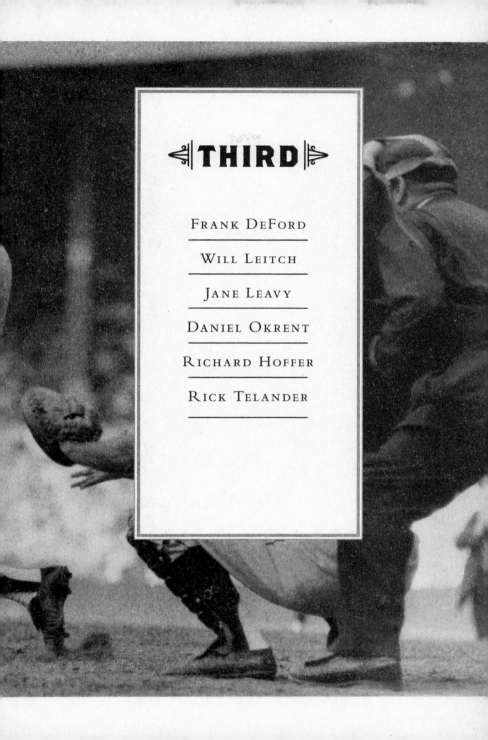

◁|THIRD|▷

FRANK DeFORD

WILL LEITCH

JANE LEAVY

DANIEL OKRENT

RICHARD HOFFER

RICK TELANDER

◄‖ *twelve* ‖►

A Baltimore Chop

FRANK DEFORD

Next to Satan and dream sequences in movies and calves' liver, I dislike the New York Yankees the most. Actually, "dislike" is probably too nice a word, because unlike Satan and dream sequences and calves' liver, the Yankees are elemental to my world, always around me, part of the air I breathe, the magnetic north on my GPS.

I did, you see, depart Baltimore, city of my salad days, land of the poor but honest Orioles, nature's noblemen, to go live in the New York metropolitan area, Greater Yankeeland. I have been there now for half a century. And counting. I love New York. I defend it to the teeth. In fact, I like just about everything about New York *except* the Yankees. It is like living in Vatican City and liking everything about the place but the Roman Catholics.

But it has made me a stronger, better person, for I know that I am a finer slice of humanity than the Yankee fans who abut and surround me. It is worse, I think, to cheer for a bully than to be ordained one. The Yankees are inherently a bully. They can't help what Beelzebub made them. Even dear Derek Jeter, who will surely be played in his bio-flick by Albert Schweitzer, didn't have a choice; he was *drafted* by the Yankees. But Yankee fans *choose* to be admirers of the ghouls in pinstripes.

Here, in no particular order, are some of the things that occur to me right now, at this random moment in time, that I happen to dislike about the Yankees:

◆ *That their manager wears the number of championships they have won on his back, with plans to change it when (not if, but when) they win again. That is so gross.*

◆ *That they're not content to just play the National Anthem at the start of the game, but also play "God Bless America" instead of "Take Me Out to the Ball Game" during the seventh-inning stretch. The Yankees don't fool me. They want you to think America = Yankees. "In a pig's eye," I say.*

◆ *George Steinbrenner. His plaque. His aura. Him. All of him. And any suggestion that he should go into the hallowed National Pastime shrine, the Hall of Fame. Ye, let the doors swing wide open for the steroid sons of bitches first.*

◆ *The Yankee mascot. Fooled ya. Yeah, I know. The Yankees don't have a mascot. They're too good for mascots. There's no crying in baseball and no laughing in Yankee Stadium.*

Okay, that's enough for now. Find and push my app tomorrow for more and different vivid examples of ugly, detestable things about your New York Yankees.

Wasn't it typical the way Yankee fans carried on about the late Bob Sheppard? I mean a nice man, yes. He went to mass every day, which is a lot more than you can say about most godless Yankee fans, but all he was was a lousy lineup announcer. All he ever said was: "Now batting, number 13, Alex Rodriquez. Rodriquez." And Yankee fans had it that he was John Gielgud.

For Christ's sweet sake.

And just for the record, I never liked that mealy-mouthed Mel Allen, either.

But, of course, everything about the Yankees has to be special. Even the guy who reads the lineups. Old-Timers' Day. Yogi Berraisms. The pinstripes. The frieze. Kiss my ass, the Yankee Stadium frieze.

The Yes Network. No.

And what ever got into Billy Crystal? Talk about drinking the Kool-Aid.

Even worse, why in the world did Paul Simon ask where that cold fish of a human being, Joe DiMaggio, had gone to? Hey, where had Fred Astaire gone? Jimmy Stewart—where did he go? Doris Day: I want to know where she is. Peggy Fleming, Arthur Godfrey, Lena Horne, Alben Barkley, Red Grange, Ferrante and Teicher—there are so many other nicer has-beens you wonder where they've gone, and that creepy little Paul Simon has us brood over a goddamn sourpuss Yankee. I swear, sometimes you think it's gotta be a conspiracy.

And all the Yankees do is: they just buy everything. The Yankees. Overpay. Hey, push comes to shove, all they are is, they're vulgar wastrels. Bottom line: Why would anyone admire smug rich people who are suckers? But, though it breaks my pure heart, I actually personally know many good and true of my Tri-State-area neighbors who otherwise profess to believe in fair play, equal justice for all, and (get this) A LEVEL PLAYING FIELD, but who still root for the Yankees. How do they look at their two faces in the mirror?

So now, to honor America, let's all cheer for the boys in pinstripes.

Yeah, a Bronx Cheer.

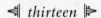

thirteen

An Innocent Abroad

WILL LEITCH

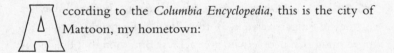ccording to the *Columbia Encyclopedia*, this is the city of Mattoon, my hometown:

> *Mattoon . . . (1990 pop. 18,441), Coles co., E central Ill.; inc. 1859. It is a processing, rail, and industrial center for a farming region. Among its manufactures are road-building equipment, paper and brass products, and springs. Nearby are many oil wells, a fish hatchery, and Paradise Lake. The farm and grave of Abraham Lincoln's father and stepmother are southeast of the city.*

Mattoon is the bagel capital of the world. This might seem curious, since, well, no one in Mattoon eats bagels, and I don't think we've had a Jewish family since the turn of the nineteenth century. But in 1990, Lender's Bagels, a huge company now owned by the Kraft Foods conglomerate, decided to move its central production facility to Mattoon. That created about a thousand new jobs, but more important, it made Mattoon the city that produced more bagels per day than any other in America.

Murray Lender himself came to town and made the announcement, and the mayor—who, in her time away from the office, was a cashier at the Mister Donut shop right off Charleston Avenue—proclaimed that August afternoon as Official Bagel Day in Mattoon. From then on, every August, Mattoon has hosted Bagelfest, a three-day celebration of the city's leading industry. On Friday, the carnival set up on the main drag, Broadway Avenue. There was a mini–Ferris wheel, a ridiculously dangerous Tilt-a-Whirl, and a dunking booth where you could drench local celebrities (high school principal, sports columnist, guy who runs the bar over at the Eagles club). My sister once entered the Little Miss Bagelfest contest, where eight-year-old JonBenét Ramsey wannabes paraded around in sashes and had their self-esteem properly trounced. This was the biggest weekend every year, the only time we could ever claim to be a tourist attraction. Every Bagelfest Saturday, I would awake at 6 A.M. and enter the Ride Around Mattoon for a Bagel contest, a twenty-five-mile bike ride beyond the city limits. Halfway through, you were rewarded with a bagel. At the end, they gave you a bagel. Then you went downtown, where you got free bagels.

Mattoon is tradition, history, comfort. We have one high school, aptly named Mattoon High School. We have about fifteen churches, all Christian, only one wild enough to be Catholic, a religion seen as dangerous and rebellious by most of the Protestant town. We have two drive-through liquor stores. We have a lake, Lake Mattoon. We have a big park, Peterson Park, where the high school baseball team and the local American Legion team play. Every Christmas the park district lights it up, spending half the county budget, and teenagers sneak over there to make out once the lights are shut off.

We have a police department, one fire station, a hospital we share with county rival Charleston. We have a Hardee's, a Mc-

Donald's, a Kentucky Fried Chicken, an Arby's, and a Burger King, but not a chain Burger King. We have the original Burger King, established before the Whopper was even imagined; because of this, no Burger King franchises can be located within thirty miles of the city limits. I'd never been inside another Burger King until college.

We have a bar where I can find half of my graduating class on any given weeknight. We have a house-cleaning service called Rent-A-Wife. We have three houses that are rumored to be haunted. We have a crazy old lady who spray-paints curses about her ex-husband on her front door. We have three trailer parks. We often are hit by tornadoes. We have three Mexican restaurants. We have one Chinese restaurant, where none of the people who work are Chinese, though one might be Korean.

We have a newspaper publisher, who has been in charge for thirty years. We have a school board that once fired my scholastic bowl coach because he was gay. We have a section of town littered with crosses, "each one representing a baby killed by its mother."

This is Mattoon, and we never change. We always think of ourselves as the underdog in everything we do. We grouse about the mainstream media, we think nothing in popular culture conveys our belief system, other than maybe *American Idol,* and we hate that every time we want to watch a game on ESPN, it's the damned Yankees vs. the damned Red Sox. We hate the East Coast bias. We are the opposite of exceptionalists. We are about our family, our loved ones, our God, and the rest of the world can take care of itself without us bothering them, or them bothering us. To each his or her proverbial own.

◆

I left Mattoon and moved to New York City in January 2000, not because I was particularly enamored of New York City but because I was a writer, and New York offers a few more employment opportunities for a writer than Mattoon does. The main appeal to me, though, was being able to meet other people who were searchers, artists, restless dreamers. All I knew about New Yorkers I learned from Woody Allen movies: I imagined everywhere I went, there would be conversations about the newest issue of the *New Yorker,* global politics, everyone smoking cloves and wearing berets, debating whether or not *Immanuel Kant's Faculty of the Understanding* allows for objective reasoning outside of one's perspective on the imperative.

I thought all of New York would be like this. And as a baseball fan, I was particularly eager to see Yankee Stadium, which I envisioned as a cavalcade of baseball intellect, distinguished gentlemen wearing tweed and smoking pipes and discussing the eternal nature of spring. They might also have a monocle.

My first game, as it turned out, was a playoff game against the Red Sox in 2003. The psychology of Yankees fans was fascinating to me. When the Yankees fell behind, no one was concerned about losing. Yankees fans just smirked; their team was coming back, obviously. The fans around me viewed the ultimate, inevitable comeback like honors students who had aced a test. When you're as smart as we are and you study up, of course you're going to get an A.

But mostly: I was just amazed they played "Cotton-Eyed Joe" during the seventh-inning stretch. "Cotton-Eyed Joe" is ear poison, a wretched faux-dance combination of two different, equally horrible musical genres. It is also the sort of junk I had left Mattoon to get away from. This was defiantly un-tweedy.

We sat in the right-field bleachers. I was amazed how well-organized and clever the fans in the bleachers were. Go to another stadium, even my beloved Busch Stadium in St. Louis, and the fans need some sort of external stimuli to fire them. Maybe it's the organist launching into the "Da-da-da-dut-dada . . . CHARGE!" song, or the public address system blaring "We Will Rock You." Or even, God help us, the wave. But not at Yankee Stadium. The cheers in the Yankee Stadium bleachers are communal comedic concertos. Everyone seems to have studied from some sort of crude handbook. When the game starts, they shout out the names of each Yankee on the field until the player waves. Anytime there's a bad call, everyone, in unison, immediately breaks into "ASS-HOLLLLE. ASS-HOLLLLE!" When the grounds crew comes out to drag the infield in the sixth inning, to the tune of the Village People's "YMCA," the bleachers make it their own song, finding someone wearing the opponent's cap and screaming, together, to the chorus: "WHY . . . ARE . . . YOU . . . GAY? HOW . . . DID . . . YOU . . . GET . . . THAT . . . WAY?" It's politically incorrect, awful, wrong, and, frankly, all-in-good-fun hilarious. Everyone was screaming, everyone was chanting, everyone was downright insane.

In particular, there was Jerry, right behind us. Jerry, probably about fifty, was wearing a beat-up old Yankees jersey with Don Mattingly's number on the back and a plastic Yankees helmet that had several cracks on each side. He also had the Yankees logo written on his face. Jerry was fired up. He ran up and down the aisles, screaming like a buffoon, carrying an old Babe Ruth jersey with "1918" and "Curse of the Bambino" scribbled on it in magic marker. The man yelled the entire game, so much so that even some of the Bleacher Creatures looked at him askance. He spent a good five minutes heckling Red Sox right fielder Trot Nixon, calling him a "homo" and asking him if Richard was his father. ("YOUR DAD FUCKED US IN WATERGATE! YOUR DAD FUCKED US IN WATERGATE, YOU HOMO!") In any other stadium, Jerry would have either been kicked out or disowned by everyone in his section. In Yankee Stadium, he was a peculiar presence everyone tolerated, even cheered alongside, when we weren't busy stifling any notions of taking offense. I tried to imagine what Jerry's life outside Yankee Stadium was like. Did he have a family? Did he live alone, calling talk radio until midnight? I imagined him living in the basement of his ailing octogenarian mother, a woman who still thinks he just needs to meet the right girl.

When the Yankees went up 1–0 in the first, with star left-hander Andy Pettitte on the mound, all looked well and secure. I heard a small voice perk up next to Jerry. "Dad, Dad, Jeter's playing too deep at short." Stunned, I turned around . . . and Jerry's children were there. One was a girl of about sixteen, glossed up in a trashy way that likely shows up in the fantasy of every kid in her algebra class. She was bundled up in a Yankees sweatshirt and a blanket. Next to her were her little brothers, probably thirteen and eleven, who, like any sons at a baseball game, were just trying to show off their baseball knowledge to their dad. "Dad, Dad, I think he's playing too shallow at second, what do you think, what do you think?" They were like little birds begging for a worm. I couldn't conceive that these seemingly normal kids were being raised by the man currently pulling up his shirt, hoping a TV camera would show the BOSTON SUX painted on his beer belly.

He would look over at them, pat them on the head, and say, in a voice about thirty decibels quieter than the one screaming about the size of Manny Ramirez's testicles, "That's right, kiddo. I think they should make Soriano an outfielder already, like you said." He'd put his arm around his daughter and whisper, "You keeping warm, honey?" He'd then head to the concession area and come back loaded with four hot dogs and four Cokes, handing them out to his kids . . . before settling in to continue his verbal assault.

I saw no embarrassment on his children's faces, and why should I have? This was their dad, and he was a Yankees fan. I imagined those kids, in twenty years, when they have kids of their own, heading to the bleachers and screaming the same things.

The game turned ugly and gnarly and twisted for the Yankees, and Jerry started jeering his own team, growling about Aaron Boone's inability to put the ball in play ("Go back to Cincinnati, you jackass!") and booing Yankees right-hander Jose Contreras, who famously defected from Cuba to play for the Bombers ("If you can make it on that boat, you can certainly strike out Jason Fucking Varitek!").

The Yankees made a comeback attempt that fell short, and a

stunned crowd, which had been amped to celebrate a World Series trip, filed out. Jerry and his kids followed behind me. One of
the boys was distraught, almost crying, asking his father, "Dad,
how could they lose? I can't believe they lost."

Jerry pulled the kid's Yankees hat over his eyes and tapped
the boy's nose lightly. "Oh, now, don't cry, kid. We'll get 'em
tomorrow. Smile. Did you have fun? You kids have fun? Come
on now . . . it's just a game, kiddo."

◆

The beating heart of this city is the blue-collar workforce—the
garbage men, the construction crews, the longshoremen, the
cops, the firemen, the ones who grew up in the remote sections
of the outer boroughs, maybe Astoria, maybe Bay Ridge, maybe
Bensonhurst, maybe Staten Island. The ones who never left their
neighborhood, the ones who married the girl of the same ethnic
background with whom they went to high school, the ones who
bust ass all day and clock out at five, pop a cold one at five thirty,
and fall asleep on the couch at eleven. The ones who maybe drink
too much on Friday nights, the ones who go to the same restaurants they went to when they were kids, the ones who have hung
out with the same five guys for thirty years.

They're the blood of this city. They sit back and laugh as the
masses move here from across the country, rattle around for a
while, making a lot of noise and accomplishing very little before ultimately deciding that life really was easier in Wisconsin,
after all, and returning home, leaving the unquenched longings
of their youth far behind them. (The interlopers who stick it out
here? They end up in New Jersey, or maybe Connecticut.) For
those who have lived here their entire life, Manhattan is referred
to as "the city," a faraway place full of traffic and drinks that are
much too expensive. (As in, "I'm not going all the way into the
city tonight.") To them, New York City is not a vast, expan-
sive playland, where twentysomethings drink and party and try

to make something of their lives. New York City is simply, and wholly, their home.

They are, essentially, just like everyone who grew up in Mattoon. They stay within their close circle, in the same hangouts, doing the same things. And family and blood are more important than anything else. In college, we would call them "townies." The rest of us just kind of pop in, hop around for a while, and drive up the cost of everything. And then we leave, and they're here, and the next group comes in. They're the ones making sure the trains run on time, everything remains calm, and the foundation for it all remains solid, consistent, secure. This is their land, and it is because of them that New York City is, as they say, the Greatest Fucking City in the World. And it's why I love it here. It's why it now feels like home.

That said, my family came to visit Yankee Stadium when the Cardinals were in town, and when the Bleacher Creatures saw my family and me wearing Cardinals red shirts, they began chanting, "DAR-RYL KILE! DAR-RYL KILE! DAR-RYL KILE!"—the name of the Cardinals pitcher who'd had a heart attack and died in a Chicago hotel room a few years earlier. It might take a while for New York to feel like home to them.

◄| fourteen |►

Sully and the Mick

JANE LEAVY

The inquiry arrived via e-mail with a note of urgency from my publisher. *You might want to take a look at this.*

Mrs. Frank Sullivan had just received a condolence call from a dear friend who had learned of her husband's death on page 162 of *The Last Boy,* my biography of Mickey Mantle. Mrs. Frank Sullivan was upset. She was also surprised, because her husband, the pitcher, #73 on the Boston Red Sox list of their top one hundred players ever, was sitting beside her on the porch in Kauai watching the sunset and sipping his favorite wine from a box. Mrs. Frank Sullivan wished to know how might I declare him undead.

I was appropriately mortified. Mickey murdered the ball, sure, but I killed Frank. My apology was prompt and profuse. I had tried to find Frank Sullivan, honest. Two teammates (at least!) and one unimpeachable online source had reported that Frank was putting his pants on one leg at a time in a better world.

I had grieved for him and, truth to tell, for myself, because Frank wasn't just another dead ballplayer. He was responsible for best line ever uttered about Mantle, maybe the best line ever uttered by a major league pitcher. Asked how he pitched to the Mick, Frank answered on behalf of the 548 badgered hurlers who faced him over eighteen years: "With tears in my eyes."

I had to use it. So I put Frank in the past tense.

"The late" Frank Sullivan e-mailed the next day:

> *Dear Jane, it would distress me big time if you were to lose a minute's sleep over this. I know I haven't. And besides, you're probably not off by much.*

Sully pitched for the Red Sox in the era before the ball club attained Most Favored Nation status. He was far better than the teams he played for, a two-time All-Star, who deserved a better fate—certainly from me. "Water off a duck's back," Frank said when I called to make further amends. "Don't forget you're dealing with a guy who was booed by thousands."

He doesn't remember when he said what he said about the Mick, what occasioned it or to whom he might have said it. Mantle had a tendency to obliterate memory. "He was spooky good," Frank says.

Theirs was a *liaison dangereuse,* a template for the complications faced by every pitcher who got involved with the Mick. It lasted nine years, on and off—27 one-night stands, home and away; 79 brief encounters at the plate (including unofficial at-bats), each preserved in box scores and encrypted in agate type.

AB	H	2B	3B	HR	BB	IBB	SO	HBP	SH	SF	AVG	OBP	SLG
61	18	1	0	7	18	0	14	0	0	0	.295	.456	.656

They crossed paths on the base paths and met in occasional headlines and hijinks. Like many baseball relationships, it has improved over time, at least in Frank's memory. "I had a lot of success with Mickey," he tells me. "He didn't like my herky-jerky motion." Which might explain why nine of the fourteen times

Frank struck him out he was caught looking. "I think he hit only four home runs off me," Frank says.

Actually, it was 7, only 1.3 percent of Mantle's 536 career home runs but enough to tie Frank for sixth place on the list of pitchers Most Victimized by the Mick. You might call it a long-distance relationship.

61 May 21, 1954, Yankee Stadium BOS d. NY 6–3
Mantle: 1-for-4, 1 R, 2 RBI, WP Sullivan

72 July 1, 1954, Fenway Park NY d. BOS 8–7
Mantle: 1-for-3, 1 BB, 1 R, 1 RBI, LP Sullivan

89 May 6, 1955, Fenway Park NY d. BOS 6–0
Mantle: 1-for-4, 1 BB, 1 RB, LP Sullivan

114 August 16, 1955, Fenway Park NY d. BOS 13–6
Mantle: 3-for-5, 1 BB, 1 R, 2 RBI, LP Sullivan

172 September 21, 1956, Fenway Park, BOS d. NY 13–7
Mantle: 3-for-5, 1 BB, 3 R, 2 RBI, Sullivan ND

205 August 13, 1957, Fenway Park, NY d. BOS 3–2
Mantle: 3-for-3, 1 BB, 1 R, 3 RBI, LP Sullivan

246 September 3, 1958, Yankee Stadium NY d. BOS 8–5
Mantle: 2-for-4, 1 BB, 3 R, 1 RBI, Sullivan ND

May 21, 1954, was a raw, dank day in New York. Frank thought the game might well be called on account of rain. Then a photographer knocked on the door of his room at the Commodore Hotel and said, "I'm here to take your picture. You're pitching tonight."

Nobody had said a word to him about making his first major league start. He was the Rookie, bearing the burden of possibility, just as Mantle had in 1951. Everything was before him. He had survived four and a half months on the line in Korea, where he rehabbed a sore arm by chucking hand grenades. "I'd just as soon have had a sore arm forever," Frank tells me.

Mantle had yet to fulfill the tantalizing promise ignited in March 1951, when he had what Yankee infielder Gil McDougald called "a spring you only dream about" and Casey Stengel prevailed upon the Yankee higher-ups to put the nineteen-year-old rookie on the major league roster after only two years in the minors. "He has more speed than any slugger and more slug than any speedster—and nobody has ever had more of both of 'em together," Stengel declared. "This kid ain't logical. He's too good. It's very confusing."

McDougald was named Rookie of the Year. Mantle's season ended with disappointment and despair in the fifth inning of Game 2 of the '51 World Series, when he tore up his right knee trying not to run into the man he called "Joe Fuckin' DiMaggio" in center field in Yankee Stadium. He would never step foot on the field again without pain. He would play the next two seasons on an undiagnosed, unstable knee and would not have surgery until November 1953. It was too little and too late to repair the damage, which was compounded by a misguided post-surgery hunting trip with Billy Martin in the winter of 1954. He was operated on again just weeks before the opening of spring training.

Mantle was limping when the Yankees reported to camp in St. Pete and would not be sound enough to play both ends of a doubleheader until June. Yankee poo-bahs fumed at his lack of maturity and his irresponsibility. The violence of his urgent left-handed swing placed extreme torque on the compromised right knee. Stengel had benched him in the eleven previous games against right-handed starters—he was batting .136 left-handed, with three measly singles. But Stengel had him in the lineup and batting third against Sullivan and the last-place Red Sox on May 21, 1954.

Dr. Bobby Brown, the Yankee infielder just back from two years in Korea (the only man ever to take medical school exams in the home locker room), was aghast when he saw the condition of Mantle's knee. He had lost two inches to atrophy. "I measured it," Brown says. "I told him, 'Your knee is going to continue to buckle until you get that quadriceps built back up where it should be.'"

Brown first saw Mantle run in the fall of 1950, when the Yankees brought him up for a late-season cup of coffee, a reward for being named MVP of the Western League. Mantle ran so hard, Brown says, "that he kicked up tufts of dirt as high as his head." Even after the injury, which cost him at least a step, he was still faster than anyone else from home to first. One night during a lull in the fighting on the 38th parallel, Brown had screened footage from the 1952 World Series for the enlisted men in the mess-hall bunker. Mantle hit the first of his 18 World Series home runs in Game 6 and broke a 2–2 tie in Game 7 with a sixth-inning homer that vanquished the Brooklyn Dodgers once again.

But that wasn't what took the G.I.s' breath away. "It was a bunt on one bounce back to the pitcher that he was out on by about a half a step," Brown says.

"Lieutenant, lieutenant, run that back again!" an enlisted man called out.

The projectionist ran it again. "Look at that 4F son of a bitch run!"

Twice Mantle had been declared 4F by army doctors because of osteomyelitis, a bacterial infection of the bone in his left shin. While Sullivan and Brown were on the front line, Mantle was in pinstripes, receiving death threats and bad PR, which prompted another physical examination in November 1952. The army surgeon general took one look at Mantle's X-ray and declared him unfit to serve, citing a "chronic right-knee defect resulting from an injury suffered in the 1951 World Series." Yet, he did not have surgery for another whole year. And, the Yankee trainer confided in Brown, Mantle hadn't done the exercises he needed to strengthen the muscles around that knee. Mantle hid the weights he had been given so he didn't have to do the prescribed exercises on road trips.

When Mantle came to the plate to face him with two outs in the bottom of the first inning, what was Frank Sullivan thinking? "Not much," he says. "I would have been throwing sliders for strikes and a fastball to get the guy out and I had no idea where the fastball was going."

Mantle wasn't an intimidating physical presence, not to Sullivan, who at six-foot-seven was the tallest pitcher in the American League. (Years later, he was traded for six-foot-eight Gene Conley, in what is still known as the biggest trade in baseball history.) Sully had made his first major league appearance as a reliever the previous July and walked Mantle the first time they met that September. But this was his debut as a member of the starting rotation. He struck Mantle out in the first inning and in the fourth and again in the sixth. "I thought, 'Where's all the press on this guy coming from?'" Frank says. "Then he hit one so far up in the bleachers in Yankees Stadium I couldn't believe it. He could hit the ball so much farther than anybody his size. Or anybody's size."

The headline in the *Times* the next morning said:

ROOKIE FANS NINE, TRIPS BOMBERS, 6–3; Red Sox' Sullivan Wins First Big League Start Despite Mantle's 2-Run Homer

Buried at the bottom of the story was this note: "Mantle, starting against right-handers again now, has more strikeouts than hits, 17–16."

By the next time they faced each other, in Boston on July 1, Mantle was hitting .313. He hit his fifteenth home run of the year in the first inning to give him the American League lead.

But the Yankees were as far behind the first-place Cleveland Indians when they left town as they'd been when they arrived, a gap they would never close and an indignity Casey Stengel would never forgive. He blamed Mantle for the Yankees' forfeiture of their rightful place atop the American League, daring him to be as good as Duke Snider and Willie Mays, his New York counter-parts, who surpassed him that year in statistics and stature. Mantle would have much to prove in 1955.

He reported to spring training as whole as he could be. On May 6, in a brief pregame ceremony at Fenway Park, the Red Sox celebrated the beginning of Mental Health Month in honor of Jimmy Piersall—"now fully recovered from a nervous break-down," the New York Times reported. Mantle celebrated his re-gained fitness by hitting his fifth home run of the year. In the first inning he defied a whistling wind blowing in hard from right field and redirected one of Sully's pitches into the Yankee bull-pen. (A week later, he would have the only three–home run game of his career, which was also the first time he homered from both sides of the plate.) Sullivan was gone by the fourth inning, having "strained his left shoulder when he fell while fanning," the Times reported.

Sullivan recovered in time to be the losing pitcher in the 1955 All-Star game twelve days later in Milwaukee, a black mark on what would be his finest season, with an AL-best 18 wins. Sully was summoned to relieve Whitey Ford with 2 outs in the eighth inning and the American League ahead 5–3, thanks to Mantle's 430-foot first-inning home run (one of only 2 he hit in 20 All-Star Games). The game had been delayed a half hour by the fu-neral of Chicago Tribune sportswriter Arch Ward, who'd conceived the Mid-Summer Classic in 1933. "I had to walk by Mantle com-ing in from the bullpen," Frank says. "He hollered at me, 'Let's get this thing over because it's getting into cocktail hour.' I didn't reply. I was nervous as hell."

Al Rosen booted a ball at third base, allowing the National League to tie the score at 5–5. Frank stayed in the game and kept it that way. By the bottom of the twelfth, when no further progress had been made, everyone was getting thirsty. "Do some-thing," Yogi Berra implored leadoff hitter Stan Musial, who hit Sully's first pitch for a game-winning home run. "I was only fol-lowing Mantle's advice," Frank said, but the memory still rankles.

Mantle, who regarded the All-Star Game as an interruption in his weekend-long cocktail party, had played all three hours and seventeen minutes. He exacted his revenge on Sully when the Yankees returned to Fenway on August 16. There was a moment of silence for the Babe—it was the seventh anniversary of Ruth's death—and then, in the top of the third, a crash: Mantle's 30th home run of the year, his 4th in three days, an opposite field shot that sailed over the 379-foot mark in left center field and hit a building across the street. Frank lasted two and two-thirds innings.

But Mantle wasn't done with him. One day, Sully isn't sure exactly when, he returned to the Kenmore Hotel, where he lived during the season, to find his VW Beetle sitting on the sidewalk, wedged tightly between a telephone pole and a brick wall. "I had to call a tow truck," he says, "to pick the front end of it up and drag the damn thing far enough so I could get in."

When Sully got to the ballpark the next day, Vince Orlando, the clubhouse man who worked the visiting locker room, told him he had overheard Mantle laughing about it with his pal, Bill "Moose" Skowron.

If Mantle's accomplishments during the 1955 season (.306, 99 RBI, and a league-leading 37 home runs) were a prelude to what would be the greatest year in his professional life, the World Series that fall was a reminder of how hard it would be for him to sustain good health and good fortune. In mid-September he tore his right hamstring trying to beat out a bunt. No one knew enough sports physiology back then to understand that a hamstring was subjected to abnormal stress—sometimes more than it could bear—when it had to compensate for a compromised knee. Mantle could play in only three of the seven World Series games against the Dodgers that year, managing 2 hits in 10 at-bats, and is widely credited with delivering a belated World Championship to Brooklyn.

By September 1956, Mantle was on the cusp of complete redemption, vying with Ted Williams for the batting title and making a serious run at baseball's elusive Triple Crown. When the Yankees arrived in Boston on September 21, Mantle was batting

.350, 5 points behind Williams, who did not yet have enough at-bats to qualify for the batting title. All the talk coming into the series was about whether the Yankees would pitch to him.

The Yankees set two major league records that day: most men left on base (20) and, thanks to Mantle, most home runs by a club in one major league season (183). Again, Sully was the victim. "Damn near broke the back wall at Fenway," Frank says. "Hit the last brick on top of the wall in dead center field. I thought it was going to wipe out the Citgo sign."

It was his 51st home run of the season. He went 3-for-5, raising his average to .352, 4 points behind Williams. The paper of record began referring to Sully as Mantle's "favorite cousin."

By the end of the weekend, he was batting .356, 6 points ahead of Boston's favorite brooder. (And Mantle would go on to win his Triple Crown, hitting .353, with 52 homers and 130 RBIs.)

◆

Sully and Mantle would soon show up in the same place once again, though neither would be obvious to the naked eye. After Sunday's game, Tom Dowd, the Red Sox traveling secretary, arrived in the losing clubhouse with orders for Sullivan, his catcher, Sammy White, and Jackie Jensen: they were to report to an artist's studio in Stockbridge, Massachusetts, the next day. No one gave them a choice and it didn't occur to them that they had one. Williams, whose presence had also been requested, was not about to drive halfway across the state to pose for anybody on his day off, in the middle of a race for the batting title, but he agreed to allow the artist, a guy named Norman Rockwell, to use his likeness.

"I didn't know who the hell he was," Frank says. "We were told by the Red Sox to take our uniforms and go. Jesus, it was a whole long way. There was no freeway in those days, three hours there and three hours back—and he served iced tea for lunch!"

Then he ushered them into his spartan studio, where a facsimile of the Red Sox spring training locker room in Sarasota,

Florida, had been created. There were makeshift lockers with handwritten nameplates and a rudimentary bench constructed by Rockwell's studio assistant, Louie Lamone. The artist littered the floor with matchbooks, crumpled paper cups, and dirty towels. He filled the lockers with liniments and towels and ball gloves. Frank hung his aloha shirt and sport jacket on a hook and put on his uniform and posed for Rockwell for an hour. He told the players where and how to sit, where and how to look. Then his photographer, Bill Scoville, began shooting.

"He just kept telling us to keep looking up," Frank says. At what? He wasn't sure. Rockwell didn't explain the composition he envisioned or the assignment for the *Saturday Evening Post,* which had commissioned the piece for its cover. "He was a little meek, pipe-smoking guy, very polite," Frank says. "He wanted me to sit there with my arm on Jensen's shoulder," affecting locker room intimacy. He stationed Sammy White on the bench to Sully's right and the bare-chested studio assistant behind him. Rockwell called him "John J. Anonymous," a stand-in for "all the forgettables who squeaked into the majors."

Then he told Frank to stand at Williams's locker and pretend he was the Splendid Splinter. He would put Ted's head on Frank's body later.

Ledgers at the Norman Rockwell Museum show that a check for $100 was issued to each of the players. "I never saw mine," says Frank, who should have gotten paid twice.

A few weeks later, on October 20, Mickey Mantle's twenty-fifth birthday, a high school senior from Pittsfield, Massachusetts, arrived at Rockwell's studio to complete the composition. Sherman Safford, who actually preferred basketball to baseball, had been recruited to pose for Rockwell as the Rookie in his eponymous painting. "Picked me out of a chow line," Safford recalls a half century later.

He was a tall, gangly, California-born boy. He had an open, expectant face that was full of promise, the look Rockwell was searching for. He called Safford's mother with a list of instructions about what her boy was to bring and to wear. He was to show up with a five-fingered fielder's glove, which he didn't own, and a bat. "He didn't want me to wear Levis," Sherm says. "He said, 'See if you can get a seersucker coat.' And he said, 'I want a straw suitcase.' My mother found one somewhere. I think it was a picnic basket."

And, Rockwell told Mrs. Safford, "For God sake's don't let him cut that hair."

"I always got it cut once a month," Sherm says. "By the end of the month it got pretty shucky."

That was the hayseed look Rockwell was after.

Safford arrived in brown penny loafers, chinos that were too short to cover his white wool socks, and a jacket whose sleeves didn't reach his wrists. Rockwell plunked his own fedora on Sherm's head. "He said, 'Here's what I want. Smile just as broadly as you can. Extend your hand. You're here to be the savior of the team. You're going to take them to the World Series. And you're just as proud as you can be.'"

Rockwell directed him to put the glove and suitcase in his left hand so he could extend a hand to the jaded vets lounging in the faux locker room—Rockwell had attached their photographs to a large sheet of plastic on which he arranged and rearranged the composition.

But, Sherm says, "There was something he didn't like." And on November 1, Rockwell called him back to the studio. The painting was slated for the cover of the *Saturday Evening Post* in March, when pitchers and catchers reported to spring training, and perhaps the artist realized that the rookie in his painting would have been too abashed to be so forward and outgoing, to present himself that way, especially when confronted by the predatory glare that Rockwell fixed on Ted Williams's uninviting mug. In an early iteration of the illustration, the Rookie, wearing a cockeyed grin and a straw boater, is recoiling from the glowering star. In the final drawing, Rockwell stationed infielder Billy Goodman (photographed separately) behind the Rookie, hand to mouth in an attempt to stifle the grin provoked by the interloping rube.

According to the museum archivist, Sherm received $15 for each sitting; Sherm is positive he got $60 a pop. He had used the money to pay off his car insurance policy when he enlisted in the army. He was in basic training at Fort Dix when the cover hit the newsstand on March 2, 1957; the Red Sox were in spring training in Sarasota. Frank noted how faithfully Rockwell had replicated their locker room—minus his aloha shirt. He got everything right but the shoes—Jensen is wearing street shoes with his uniform—and Ted Williams. "Looks awful, doesn't it?" Frank says.

Certainly, it didn't look anything like Ted Williams. But the title character in *The Rookie* looks very familiar. In fact, he looks just like Mickey Mantle did when he showed up in the Yankees locker room in 1951, carrying a straw suitcase and, in the recollection of the late Hank Bauer, "wearing hush-puppy shoes and white sweat socks all rolled up." Like Rockwell's Rookie, he was met by a glowering superstar glare. Joe DiMaggio was not happy to make his acquaintance. Like Rockwell's Rookie, Mantle's face was unclouded by doubt and freckled with possibility. "That face was special," Sully says. "You've never seen another face like that."

There is no allusion to Mantle in the archives at the Rockwell Museum in Stockbridge, Massachusetts. But Rockwell, who grew up rooting for the Dodgers, was no doubt aware of Mantle's ineffable smile. By the spring of 1957, Mantle had become an American archetype. His image and his myth had become part of our collective consciousness. Perhaps that explains why *The Rookie,* one of Rockwell's 321 covers for the *Saturday Evening Post,* remains one of his most ubiquitous and merchandized illustrations. Frank has a *Rookie* magnet; Sherm's boss saw *The Rookie* on a wallpaper border at a home-improvement megastore.

The Rookie can be pieced together in a 1,000-piece jigsaw puzzle or assembled from a 500-piece puzzle in a tin. *The Rookie* adorns a 100-percent silk tie sold at the Rockwell museum in Stockbridge and a 4¼-inch collectible plate sold at the Rockwell museum in Vermont. The Museum of Fine Arts in Boston sells a "Rockwell Rookie Single Coaster" for $5.95 ($19.95 for a set of four), a mouse pad for $18.95, and a set of two key chains for $2.99. That's where Sully, the sole surviving ballplayer on Rockwell's canvas, saw the original painting in 2005, and when he saw his first major league baseball game since the Minnesota Twins put him out to pasture in 1963. He was inducted into the Red Sox Hall of Fame three years later.

◆

Sully faced Mantle for the final time in the summer of 1962 after the Phillies traded him to the Twins, his third and last stop in the majors—Frank walked him, just as he had the first time they met. Frank was "in the twilight of a mediocre career"—a line he says he stole from Rocky Bridges. Soon Mantle, too, would be in decline. After 1964, he no longer "had it in his body to be great," as Stengel once put it. Mantle told me he should have quit after 1965. But he played another three years because he didn't know how to do anything else and the Yankees didn't know what to do without him.

Frank moved to Hawaii in order to get as far away from baseball as possible. If he had to dig ditches for a living, he didn't want anyone see him doing it. He didn't want to be "just another stupid jock hanging around a game he could no longer play." He worked for a company that built helicopter pads and golf courses on Kauai; he became a golf pro and sailed boats throughout the seven seas; he wrote a damn good book called *Life Is More Than 9 Innings*—a lesson Mantle didn't learn until it was too late.

Mickey's star burned hot and bright, and burned out too soon; Frank's still twinkles. Mantle became a legend. Sully survived. "I'm glad you're alive," I told him, still repentant after we'd gotten to know each other better. "And I'm glad you're alive," he replied, which was generous, considering that I'd inadvertently killed him off in my book.

"If I knew I was going to live so long, I would've taken better care of myself," Mantle liked to say, a throwaway line he delivered often while throwing his life away.

"I had no idea of the misery and suffering the poor bastard went through," Sully wrote after he finished reading the book. "If I'd known how tough Mickey's life had been, I would've thrown a few fat ones over the plate."

(From left to right:) *The three Red Sox, Sammy White, Frank Sullivan, and Jackie Jensen, modeled for Norman Rockwell as he prepared to paint* The Rookie, *the subject of which bears more than a hint of Mickey Mantle's hayseed spirit.* THE NORMAN ROCKWELL MUSEUM

fifteen

The Deal of the Century

DANIEL OKRENT

In the late 1970s, on my very first assignment as a baseball writer, I found myself in the press box at the Yankees' spring training home in Fort Lauderdale. On one side of me sat Murray Chass of the *New York Times,* fairly early in his own career as the most prolific and most boring baseball writer in the paper's (maybe any paper's) history. On the other side my seatmate was Maury Allen of the *New York Post.*

It was only an exhibition game, but I had never been paid to watch baseball before, and even the cramped little press box in Lauderdale seemed like some sort of heaven to me. I gurgled something about this being my first professional gig as a sportswriter, and Chass looked at me briefly, emitted a noise composed entirely of consonants, and went back to his crossword puzzle. Allen was friendlier. He introduced himself, shook my hand, wished me luck, and spent the first couple innings chatting amiably about his life as a sportswriter. Around the top of the third, he paused in mid-anecdote, looked at the field briefly, and tapped a pencil on the arm of his chair. "I love everything about the job," he said, "except the fucking games." Then he got up and left.

It would be cheap to contradict the defenseless Allen, who died in 2010, and point out that his role in what was almost precisely a fucking game may have been the most exciting moment in his career. In the summer of 1972, the biggest trade in Yankees history originated at a party at Allen's house in Westchester County, when pitcher Mike Kekich drove home with the wife of pitcher Fritz Peterson, and Peterson drove home with Mrs. Kekich.

Several months later, the *Times* splashed a headline across four columns: "2 Yankees Disclose Family Exchange." In separate interviews, the men explained that Peterson had moved in with Mrs. Kekich and the Kekich kids, and Kekich had unpacked his bags chez Peterson. Even Chass, who wrote the piece, couldn't make this one boring. Every newspaper and broadcast news show in the country was on the story in minutes, displaying a previously unacknowledged interest in the sex life of professional athletes. Fritz and Mike tried to make the point that they had swapped lives, not wives, but Commissioner Bowie Kuhn nonetheless declared that he was appalled. (Peterson replied, "He didn't like the fact that I was teaching billiards, either.") Manager Ralph Houk first made a whooshing sound, and then said he didn't think any of it was Kuhn's—or anyone else's—business. The Fat Boy from Cleveland, who had just bought the club, hadn't yet learned that newspapers might actually print whatever he had to say. So he said nothing.

But the Susanne Kekich–Marilyn Peterson trade was undoubtedly the most memorable thing that happened to the Yankees during the grim years of Horace Clarke and Frank Tepedino. Back then, the only other thrills came during those on-field fights that featured Joe Pepitone running desperately toward the dugout, terrified that a brawler from the other team might unstick his toupee. (Pepi actually had two hairpieces: one for civilian life, and a more compact number especially designed to fit under his baseball cap.) As it turned out, Kekich and Marilyn Peterson couldn't make it work, while Peterson and the former Susanne Kekich have been married for thirty-seven years. In other words: two relationships just like a million other relationships, except this one was played out in public, in pinstripes.

◆

For all its tabloid oomph, the Kekich–Peterson tag team match was much more decorous than most of the sex-tinted sagas that had previously escaped from clubhouses and dugouts and into the public consciousness. Anyone who came even close to the fringes of baseball in the twenties knew that Babe Ruth's appetites were not confined to beer and steaks. In 1949, a deranged fan named Ruth Ann Steinhagen shot Phillies first baseman Eddie Waitkus; Ruth Ann's mother said her daughter was attracted to Waitkus by his "Lithuanian heritage," surely the most original euphemism in the annals of baseball and romance. But indirection had long been the favorite literary mode for public discussion of athletes' romantic foibles. A few years after the Waitkus incident, in a piece about a great prizefighter from the early part of the twentieth century, John Lardner wrote, "Stanley Ketchel was twenty-four years old when he was fatally shot in the back by the common-law husband of the lady who was cooking his breakfast."

Indirection finally gave way to candor when the players themselves began to do the talking, around the same time that the rest of the culture was beginning to absorb the aftershocks of the sexual revolution that had begun in the 1960s. In 1970, Jim Bouton—as it happens, Fritz Peterson's best friend in baseball—published his epochal *Ball Four,* which lifted the window shade on the habits of men whose behavior, whenever they were in proximity to women, would have embarrassed the frat boys of *Animal House.* The alpha animal at the head of the Yankees sex pack was undoubtedly Mickey Mantle. I own a photocopy of a form filled out by Mantle in 1973, when ex-Yankees were asked to add their two cents to the Stadium's fiftieth anniversary plans by recalling their "outstanding event at Yankee Stadium." Mantle wrote, "I got a blow job under the right field bleachers by the Yankee bull pen."

Fritz Peterson was no Mantle, nor was he even teammate Gene Michael, the shortstop (and later general manager) who was known as "Stick" neither because of his body type nor his bat. By Peterson's own description, his libido was lower than his ERA, and he had the lowest lifetime ERA of any New York pitcher in the history of the old Yankee Stadium. In a memoir published in 2009, he relates how Marilyn, pre-swap, had bought him a book called *The Marriage Art,* "a sort of 'how-to' book. I realize now that she was trying to tell me that I didn't 'have it.'" Kekich, on the other hand, must have had quite a lot of it.

◆

In a paragraph about how they used to sing together, Peterson writes, "Mike could even yodel with the best of them," and I'm still wondering whether "yodel" had a secondary meaning among the ballplayers of the seventies and eighties. Once the press had established its interest in ballplayers' sex lives, and ballplayers had stopped pretending they were Boy Scouts, the game developed layers of subterfuge to protect the guilty. Some equipment managers carried a special cigar box, where wedding rings were deposited on road trips. Occasionally teams would talk about barring wives from the team plane, citing all sorts of flabby excuses to disguise the real reason: the players' conviction that a teammate's traveling wife was a spy for all wives (the Brewers of the early eighties referred to the road-tripping Mrs. Paul Molitor, grumpily, as "the twenty-sixth man"). Recovering in Cleveland from a back injury, Indians outfielder Rick Manning yodeled Dennis Eckersley's wife whenever the team was on the road. Wade Boggs called himself a "sex addict" when a sensational lawsuit revealed his years-long affair with a California mortgage broker named

Margo Adams, whose mortgage business was going so well she had been able to join Boggs on sixty-four separate road trips.

Yet neither Manning's nor Boggs's extramarital adventures—or, for that matter, Ruth's, or Mantle's, or any other ballplayer's—had the staying power in the popular imagination that has accrued to the story of Fritz & Sue & Mike & Marilyn. Kekich has changed his name and lives in semi-seclusion, Marilyn Peterson has disappeared from view, and even though Fritz and Sue are still married, not once does Peterson refer to her by name in his 220-page book. Yet early in 2011, Ben Affleck announced that he was making a movie about the affair, and once again the names Peterson and Kekich were suddenly familiar.

Peterson's book, by the way, is to a large degree a religious tract addressing whether certain ex-Yankees will or will not make it into heaven. Such is the power of redemption that he believes that Mickey Mantle, who accepted Christ on his deathbed, is all but a lock. Mike Kekich? Peterson says no, which at the very least seems ungrateful.

⊰| *sixteen* |⊱

Death by Baseball

RICHARD HOFFER

When the Yankees arrived in Miami for spring training in March of 1920, a band met them. No wonder. Even before they bought the reigning home run king from the Red Sox, the Yankees were loaded with big bats, but with Babe Ruth now in the fold, and never mind the cost, they were almost certain to make a run at their first pennant. They'd been assembling quite a collection of All-Stars, getting the always-disgruntled pitcher Carl Mays from cash-poor Boston the year before, and had just added sluggers like Duffy Lewis and young Bob Muesel to a potent lineup that already included Ping Bodie and Wally Pipp. Home Run Baker insisted he was retiring but the Babe could more than make up the difference. Home Run Baker? Ten home runs? The Babe had hit twenty-nine the year before.

Expectations were so high that no fewer than thirteen scribes went south with the team for the exhibition season. Boston, with owner Harry Frazee selling off assets to meet his Broadway debts (he got $125,000 for Ruth), was not going to be contending any time soon, after a run of four pennants in eight years. The White Sox, who had played so curiously in losing the 1919 World Series, were suspect, and so were the Cleveland Indians, whose aging player-manager Tris Speaker was coming off his first sub-.300 season.

But dynasties are not so easily wrought, and the euphoria of the winter gave way to one distraction after another. The scribes had little time to attend to their narrative of an American League cakewalk as these Yankees became newsmakers of a different sort. Ruth, in particular, was the source of much of the copy, struggling at the plate and with various off-field run-ins, including one with a tree that knocked him unconscious. He and Mays were always glowering at each other, too, their mutual resentment about contracts carrying over from their days as Boston teammates. Mays, the team's best pitcher if one of its least popular players, was also at odds with manager Miller Huggins, who had borrowed Mays's car one afternoon and returned it without filling the gas tank. Of course, hardly anyone got along with Mays, "a man with a permanent toothache," a teammate once complained.

And then, just as the exhibition season was winding to a close, Chick Fewster, the Yankees slender leadoff man, was hit in the head with a pitch. This was nothing unusual, of course. Hurlers, with their peculiar deliveries and odd applications to the baseball, could be quite unpredictable. The ball could go anywhere. And even those pitchers with good control might "dust off" a hitter on a whim.

Still, if a hit batsman was a common and mostly harmless occurrence, this particular case was unnerving. Fewster sank to the dirt, quivering, and didn't come to for ten minutes, and when he did resume consciousness, he couldn't speak. Nobody had seen anything quite like this. Fewster would eventually regain his speech and return to the Yankee lineup, but not before he'd undergone surgery and spent a couple months recovering, including some time in a wheelchair, a mute reminder that teams of destiny do not simply snap together like puzzle pieces. When the Yankees broke camp, they were just happy to get out more or less alive.

◆

For all the expanse of a baseball field—it's called a park, you know—the important action is surprisingly concentrated. Try to remember this, even as you watch the balls gathered up on the base paths, the balls run down on the lawns of the outfield, the long fly balls unspooling into the air above the grassy park or escaping its confines altogether.

The fun of the game is that the ball can go anywhere at any time. Yet it mostly has to go here, *right here,* through the strike zone, an almost absurdly tiny volume of air, seventeen inches wide, from a batter's knees to his elbows. Think about that, as you examine the vastness of the park, the mostly empty area spread before you. Most of the players spend their time chasing the ball, guessing where it might land, somehow capturing it. That, as we say, is the fun of the game. The business of baseball, though, the preponderance of action takes place in this strike zone, a deadly serious, ferociously contested slice of the ballpark atmosphere.

It's not quite as much fun to watch the pitcher make his living, battling away, nibbling at corners, trying to get that ball past the hitter, who's got a wooden cudgel in his hands, for God's sake! Nor is the batter all that entertaining at the plate, checking his bat, his spikes, his gloves, daring the pitcher to deliver something down the pike. The fun doesn't really begin, not for you, until the wild scramble is on. Yet, as we say, important action here. Work is being done.

And not just work, but extremely hazardous work, the ball whizzing by a batter's chin at 90 mph. How is it that more harm doesn't come of all this? Baseball is all about margin of error; the ball doesn't have to land anywhere special to produce a hit, after all, just somewhere between the wide chalk lines. But the strike zone, with its demand for precision, is an accident waiting to happen. The pitcher stands more than sixty feet away, rears back, and lets it fly with all his might, hoping to control the ball but hardly able, from that distance, to guarantee its destination. The batter stands more or less in its way, ignoring the unthinkable, hoping for cosmic forbearance, if not the pitcher's mercy. Something seems to tickle his whiskers.

Everybody else on the field—in the park—is having a carefree time, gamboling around on the lawn, and these two are engaged in the kind of one-upmanship the subtext of which is basically a criminal act, assault with a deadly weapon. The pitcher, of course, has the upper hand here, able to use the element of surprise and location, along with velocity, to establish the proper respect. It's in his professional interest to keep the hitter off balance physically, but psychologically as well. He could hit the batter behind the ear with a baseball if he wanted. It's entirely up to him. All the batter can count on, really, is that the pitcher will honor the game's unwritten contract: to come close, but not so close as to make their little duel a gladiator sport. You know, not kill him.

Only once, in the long history of the game, has that contract ever been fully breached, has anybody ever been killed by a pitch. The odds suggest it should happen more often, perhaps regularly, so many pitches dealt, with such uncertain intentions. But, no, it doesn't. Brush-back pitches, sure, setting off some of baseball's more comic set pieces, the charging of the mound and some of the least convincing tussles this side of professional wrestling. An occasional rib-plonk, the batter stoically refusing to rub the spot as he trots to first. Every once in a while, a warning to the pitcher, lest calls for payback plunge the game into an interminable feud. But kill pitches? In the history of baseball, just one. In 1920.

The regular season that year, once it began, went according to plan, the Yankees as strong as advertised. They were slow starting, but once Ruth and Mays found their grooves in midsummer, the Yanks were a force to be reckoned with. Mays silenced early-season speculation that he was washed up—he was only twenty-nine—by winning eight straight games before the end of July. Ruth, having survived yet another collision—this one in a car (the newspapers initially reported him dead)—was crushing the ball with such frightening regularity that pitchers were complaining of a "fixed up" ball. Reacting to the concerns of cost-cutting team owners, umpires were increasingly reluctant to retire the $2.50 baseballs from the game, scuffed or not, though it didn't seem to matter what kind of ball was served to Ruth.

Still, what nobody had planned on was a resurgence of the Indians. The Yankees simply could not shake them. Tris Speaker had regained his form at the plate, flirting with the .400 mark well into July. And Ray Chapman, who had gotten married the previous year and had to be cajoled into staying in baseball, was having the season of his life. Everybody loved Chapman, maybe the most popular player on the team, a talented singer who often organized his pals into one vocal quartet or another. A slick-fielding shortstop known primarily for his speed, Chapman was even hitting above .300.

The two teams went back and forth in the standings, neither able to gain any distance on the other. In early August, the Yankees came into Cleveland trailing the Tribe by four and a half games and swept a four-game set, with Mays winning one game, saving another on two days' rest, and even chipping in at the plate.

Cleveland held on to its remaining half-game lead over New York until they met again, just three days later, at the Polo Grounds. The season was withering away in the August heat and head-to-head meetings were becoming increasingly pivotal. Cleveland could not afford another collapse, all too reminiscent of seasons past. And the Yankees, with their enormous payroll, could not afford anything short of a World Series. More than twenty-three thousand fans crowded the stadium for the opener, hoping to see New York finally charge ahead in the standings.

With Mays on the mound, they had reason to be encouraged. The Yankees' submariner had won ten of his last eleven games and was shooting for his hundredth career win. Considering his performance in Cleveland the week before, the Indians were wary, none more so than Chapman, who had never found a solution to Mays's underhand delivery. On the way to the Polo Grounds that day, when reminded by teammates who was pitching for the Yanks, Chapman simply laughed and said, "I'll do the fielding, you fellas do the hitting." And then, according to Mike Sowell's *The Pitch That Killed,* he led them in a rendition of "Dear Old Pal o' Mine," his tenor voice rising above the racket of the elevated train, the entire club finally joining in.

The game, played in withering humidity that intermittently turned into a mist, was every bit the struggle the standings would suggest. Perhaps buoyed by their subway serenade, the Indians chipped away at Mays, a bunt here, a sacrifice there, finally a solo home run, to build a 3–0 lead. As he had predicted, Chapman was having no luck with Mays, didn't even seem to be trying, really. He had squared to bunt in his first two at-bats and, here, to lead off the fifth inning, he was squaring up again. It seemed his only move against Mays.

What happened next was plain to see, to hear even. But why, nobody could say. Had the balls become harder to see, scuffed and darkened as umpires hesitated to replace them? Had the pitch, which originated so low that Mays's hand seemed to drag across the mound, simply gotten away? Or had Mays, who had hit forty-four batters in the previous four seasons, just gotten tired of these Indians pecking away at him? Did it even matter?

For the rest of his life, Mays insisted the pitch he threw to Chapman was a strike. He had sensed Chapman shifting in the box—another stupid bunt!—and modified his delivery on the fly, directing the ball high and tight to foil the attempt. Yet Chapman failed to modify his stance, and instead remained frozen in his crouch, as if he'd been hypnotized by Mays's motion. It was strange. He just stood there, anticipating a change in the ball's course, an event that simply wasn't going to happen. The pitch continued on its straight line, taking the 400 milliseconds or so (the average blink of an eye) to travel from the mound to that tiny zone of contested space. It struck Chapman in the left temple, unprotected by anything but a flannel cap.

The ball rebounded so hard—it made a noise that could be heard throughout the stadium—that it bounced nearly all the way back to Mays, who thought it must have hit the bat handle. He fielded it and threw it to Wally Pipp at first, who was about ready to send it around the infield himself when he glanced toward home and saw Chapman crumpled there. Chapman had fallen and then, with blood coming out of his ear, was trying to square himself on his seat. He was conscious, but it didn't look good. "Is there a doctor in the house?" umpire Tommy Connolly called. Speaker ran to the plate, where it seemed to him that Chapman was trying to regain his feet, possibly to charge Mays. It didn't look good at all, but it was still a familiar scene. And, finally, after several minutes, just as it always happened before, Chapman was raised to his feet and was able to leave the field, unassisted at first, but then carried when his knees gave way. The crowd cheered him as he passed into the dugout.

These duels were commonplace, although it was always a shock to see a player hit in the head like that. But no permanent harm had ever come of it. Speaker had once been hit in the head and, while he was out of the lineup for ten days, he came back without a problem. And look at Chick Fewster. Wasn't he back in the Yankees' lineup for the pennant stretch? Baseball was largely a pastoral game, its incredible languor seemingly enforced from on high. There might be discomfiting incidents—a collision at home plate, spikes high on the base path, or even a player getting beaned like this—but they never amounted to anything more than a temporary and quickly forgotten disturbance. This wouldn't be any different; the entire history of major league baseball insisted upon it: nobody ever killed in all this time.

The two teams returned to the job at hand. Inside the visitors' clubhouse, meanwhile, a pair of doctors was taking a different view of Chapman's injury, even calling for an ambulance, suspecting that surgery might be required to reduce pressure on his brain. Chapman remained conscious, although he could not do much more than mumble. Outside, unaware of Chapman's condition, Mays was regaining his composure, giving up a run in that fifth inning but settling down to retire Cleveland in order the next three innings. It was a decent outing, all things considered, though it would go down as a loss. Inside, Chapman was frantically tugging at his ring finger, utterly frustrated in his efforts to communicate. The team trainer suddenly realized he was signaling for his wedding ring, which Chapman had given him for safekeeping before the game. He put it on Chapman's finger before the ambulance arrived. It seemed to the trainer that Chapman sank back in relief.

Chapman—Chappie, as he was known in the clubhouse—died at 4:40 the next morning after surgery to relieve pressure from cerebral hemorrhaging and a fractured skull. He was twenty-nine.

The shock was immense. How was it possible for somebody, much less somebody as popular as Chapman, to die at the game of baseball? This was not a gladiator sport, like football, in which players were so routinely sacrificed that a president nearly abolished the game some years earlier. This was baseball, a civic entertainment on a par with opera. More like ballet, actually, a strictly choreographed exercise that had the advantage of slightly unpredictable outcomes and the smell of roasted peanuts. This no-man's-land at home plate was an acknowledged danger, yes, but not a death trap. Nobody dies at baseball.

In Cleveland, the front-page news of Chapman's death was accompanied by a letter from the mayor, as if the city's mourning was an official affair. But all across the nation, and certainly throughout baseball, the reports were morbidly disturbing. This was a game children played. But its charm, in that instant of an eye-blink, was proved fragile, an illusion made possible only by this unspoken agreement, this contract, this vague and nonbinding treaty between the pitcher and the batter. If this wasn't going to be observed . . . well, what possible future did this game have?

There was immediate talk of banning Mays, possibly prosecuting him. But it was just talk. The game, it turned out, had an overarching structure that could accommodate even the grisliest interruptions. The season was long, full of enough distractions, given time, to cloud even this tragedy. It was not convenient to the pastime to now make it a death sport; this was sad, but it simply could not be incorporated into the range of the game's possibilities. Even if the players knew the danger that turbulent strike zone represented, it could not be acknowledged. Baseball would no longer be possible unless this incident—let's call it that—was consigned to the category of anomaly. Ray Chapman could just as easily have been struck by lightning that day.

Which is to say, the pennant race quickly resumed, all of baseball did, the batters digging in as always, the pitchers shaving away at the corners. Mays was badly shaken, sure, as much by the event as by the animus he seemed to have created, and dropped out of sight for a while. But he was soon back on the mound and back to his old form, winning four straight games, finishing the season with 26 victories. Alas, he did not finish the season in the World Series. Even with his steady hand and Ruth's big bat (he ended with an unthinkable 54 home runs), the Yankees could not lock up the pennant, fading right at the end. The Indians rebounded from Chapman's death with a resolve of their own, finished the season strong, and won the American League pennant going away.

It was a stunner, given where the Yankees and Indians had started the season and, even more, what had happened that day in the Polo Grounds. But baseball was funny that way, rewarding serendipity more reliably than any logic. That was the fun of the game, then and always, this peaceful little recreation, its potential for surprise as wonderful as it was—once, one time only—tragic. The Cleveland Indians, of all people, were going to Brooklyn for the World Series that fall. Almost all of them, anyway.

seventeen

One True Pitch

RICK TELANDER

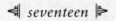

D o you know when your Jim Abbott story ran?" my old
Sports Illustrated editor asked.
I wasn't sure. Sometime in the early or mid-nineties, I
thought.

But exactly when? What issue? I can remember every one of
my *SI* articles by the subject of the cover that encased it, be it a
jockey, an Olympian, an NBA star, a boxer, a championship dog,
sometimes even the character in my own piece. Lots of stories,
spun over a quarter century, burnished in my gut. But this one
was vague. Odd. I couldn't explain it.

The editor (who is also the editor of this book) checked with
friends at the mag. They searched the library, the archives, the
covers. Nothing. Nobody could find a Jim Abbott story, not by
me, anyway.

But I wrote one, didn't I? Abbott, the pitcher who was born
without a right hand. The guy who never gave up, who developed his own way to play the game. How could I forget that?

Even my *SI* editor believed I had written the piece. He mentioned anecdotes I had told him about Abbott while I was reporting the story. And I remembered traveling with Abbott, meeting his wife, riding in his car, eating a meal at his home. I went to one of the filing cabinets in my office at home, the four big metal cubes that house pretty much everything I have ever worked on in my journalistic life. The files are my brain, only alphabetized.

There under "A," behind only Aaron, was "Abbott, Jim."

The file was thick. I pulled it out, laid it on my desk, and opened it. A sheet of white legal paper was on top, hand-printed in black ink marker, a fax I had sent more than seventeen years ago. It read, "To: Rob Butcher, N.Y. Yankees. From: Rick Telander, Senior Writer, *S.I.*" Below that was taped my business card, and below that, "Request credentials for games for Jim Abbott feature. Will be at Friday's game. Thanks," and my signature. It was dated 4-7-94.

Butcher was then the Yankees PR man, and I knew he was now with the Reds, because I would say hi to him when Cincinnati visited the Cubs at Wrigley Field during my new life as a sports columnist for the *Chicago Sun-Times*. I must have been following protocol by faxing the credentials request after we talked on the phone, which I knew we'd done, because we talked about children and baseball and about the meaning of Yankee Stadium in the lore of our country and the fantasies of youth. "If you ever want to bring your son or daughters to a game, just let me know," Butcher had said. And I had envisioned a big family trip to New York, and me explaining Ruth and Mantle and the monuments and even Steinbrenner to my kids, then ages eleven, nine, seven, and three, in a revelatory moment without boredom or brawling. Time went by, it never happened, but the image lingered.

Under the fax were several lineup cards, including the one from Wednesday, April 13, 1994, a Yankees–White Sox game at U.S. Cellular Field in Chicago. Pitching was Jim Abbott. His record coming in was 1–0, his ERA was 0.00.

Did I go to that game? I live in Chicago. I must have. Didn't I? I knew I went to a game or two at Yankee Stadium. Then where was my Abbott story?

My mind wandered. I looked at that lineup card. Abbott was obviously off to a good start. What else? Ozzie Guillen and Joey Cora were together, the chatty White Sox middle infield, Cora playing second and leading off, Ozzie at short and hitting eighth, and now Ozzie was the White Sox manager and Cora his bench coach. The Sox DH was Frank Thomas, "the Big Hurt," batting .346 with 2 home runs and 7 RBIs in seven games, a sure Hall of Famer, and the Yankees third baseman was Wade Boggs, another superstar, hitting .522. Danny Tartabull, the DH for New York, was at .346 with 2 homers and 8 RBIs in six games. The umpire crew chief was Don Denkinger, who famously blew that call on the Royals' Jorge Orta at first base in the 1985 World Series, the one that cost the Cardinals Game 6.

But Abbott—where was my story about him? Normally, in these files I keep a copy of the completed manuscript I would send off to the editors in New York, whether it was a printout or a typed original or a blue carbon copy or—this shows my early journalistic skill set—handwritten sheaves of school tablet paper. But nothing like a finished copy was here. Not even a rough draft. There was, however, a penned outline, the kind I created before every story I wrote. And I'd made check marks partway down the side of this one as I went through the topics, one by one, as I always did. But there was no manuscript.

So I pondered. It was early in the '94 season, and often *Sports Illustrated* got excited about a player who began a year on fire, but then held the story when he smoldered, and waited for the player to come aflame once more, and sometimes the piece would never run at all. Looking through my notes, I could see that as I tailed Abbott through April, he did indeed start to cool a bit, as pitchers with a perfect ERA tend to do. Regardless, I should still have a manuscript. Then it hit me—1994. The strike was coming. Not until midsummer, but the hum was in the air. It was going to be a bad one, insiders said, making up for a century of distrust.

Yet what could be more inspiring than a story about a young man like Abbott? What could be sweeter than a tale about the kid working so hard that he became a pitching sensation at the University of Michigan, the gold-medal-game winner for the USA at the 1988 Summer Olympics, the Sullivan Award winner as the best amateur athlete in America, the first-round draft pick of the California Angels, and then a New York Yankee who, in the heat of the '93 pennant race, threw a no-hitter at Yankee Stadium, the team's first in ten years? Not much. And what can be more deflating than a strike? Not much. So baseball stories were getting killed at *SI*. And that was the answer: the strike got my Jim Abbott tale. I must have started with the feel-good piece and had it declared dead in mid-paragraph. That would explain the marked-up outline. That would explain why I'd tossed what I'd written in the Delete can. That would explain why, even now, I have the ghost of a story in my mind.

◆

Roman numeral I of my outline had this next to it: "He's not handicapped. They keep giving him 'Courage' awards. 'It's so easy,' he says."

I remembered that well. When I first talked to Abbott, it had been so relaxed, so normal, as if we had known each other for years, that he quickly got past the notion of being something special and talked about the inverse, about how much he thought he was no big deal, about how strongly he felt that. One of my file clips from an *Atlanta Constitution* story quoted him as saying, "The curiosity, the one-handed issue, I guess it'll always be there . . . A lot of people are tired of hearing about it. I like that, too. I'm tired of hearing about it." He was nineteen when he said that. The article made it clear that the young Abbott hadn't said this in a scornful way but simply as fact.

Before we met, I had scoured the '94 Yankees media guide.

The booklet informed me that reliever Steve Howe had dealt with drug issues, infielder Mike Gallego had survived testicular cancer, and pitcher Bob Wickman was "missing the tip of his right index finger." But there was no mention of Abbott having been born with only a nub for a right hand.

"I don't know why it's not in there about Jim," Butcher had said when I questioned the bio. The PR man's response was written in my notes, and it all started to flood back to me as I read his words. "I think he doesn't want to be thought of any differently. To him it's what he is, no big deal. But, you know, I've never spoken to him about it."

At that first meeting with Abbott, which I see from my notes was at Yankee Stadium, I had been flummoxed as I stood before him, reaching out first with my right hand to shake, then pulling it back, then starting to extend it again, then—not knowing what to do and making far too much of this—I offered my left hand and we shook that way, though I could tell Abbott was waiting for me to relax and be normal and had been through this embarrassing dance a million times.

Embarrassing for people like me, that is. But the deformity was there, and it had to be taken into consideration. Besides having no right hand for fielding, Abbott had to do an astoundingly quick and facile glove switch from right to left hand every time he threw a pitch, then switch again after he fielded the ball and had to make a throw. And he could not hide the ball and mess with it before pitches the way two-handed pitchers could. As White Sox manager Gene Lamont told me, "He can't throw a split finger. I mean, he can, but he might as well announce it."

Yet the six-foot-three, 210-pound Abbott had sailed through all the difficulties you can imagine—the taunting as a youth, the staring and questioning, the necessity of learning new ways to do things that are so common yet mundane that we barely consider them, such as clapping or swinging a bat (Abbott batted .400 in high school) or tying your shoes, and when he threw the no-hitter against the Indians on September 4, 1993—in the thick of that pennant race, remember—he felt that was proof that he was just a damn fine ballplayer who on that Saturday afternoon was *on*, not some freakish roadside miracle. You don't shut down a Cleveland lineup that included Kenny Lofton, Albert Belle, Carlos Baerga, Manny Ramirez, and Jim Thome because Disney thinks it makes a swell story.

"There aren't many days, period, when I don't think about how lucky I was," Abbott said of his upbringing. Born and raised in Flint, Michigan, Abbott had two doting parents who helped him become whatever he knew he should be. "And as a kid there were things I really, really, really wanted to happen. Like Christmas, and playing in the major leagues. Now I look back and wonder if I had the right—I mean, I'm a competitive person, but, honestly, a lot of my drive comes from wanting to be normal, accepted. Not having a hand, I used sports to get in good with the other athletes at school, with the cool guys."

Abbott had a hook on his right stump for a brief time as a small child, but some kids wouldn't play with him because they were frightened, and others teased him and called him "Mr. Hook," and after a while he refused to wear it. In second grade he had surgery on the limb, "because some bones were wrong or something," and after that he just competed as an able-bodied human, sympathy be damned. He played basketball in high school and quarterbacked the football team.

"I am fortunate," Abbott said. "I can lift free weights. I can do bench presses." Indeed, as we spent time together, I saw that by having just a part of what could be called a reduced palm and the bare essence of a finger, Abbott was able to do what he likely could not have done had his right arm ended at the immobile junction of the radius and ulna. The developmental defect, which occurs at a certain time during gestation, was a problem for Abbott, yes, but not an insurmountable one.

He talked about the terrific coaches he'd had, about his mom and dad marrying at eighteen, having him only months later, and still continuing their way to success—his mom made it through law school; his dad, a machinist, "was a great father, he instilled in me a real sense of security, he was always naturally very positive"—and how his dad inspired him by telling him, before he left for school every day, "Be a leader, don't be a follower."

Even as I am writing those words now, it flashes in my mind that I repeated that slogan to my own kids almost every day as they left for school from 1994 on. It became a habit, a corny nugget of advice to which they usually responded, "Yes, Dad," or not at all. I had forgotten I picked up that saying from Abbott, and thereby from his father, just as I had forgotten that I'd never written this story at all.

I had talked to Jim's dad, Mike, back then and I remember thinking how cheerful and rooted he was. His mom, Kathy, too. They were only forty-five, and their son Jim was almost twenty-seven, and that was pretty odd, but ultimately irrelevant.

"Any kind of positive affirmation a kid gets, it will help him," said Mike. "If we all got the support Jim had, who knows what we could be? Love. A place to come home to. A place to emerge from with confidence. He was never a problem. The teachers went out of their way to do nice things for him. I guess he is blessed."

Still, Mike didn't say it was easy for his son. "To this day buttoning his shirts is hard for him, and tying ties. But when he became a man, I quit doing it for him. To tie his shoelaces, well, he did it. Make a fist and try to do it. It still amazes me."

◆

And now I am transported back to Yankee Stadium, and it is April 8, 1994, and this is Abbott's first start of the season, against the Tigers. His black glove is on his right forearm, held easily on his hip as he looks in for the sign. The ball is behind him, circling like a bearing in his left hand. He goes into the stretch, raising the glove high, holding it on his stump by pressing the ball against it, and even as he enters his follow-through, his left

hand is seeking the glove, which always is in perfect position for
him to slip on. By the time the batter can swing and before the
umpire can make a call, Abbott is wearing his glove on his left
hand. If he has to field a batted ball, he will make the switch
again after catching the ball, this time pinning the glove against
his belly with his right wrist, yanking his left hand out of the
glove and snatching the ball from the pocket in one swift motion. He is in control in this game, and he will win 4–0, going
seven innings, striking out eight, giving up three hits and three
walks, and establishing that 0.00 ERA. It's hard to believe that
his jersey was pre-buttoned for him so he could slide it on in the
locker room.

"I swear to God I don't even think about it no more," Tigers
manager Sparky Anderson told me of Abbott's defect. "He's made
himself an *ordinary person*." The garrulous skipper shook his head
with passion. "If he isn't as miraculous an athlete as I've seen—I
mean, when you gonna see something like *that*? If that doesn't
show something to kids who sit around and cry about little problems. Think about the crybabies you see today. We're talking
about a guy with so much courage. Hell, *I* could write that story!"

He could have, I dare say, even if somebody had to translate it
from Sparky-ese. But Abbott still wouldn't have liked the special
attention.

"There's nothing courageous about what I do," he will keep
insisting to me. "I know there is a role for my play, that there are
people who are challenged. They may need somebody pointing
to me, saying, 'He pitches with one hand.' But if they only knew
how easy it is!"

What Abbott meant was that he was not truly impaired, that
he was, in an athletic and social sense, as his dad said, quite gifted.
Everybody who plays in the bigs is lucky, and good. Yet he did
charitable events ceaselessly. Owner Steinbrenner had even said
snidely—he later called it jokingly—that maybe Abbott should
concentrate more on baseball than on helping people with their

ailments. There were so many of those wounded kids (and adults) that Butcher and others had to sift through the requests so that Abbott didn't have to quit the game entirely to help out.

What he would usually do was sign autographs under the statement, "Your handicap is only a handicap in the eyes of others." He was unfailingly nice and ceaselessly encouraging. But still, he was a ballplayer. And by 1994 his fastball had lost two or three mph, and sometimes he only clocked in the high eighties. He always received rousing ovations at ballparks on the road, but at Yankee Stadium it was, basically, what have you done for us lately? Abbott knew the Big Apple crowd was different when, while still with the Angels, he was warming up at the Stadium and a fan yelled, "F—k you, you one-armed bastard!"

"New York has been unbelievable to me," Abbott insists. "But I knew by 1991 when I was in L.A. that the focus isn't on the hand, that there's no sympathy. People want results." In 1991 Abbott had finished third in the Cy Young voting, going 18–11, with a 2.89 ERA. That would be his best season, although the following year he would pitch 211 innings and finish with a stellar 2.77 ERA, but, oddly, a 7–15 record. His run support that season was zip. But the win-loss differential was a harbinger of the gradual decline ahead and of a fastball that would slowly lose its sizzle. In six more seasons Abbott would never have an ERA better than 3.70.

But that year of 1994, he was on the cusp of something—neither here nor there—and no one knew for sure if he was headed up or down. Was that no-hitter his apex? Was that more than enough from this man who fielded bunts down the third base line in a way that nobody could believe, in a way that nobody else in the world could do?

There in that game against the Tigers, I can see it now, see it as vividly as if I'm still in the open-air press box behind home plate: It's the fourth inning. The Yankees are up 2–0. Travis Fryman is on first base. The count is 1–2 on Alan Trammel, the potential tying run, when Abbott abruptly calls time-out. He kneels down calmly there, just behind the pitcher's mound, and ties his left shoelace. This is not for effect; the laces are truly undone. The TV cameras zoom in, and it doesn't look possible, but it takes only a few seconds, his left hand moving like a frenzied tailor's as the right hand nub serves as an anchor, and then he is pitching again.

Later, at his house in Greenwich, Connecticut, I will marvel at the ease with which he had turned the ignition key in his car, reaching around the steering column and down with his left hand as though it were simple and normal, but I won't say anything. The house is rented, "until the end of the season," Abbott says with a chuckle, because he doesn't know if the Yankees will re-sign him, whether he'll be here or somewhere out on the baseball frontier. In fact, this will be it for him as a Yankee, but he doesn't know that yet.

His wife, Dana, tall and pretty, a former college basketball player, says hello and we eat dinner—order-out Mexican—and we talk lightly about how crazy it is that they, young people in their midtwenties, are here in a stately stone-and-timber house overlooking Long Island Sound, in one of the wealthiest suburbs in the world, millionaires. Dana laughs. She went to UC Irvine, and the school's mascot is the anteater. "'Zot!' was our cheer," she says. I ask her if she and Jim ever compete in sports.

"We don't play basketball," she answers. "We don't play anything."

Abbott looks at her. "There's something about that smirk when she lays down the last card," he says.

Jim and I then chat about the books he is reading, mostly Hemingway lately, though he is a huge fan of Abraham Lincoln and at one point gets a good start on quoting from memory the entire Gettysburg Address. Dana sits on the couch in the living room, reading her own books. Hem, Abbott feels, has much to say about life, just through his simplicity. Abbott goes to a book-shelf and comes back with *A Moveable Feast*.

"In this book, there's a part where he's talking about Dostoyevsky, and he's saying what a bad writer he is. He's saying this to Ezra Pound. 'How can a guy never use the right word and yet his characters are so alive?' "

Abbott smiles. "He talks about writing a lot in the book, but I could say it applies to pitching, too. He says, 'Write one true sentence.' And when I'm between starts I need to remember that I pitched before and I'll pitch again, and I always need to throw one more pitch. A true one."

◆

These days Abbott is a highly sought-after motivational speaker who lives in California with Dana and their two kids. He is a different person now from the one he was then. He has to be. I look him up on his Web page, see his chunkier frame, his fleshier though still kindly face, watch his videos, and memories come flooding back. I look at my interview notes, the stories they tell. "I worry about having surgery on my left arm," he said. "I'd be hopeless." What a thought. But Abbott was the first and only one-handed pitcher in major league history, and he had thoughts none of us could have. He was not a sideshow like one-armed, wartime outfielder Pete Gray, nor a gimmick like tiny Eddie Gaedel. He was a damned fine ballplayer.

His story back then, in the Yankee season after his no-hitter, would have been a poignant and inspiring one, I think. But baseball would end prematurely that season, and for the first time in the history of American sport, a league's postseason play would be canceled because of a labor dispute. The 1994 World Series was flicked away like lint.

We always say that innocence died here or there, everywhere. But major league baseball did lose something in 1994. It would be "saved" a few years later by the dubious forces created through steroids and HGH and wondrous BALCO elixirs, and it's still paying the moral price for that. Back then nobody knew nothing, weightlifters cavorted at the plate like cavemen with clubs, and chicks, of course, dug the long ball.

There never was a time before avarice or cheating. But I wish the Jim Abbott story had worked out, wish I had finished it, and it had run that summer in *Sports Illustrated*. There was something pure about the guy, something we could have used in that sad summer, something clean and never-ending.

Derek Jeter won the fourth of his five Gold Gloves in 2005, long before he made history at the plate as the first Yankee to amass three thousand hits.
STEVE GRAYSON/WIREIMAGE.COM/GETTY IMAGES

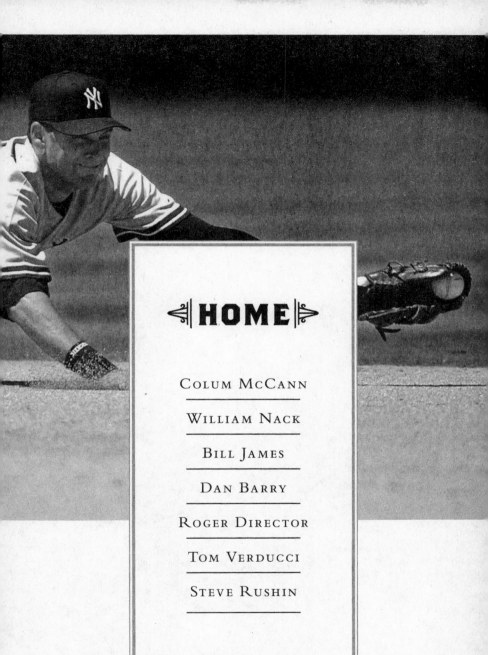

⊰| HOME |⊱

COLUM MCCANN
―――――――――

WILLIAM NACK
―――――――――

BILL JAMES
―――――――――

DAN BARRY
―――――――――

ROGER DIRECTOR
―――――――――

TOM VERDUCCI
―――――――――

STEVE RUSHIN
―――――――――

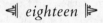

eighteen

The Long Way Home

COLUM McCANN

It was long before baseball ever enchanted me, and long before I ever knew anything of the Yankees, and long before I learned that a pitch could swerve, yet it came back to me, years later, sitting in the bleachers at Yankee Stadium, a curveball from the past.

It was 1974 and I was nine years old. I stood on board a ferry in Dun Laoghaire harbor. I was traveling with my father to England for the weekend. We crossed the high waves of the Irish Sea, the night blanket-black above us. On deck, men in flat caps worked hard at their coughs. In Liverpool, dawn rose in increments of gray. We boarded a train for London. I had to hush. We were Irish, after all. There were bombs going off in Britain in those days. We sat quiet together, my father and I, as the train made its way through a landscape that seemed exotic and familiar by turns. London, then, was a confusion of red postboxes and low white-terraced houses and chimney stacks and lavish litter caught on the breeze.

We made our way out to Highbury Road, where my favorite team, Stoke City, was playing against the mighty Arsenal. Portions of the game still decorate my memory with splinters of joy and despair—my team played to a 1–1 draw—but it is not the game that later made sense to me. On the way out of Highbury, in the throbbing crowd, my father took my hand. It was not an unusual gesture, but I recall the tightness with which he held me. We made our way to an off-license, where he bought a bottle of Powers Whiskey. He seldom drank, my father, and the purchase surprised me. We stopped, then, to buy a carton of Player's cigarettes, and I knew that the world was shifting somehow: my father never smoked.

"How'd you like to see your grandfather?" he asked.

I had never met my grandfather, Jack McCann. He was, I knew, a character—a man given to the Irish trinity of drink and song and exile. He had left my own father behind at a young age, but my father seldom mentioned it. Those had been the days, the times, the expectations.

We took a bus to the Pimlico Road, tramped up the wide staircase of a decrepit nursing home. I followed my father and stood in the doorway of the room. My father handed me the bottle of whiskey. "Go on in and give that to your grandda," he said.

A shadow in the bed. All hollowed and whiskered. He glanced up and said, "Ah, another feckin' McCann." But he perked up when he saw the bottle, reached out and tousled my hair. He was a fabulous ruin, my grandfather, a man who had fought in every available war, country, bar, and kitchen. He was dying now of gangrene from a badly clipped toenail. The small ironies.

That evening I sat on the bed beside my grandfather and—suddenly glamorous with whiskey—he told his stories. The greyhounds. The horses. The days with Big Jack Doyle. I sat in my red-and-white Stoke City shirt, stunned that this was a history that could belong to me. Present, past, future. The world was growing wider, deeper, longer.

He fell asleep in the middle of a story.

What I recall is my father lifting me on to his shoulder, down the staircase of the nursing home, out into the night, then toward the railway station, and home. A number of stray soccer fans were still singing under the eaves of the railway station.

◆

Three one down. Bottom of the ninth. One on. Nobody out. The Yankees against the Minnesota Twins. Game 2 of the American League Division Series, October 2009. A-Rod is at the plate. The air has that chewy sense of hope. There is always call for a miracle.

"It's gonna happen, Dad."

This is what baseball can do to the soul: it has the ability to make you believe in spite of all other available evidence. My son, John Michael, is ten years old. A true Yankee fan. We are in the bleachers. He leans into me and says that the pitch is going to come in high and fat. It's still a new language to me. The pitch is thrown and indeed it does—it comes in high and fat and 94 miles per hour. A-Rod leans into it like he's about to fell a tree and he catches the ball and it soars, that little sphere of horsehide rising up over the starless Bronx, and it is a moment unlike any other, when you sit with your son in the ballpark, and the ball is high in the air, you feel yourself aware of everything, the night, the neon, the very American-ness of the moment.

And then it strikes you that the ball has an endless quality of fatherhood to it.

We all know these moments. They don't come along very often, but when they do they open up your lungs to bursting point. It's not simply me sitting with my son in the Bronx, but it's my father sitting with me in London, too, and maybe him with his own father in Dublin, and it all comes back to me, the pure and reckless joy of the past, Arsenal, Stoke City, the dark corners of a nursing home, the slippery deck of a ferry boat, and how every moment is carried into other moments.

I stood there in the bleachers as A-Rod rounded the bases with that slightly nonchalant grin: a Dominican kid from Washington Heights had just brought me all the way back to Ireland.

◆

Baseball is so often talked about as the American game, but there is something wildly immigrant about it, too. No other game can so solidly confirm the fact that you are in America, yet bring you home to your original country at the same time. It is so much more local than soccer. If soccer is the world's game, then baseball belongs to those who have left their worlds behind. This is not so much nostalgia as a sense of *saudade*—a longing for something that is absent.

I have been in New York for twenty years. Every time I have gone to Yankee Stadium with my two sons and my daughter, I am somehow brought back to my boyhood. Perhaps it is because baseball is so very different from anything I grew up with. The subway journey out. The hustlers, the bustlers, the bored cops. The jostle at the turnstiles. Up the ramps. Through the shadows. The huge swell of diamond green when you crest the stairs. The crackle. The neon. The billboards. The slight air of the unreal. The guilt when standing for another nation's national anthem. The hot dogs. The bad beer. The catcalls. Siddown. Shaddup. Fuggedaboudit. The theater of it all.

And yet it is the difference that confirms the belonging. There is something so very affirming about bringing your children to a ball game. Learning baseball is learning to love what is left behind also. The world drifts away for a few hours. We can rediscover what it meant to be lost. The world is full, once again, of constant surprise. We go back to who we were.

There is seldom a night at Yankee Stadium when I don't recall my own father taking me out to the soccer games of my youth. He told me once that it made him feel young.

It was my daughter, first, who brought me out to the stadium in the Bronx. She was four years old on a school trip. Then the boys followed suit. I was bored at the games at first, but bit by bit, I began to learn. I slipped into the metropolis of Americana. The intricacies of the game. Batting practice. The hitting of fungoes. The signals, the steals, the squeeze plays. The pure mathematics, the vectors, the percentages, the gradations. Then there were the beanballs, the curveballs, the screwballs. There was all that showboating going on. All the little ritual exchanges that carried on deep into the night. The pageantry. The lyrical cursing that unfolded across the bleachers.

John Michael began listening to the radio late at night, under the covers. There was something gloriously tribal about the Yankees for him. He learned to imitate John Sterling, the radio announcer. It is high, it is far, it is gone. That one's outta here. It's an A-Bomb from A-Rod. He began playing the game, too, and so I would walk along Eighty-Sixth Street, toward the park, with a baseball bat in my hand. (How curious that the only baseball bats I knew in Ireland were ones that were used, in Belfast, for punishment beatings: how quickly the world turns.) Now I had to try to catch and bunt. I had to learn what a sacrifice fly was. I had to try to intuit the arc of a pitch. How far was my own father on the street behind me, juggling a soccer ball at his feet? How far was my dead grandfather?

John Michael began to study history through baseball. The history of the Negro Leagues fascinated him. It became a way to talk about Civil Rights, which in itself became a way for me to talk to him about Northern Ireland. He began to question his religious upbringing using baseball imagery: Wasn't Judas around in the ninth inning? He could make sense of mathematical problems by converting them into baseball questions. So much of how he negotiated his younger years came down to baseball. He grew smart with it, and curious, and provocative.

We become the children of our children, the sons of our sons. We watch our kids as if watching ourselves. We learn from them.

We take on the burden of their victories and defeats. It is our privilege, maybe our curse, too. We get older and younger at the same time.

I never meant to fall in love with the art of baseball, but I did. I learned to realize that it does what all good sports should do: it creates the possibility of joy. What better joy than hanging out with your son, or your daughter, and understanding that they have allowed you to become what you have become?

Sometimes, when walking home from the subway, after being at Yankee Stadium, I have the feeling that a whole country has been knocked around inside me. I am an Irishman, but I am also an American father, whether I want to be or not. I cherish these moments. They are majestic. It confirms that life is not static. There is so much more left to be lived. There are times that my own boys are so tired that I have to put them on my shoulder and carry them. They are brought forward by the past.

I still recall the night of the ALDS game against Minnesota. A-Rod tied it up in the ninth. Teixeira closed out the game in the eleventh. My son beamed, ear to ear. I think the stars over the Bronx shook that night. The potholes on 161st Street applauded. The 4 train exhaled oxygen. The heating units made champagne from steam. Everything was electric with possibility.

And me, well, I took a little journey a long way home.

nineteen

Day of the Locust

WILLIAM NACK

Newark seemed on fire down below, the end of some ancient holocaust, the flames from oil refineries licking at the hollows of the morning, a scene quite as surreal as the year had been so far, 1977—the year they shot Gary Gilmore in the abandoned cannery of the Utah Prison as the inmates catapulted balls of ice at newsmen gathered vulture-like outside the concertina fence, I among those hungry birds duly poised to turn the day's cold carrion into tonight's hot news. The year had by now been a lengthy glimmer of farewells—to Elvis and Groucho, to Bing Crosby and James M. Cain, to Maria Callas and Vladimir Nabokov, to Robert Lowell and Li'l Abner—and they were still counting the bodies that the Son of Sam had left behind along the sidewalks of New York.

How strange it all seems now, looking back, memories as dark and haunted as Billy Martin's eyes, circled in raccoon black. This was the year the Bronx was burning, the year of the blackout and the looting and the fires, the season when the Yankees were in a state of turmoil of their own, a twisted symbol of a twisted

town. Reggie Jackson had started it before the season even began—a few months after George Steinbrenner had signed him to
a record five-year, $3.7-million contract that had infuriated team
captain Thurman Munson—when Jackson told a *Sport* magazine
writer, over beers at the Banana Boat in Fort Lauderdale, "This
team, it all flows from me. I'm the straw that stirs the drink. It all
comes back to me. Maybe I should say me and Munson, but really
he doesn't enter into it . . . Munson thinks he can be the straw
that stirs the drink, but he can only stir it bad." When that story
appeared at the start of the season, Munson was seen walking
around the Yankee clubhouse and waving it in the air, howling
incredulously, "Can you believe this? *Can you believe this?*" When
reserve catcher Fran Healy, a friend of Jackson's, tried to soften its
impact by telling Munson that surely some things in there were
taken out of context, Munson said the funniest thing that Fran
had ever heard the catcher say: "For four pages!?"

Jackson became a prisoner of those lines, confined in solitary
everywhere he went—outside his locker, inside the batting cage,
in the dugout. "He just didn't fit in with these guys," Ron Guidry
would say. "I didn't know how to talk to him. He was him and
we were us."

His anguishing struggles with Martin grew uglier as spring
peeled off into summer. On June 18, in a nationally televised
game against the Red Sox at Fenway Park, Boston's Jim Rice hit
a blooper to right that dropped in front of Jackson, who fielded it
so lackadaisically that Rice, a slow runner, galloped unmolested
into second. Martin went into a fury. He sent Paul Blair to replace
Jackson in right field before the side was retired, and when Reggie jogged over to the dugout, Martin met him there and they
had words. In a rage, Martin lunged at Jackson, and it took two
former Yankee catchers, Yogi Berra and Elston Howard, to pry
Martin away. Red Sox fans by the thousands, witnesses to the
drama, cheered with delight at the show, at the Yankees appearing to dissolve before their very eyes, and NBC cameras beamed

it all across the land. Ignored by his teammates, despised by his manager, alone in that Ruthian house of pinstriped men, Reggie came to hate that drive to work through Harlem, the bridge to the Bronx, the walk from the car into the yard: "I was the center of the storm. It was every moment of every day. It was a coldness in the clubhouse, a coldness on the field, a coldness from the stands. *Every day. Every day.* It was a horror."

It was as though that team, and Jackson as its falling star, had a psychic bond with New York City, mirroring its travails the summer long.

Now it was 5:30 A.M. on October 10 as the plane approached the airport over Newark, the one carrying all those rollicking New York Yankees. They were standing in the aisles as the plane banked left over New Jersey and swung in low.

The party was nearly over.

Just six hours earlier, in the fifth and final game of the 1977 American League Championship series, the Yankees had beaten the Kansas City Royals to win the pennant. Mickey Rivers had cracked the game-winning hit in a 5–3 victory, and in the ensuing tumult the celebration had begun. Aside from one heroic at-bat by Paul Blair, fighting off and fouling away one Dennis Leonard heater after another, it had not been an especially inspired performance on either side—Jackson had just two singles in sixteen at-bats for the Series, a batting average of .125—but the Yankees had won the pennant in the end, and for the moment this was all that mattered. The corks began caroming off the ceiling in the Yankee clubhouse, and from the stadium the party moved by bus to the airport outside town. There the festivities finally climbed to 37,000 feet, reaching speeds of 600 miles per hour, and pitched up and down the aisle of the DC–8. Music was playing. Stewardesses sat on Yankee laps. Hands reached out and slapped Rivers on the back: "You are the Mick!"

"Outta sight, a beautiful night," cried pitcher Mike Torrez, sitting at a table near the back of the plane. "I pitched six innings on Friday night, five tonight, so that's eleven innings I pitch in two days. When I finish tonight Thurman told me, 'You're an *outstanding* fucking Mexican!' "

This went on for hours, from two to almost half past five, and it ended only as the plane turned and whined to a stop on a runway facing a bleak, squat building that appeared suddenly ominous on this dark October morning. Ballplayers sitting by the port windows watched in silence as hundreds of people, part of a waiting airport mob numbering five thousand, leaped police retaining ropes and raced madly toward the plane and up the landing ramp. You could hear them chanting through the open door. They beat on the backs of players coming off the plane. They had been drinking for hours and they smelled of beer and weaved in circles on the tarmac. Ron Guidry, who had thrown a three-hitter over nine innings to beat the Royals in the second game, 6–2, could barely move in the swarm of bodies as he sidled his way through the crowd. He was holding a satchel in one hand and his ten-month-old daughter, Jamie, tight to his chest in the other. Bonnie Guidry held her husband's belt from behind. I was a columnist with *Newsday* at the time, covering the team, but Guidry looked pale and worried with the baby in his arms, and so I switched roles, turning to him, telling him, "Hold on to my coat. I'll lead the way."

We picked our way toward the low-slung building. At times it was impossible to move. People hollered at Guidry and slapped him on the back. Someone reached for baby Jaime, saying, "A star of the future." Guidry turned away from him, his face a tightened mask. We walked on. The smallness of the child, the beery shouts and pressing of the bodies all around, painted the moment in a surreal glow. Bonnie Guidry rubbed her fingers nervously and appeared near tears as the mobs grew pushier around them. Catfish Hunter was ahead, holding a bottle of champagne in one hand and his wife's hand in the other. The Cliff Johnsons were not far behind, and with them were the Roy Whites and their nine-year-old daughter, Loreena, and then Ken Holtzman and the first base coach, Bobby Cox, and not far from Bobby came pitcher Don Gullett and his wife, Cathy, looking very solemn, and out of nowhere came pitcher Ed Figueroa and Ed's brother, Sam. Mickey Rivers trailed Catfish and winced when he heard voices call his name: "Mickey, don't leave us! Please don't leave us!" He muttered something to himself and rolled his eyes and walked on.

The center was not holding in Newark. It was growing late early and you could feel the tension in the crisp morning air. The mob swelled. Many men, loud and boisterous, were following the players and yelling their names in deep, insistent voices, a chorus laced with profane shouts. Nearby a siren whined and faded away. This little band of Yankees and their families had somehow gotten lost in the crowds around the airplane, separated from the main body of players, and now they were wandering unescorted toward a remote corner of the airport, looking for a place to hide. Two buses filled with Yankees and their wives had been stopped by crowds surging from the main terminal. They surrounded the buses. Fueled by beer they clambered onto the roofs while those gathered around them began to rock the buses and yell for the players to come out. The buses could not move, and the nightmare had just begun for the lost tribe.

Catfish and his wife, Helen, finally reached the lone building. He forced his way through the crowds pressing around him and stepped out of their reach through a half-open door. Helen Hunter held two carnations that had come with dinner on the flight home from Kansas City. They were standing in a hallway just inside the door and waiting for the others to come through the crowd.

The trouble arrived by foot a short time later. He was large and burly with a face bewhiskered and florid as a plum, and we could hear him baiting Catfish in a nasty, angry voice. "Talk to me, Hunter, goddamn it! Who do you think you are? Where's

Reggie? Is Reggie in there?" Hunter ignored the man and that only made him madder. The crowd was egging him on and he was drawing courage from them.

"Answer me, Hunter!" he yelled. "We paid three million bucks for you . . ."

Hunter stared impassively ahead, a sentry at the door. He saw us coming and opened it for us. Guidry moved very carefully with the baby in his arms as he worked his way through the crowd toward the door. One by one we picked our way through the crowd and slipped inside—the Guidrys and the Gullets and the Johnsons and the Whites, and Mickey and Bobby and Ken, and then Ed and Sam Figueroa. This was an eerie replay of that final scene in Hitchcock's *The Birds,* when Rod Taylor leads Tipi Hedren from their besieged house and quietly, so as not to startle or provoke them, through a menacingly quiescent flock of predatory gulls, who are clucking and picking at their feet.

By now the crowds had circled to the back of the building and had made their way into the office just off the corridor. That back door was locked and they started pounding on it to get into the corridor. "Let us in!" one howled. This hallway was our refuge, our sanctuary. The bewhiskered man grew more belligerent. He was still outside the front door but Catfish, now holding the champagne bottle by the neck, would not let him in.

"I'm coming in there!" the man said.

"Don't move," Hunter said.

The man pushed open the door and started through.

"Get out of here!" Catfish warned.

The man took one more step. Hunter went for his throat. At once a loud explosion, like a mortar shell, struck like a bolt of thunder through the room. Heads ducked. The women screamed. Hunter had dropped the bottle of champagne and it had exploded in shower of bubbly and glass. His hands free, Hunter missed the man's throat but grabbed his collar. The man spun in a half-circle to break free. Another man came into the room. Arms were flying in the air. Holtzman charged forward, fists pumping like pistons. The bewhiskered man reached out his hand and clutched Hunter's face in it, twisting and pinching it, and for an instant they looked frozen there—the man wringing Hunter's face, Hunter holding the man's collar, and now Helen Hunter stepped forward screaming:

"Jim! Jim!"

Hunter pried the man's hand off his face and threw a long right, bringing it over the top, like a fastball. It landed on the left side of the man's face and the voice of Don Gullett yelled, "Catfish, your arm! Watch your arm!"

Hunter went after the man again but two others pulled the man away. He was screaming and cursing. "I'll get you, Hunter! You can't do this to me!" Catfish turned away, straightening his vest and tie.

The man was gone but you could hear him cursing in a rage. "Let me back in there, I'll kill those fuckers!"

Gullett handed his leather coat to his wife. "Here," he said, "hold this."

"Why?" Cathy asked. Her voice was thin and dry.

"Just hold it," he said. Reluctantly, she reached and took her husband's coat and folded it neatly over one arm. Gullet was stripped to do battle now. He walked to the door. Hunter stepped back from it. He was breathing heavily. Helen appeared much shaken. She was still holding the carnations but they were already wilting in the heat of the corridor and Bonnie Guidry did not look well, either, standing in the pale light and broken glass of that morning.

"These are fans?" she said.

The mob kept pounding on the locked door, demanding to be let in, and for what seemed an age we were locked together in fitful stir. The pounding faded and went away. It was silent in the corridor when a security guard knocked on the door and told us that a bus was coming to pick us up. It arrived five minutes later at the back door. Those hundreds of pecking, predatory gulls had left by then, but the airport guards were taking no chances. They drove us to a distant corner of the airport and parked out there. They told us how the mob had mounted and rocked the buses carrying the rest of the team and would not let them leave. There were still unruly crowds around the terminal, the driver said, and we'd stay parked out here until the danger passed. Just relax. No one will find us out here. So we sat for thirty minutes in that bus and watched a bloodred sun climb the sulfurous sky. The players joked and reminisced about the fight. Holtzman sat turning the wedding band on his finger. "I bent my ring, but I got some licks in," he said.

Helen Hunter was quiet. Catfish wrapped his arms around his chest. He leaned back and spoke in almost a whisper to her. "You've never seen me fight like that, have you?" he said.

No, she said. She turned the stems and watched the flowers turn. "I never have," she said. "For as long as we've been married, I never have."

◆

That morning in New Jersey seemed at the time a final, fitting curtain to a year gone haywire in the Bronx, and a Yankee victory, over the loathed Los Angeles Dodgers in the World Series, seemed the only way to calm the growling stomach of the city. It had been fifteen years since the Yankees, the '62 gang of Mantle and Boyer and Tresh, had whipped the Giants for the world title. The Yankees won the Series opener in Yankee Stadium, behind Gullett and reliever Sparky Lyle, but they lost the second in New York in a game that seemed to conjure from the smoke a final signature moment for both the Yankees and the city in 1977. Some city landlords, caught in the squeeze between high taxes and deteriorating tenements, were recouping their losses by setting fire to their own buildings to collect the insurance money. During that second game, an ABC television camera was hovering over the Bronx, shooting down at burning buildings, when Howard Cosell intoned, "There it is, ladies and gentlemen, the Bronx is burning."

In the end, as this most complicated of story lines played out, there was but one man able to still the tempest on that team and that was the man who had first stirred them with his straw at the Banana Boat, seven months before. He became the deus ex machina in his own implausible drama, a figure right out of classical Greek theater, writing the most improbable of all endings to its tangled plot. It began in Game 4, when he scored two runs, one on a solo homer in the sixth in L.A., to help Guidry win it, 4–2, behind a sterling four-hitter spread over nine innings, and it culminated in Game 6, at Yankee Stadium, before 56,407 souls.

Jackson had hit his second home run of the series in his last at-bat at Chavez Ravine in Game 5, driving Don Sutton's first pitch into the seats and setting up the grandest of all baseball finales. In Game 6, he walked on four straight balls from Burt Hooton in the second inning, but in the fourth and with a man on, against Hooton, he swung at the first pitch and smashed it on a line into the right-field seats, giving the Yanks a 4–3 lead. In the fifth, against Elias Sosa, he swung at the first pitch again and drove an even harder and faster rope into the same seats, a two-run shot that made it 7–3.

By the time he came to bat in the eighth, there was a crackle in the air and Yankees were off the bench and leaning toward the plate and thousands in the stands were on their feet and chanting as he walked to the plate: "Reg-GIE! Reg-GIE! Reg-GIE!" These were the players who had shunned him all year and these were the crowds who had booed him all year—they had numbed him in their coldness *every day, every day*—and now here they were, aglow in the penumbra of his sudden magic, and on their feet and cheering as he whipped the bat around like a lash and drove Charlie Hough's first pitch, a lazy knuckleball, on a high arc into the centerfield black, 475 feet away. It was a titanic blast. Jackson circled the bases with the beam of a smile on his face, a large straw stirring a much larger drink. Jackson had homered four times on the first pitch thrown by four different pitchers, four prodigious clouts on four swings of the bat, and in the doing he made history.

Mike Torrez threw eighteen innings in that World Series, winning Games 3 and 6, and he truly was, in Munson's words, an *outstanding* fucking Mexican. But it was Jackson, at the plate, who resolved the complex, season-long drama with three improbable swings of the bat. It was a twisting plot that ended classically, with a full Greek chorus chanting the vindicated hero's name: *Reg-GIE! Reg-GIE! Reg-GIE!*

twenty

My Season's Better Than Your Season

BILL JAMES

D id you ever find yourself wondering which season was the greatest ever by a Yankee catcher? This question is not quite as strange as it might seem; it's unavoidable, in fact, once you start to make All-Star teams. To make an All-Star team of the greatest seasons ever by a Yankee, you have to choose a catcher. Once you are interested in the greatest season by a Yankee catcher, you're halfway to being interested in which was the second-greatest season by a Yankee catcher, and once you have that worked out, you are well on your way to being interested in the third-greatest season by a Yankee catcher. The rest, as they say in another context, is history. True, you have to work it for a while to develop an interest in which season was the fifty-ninth greatest by a Yankee catcher, but I'm there—way past there, in fact. If I knew when to stop, I'd be working for the post office.

1. Yogi Berra, 1950 (.322, 28 homers, 124 RBI)

Yogi Berra in 1950 was the only catcher in Yankee history to score 100 runs in a season; he scored 116. The only catcher to score more than that for any team was Mickey Cochrane, with 118 for Philadelphia in 1932. Yogi also drove in 124 runs and struck out only 12 times all year. He threw out 57 percent of attempted base stealers, although, at the time, stolen bases were so rare that most of them were reported stolen after the game by actual burglars.

2. Bill Dickey, 1937 (.332, 29 homers, 133 RBI)

Dickey's 133 RBI in 1937 is the record for a Yankee catcher. On June 10, 1937, Dickey was hitting just .229, and the Yankees were tied for first. From June 10 to July 5 he hit .452 with 11 homers, 37 RBI in 24 games, and the Yankees pulled five and a half games ahead.

3. Jorge Posada, 2007 (.338, 20 homers, 80 RBI)

Jorge hit 42 doubles that year, a record for a Yankee catcher, and played in the All-Star game for the last time. With a .338 average and a .426 on-base percentage, he would have had a good year if he'd hit 15 doubles.

4. Yogi Berra, 1956 (.298, 30 homers, 105 RBI)

Although overshadowed by Mickey Mantle's triple crown and his own three MVP Awards (in '51, '54, and '55), Berra had one of his best seasons in 1956, matching his career high with 30 homers and posting a career-best .534 slugging percentage, just missing his career highs in walks (65; his high was 66) and on-base percentage (.378; his career high was .383).

5. Bill Dickey, 1936 (.362, 22 homers, 107 RBI)

The only season by a Yankee catcher with a 1.000 OPS. Prior to the 1936 season, Dickey had been in the majors for seven-plus seasons, and had shown few signs of being a Hall of Famer, although he was a good player and a .300 hitter. He had never hit more than 15 homers in a season, had never driven in 100 runs, never scored more than 66 runs. In 1936 he learned how to pull

the ball, and launched a run of four tremendous seasons that put
him in Cooperstown. His .362 average was the highest for any
American League catcher until Joe Mauer hit .365 in 2009. Although Dickey had an immense home-field hitting differential in
some other seasons, in 1936 he actually hit .371 on the road.

6. Yogi Berra, 1954 (.307, 22 homers, 125 RBI, MVP)

Yankee catchers have won five MVP Awards, but this is the first
one on this list, and it came in a season in which the Yankees
didn't win after the Indians sprinted to a five-game lead by mid-
June. Berra played a career-high 149 games at catcher, threw out
34 of 62 would-be base stealers, and hit .343 with runners in scor-
ing position (RSP).

7. Elston Howard, 1961 (.348, 21 homers, 77 RBI)

Howard and Bill Dickey are alike in this way: both were in the
majors for a long time before their careers really took off, then
both had incredible four-year runs, Dickey from 1936 to 1939,
Howard from 1961 to 1964.

8. Yogi Berra, 1953 (.296, 27 homers, 108 RBI)

This wasn't an MVP season, either. Though Yogi won three
MVPs, we've listed four of his seasons now, and only one in
which he was the MVP. No other catcher in history had as many
great seasons as Yogi Berra.

9. Elston Howard, 1963 (.287, 28 homers, 85 RBI, MVP)

I am a huge fan of Elston Howard. If you had put Bill Dickey and
Elston Howard in the same park in the same years, a symmetrical
park, Howard would have been a far better hitter than Dickey. A
left-handed hitter, Dickey was helped enormously by Yankee Stadium; a right-hander, Howard was hurt enormously by the park.

This is not to say that Howard *was* better than Dickey; "could
have" is not the same as "did," and "would have been" is not the
same as "was." But if Howard had come up with the A's or White

Sox or Senators in 1952, where he wouldn't have had to battle Yogi for playing time or the park for home runs, he would be in the Hall of Fame today.

10. Bill Dickey, 1938 (.313, 27 homers, 115 RBI)

Bastrop, Louisiana, where Bill Dickey was born, was founded in the late eighteenth century by a Dutch con man who had fled to Louisiana to escape prosecution for using tax funds for personal gain. He called himself the Baron de Bastrop; his real name was Philip Hendrik Nering Bogel, and there was nothing "noble" about him. He got a land grant from Louisiana to establish a colony, failed to attract a sufficient number of settlers, and eventually lost the grant. He moved on from there to establish Bastrop (and Bastrop County) in Texas. In America, we only honor the best.

11. Yogi Berra, 1952 (.273, 30 homers, 98 RBI)

This one isn't an MVP season, either. That's what's remarkable about Yogi: his three MVP seasons actually weren't any better than any of his other seasons. Roy Campanella won three MVP Awards, too, but Campanella's MVP seasons are like a hundred times better than his other seasons. With Yogi, they're just random years; you can't even identify them just by looking at his record.

12. Bill Dickey, 1939 (.302, 24 homers, 105 RBI)

To illustrate the earlier point about Dickey and Howard: if you combine 1938 and 1939 into one "home" season and one "road" season, Dickey hit 42 homers and drove in 143 runs (over the two years) in Yankee Stadium, whereas he hit 9 home runs and drove in 78 runs on the road. He was a great fielder, wonderful agility and arm, excellent handler of pitchers, good hitter, but most of his power was just lining shots into the right-field porch.

Elston Howard in 1962, by contrast, hit 3 homers and drove in 31 runs in Yankee Stadium, whereas he hit 18 homers and drove in 60 runs on the road. In 1964 he hit .279 with 3 homers, 35

RBI in Yankee Stadium, whereas he hit .344 with 12 homers, 48 RBI on the road.

13. Yogi Berra, 1951 (.294, 27 homers, 88 RBI, MVP)

What will you give me if I can make it through this entire list without saying anything about the things Yogi supposedly said?

14. Yogi Berra, 1955 (.272, 27 homers, 108 RBI, MVP)

15. Jorge Posada, 2000 (.287, 28 homers, 86 RBI)

Posada in 2000 had almost exactly the same Triple Crown stats that Elston Howard had in 1963, when Elston was the MVP—same batting average, same home runs, a difference of one RBI. Other than the Triple Crown stats, however, the seasons are as different as any two seasons one can imagine. Howard had only 35 walks; Posada had 107. Howard had only 68 strike-outs; Posada had 151. The American League ERA in 1963 was 3.63; in 2000 it was 4.92. Howard allowed only 22 stolen bases; Posada allowed 70.

16. Jorge Posada, 2003 (.281, 30 homers, 101 RBI)

Peter Jackson's interminable *The Lord of the Rings,* released in December 2003, grossed $377 million, the top movie of the year, while the Clint Eastwood classic *Mystic River* grossed only $641,000 in its opening weekend, and staggered to $90 million total, the thirty-third-highest take of the year. What in the world was wrong with those people?

17. Mike Stanley, 1993 (.305, 26 homers, 84 RBI)

There have been five great catchers in Yankee history—Dickey, Berra, Howard, Munson, and Posada. It seems totally wrong to list Mike Stanley before we get to any of Thurman's seasons, but it's a list of good seasons, not good players.

I like to think of 1993 as the season of the "real" Mike Stanley. Stanley was a very talented player who had a mixed-up career.

He got to the majors in 1986 in Texas, having worked very few innings behind home plate, and he had a nightmare of a pitching staff to work with in Texas, including knuckleballer Charlie Hough and super-wild hard throwers Mitch Williams and Bobby Witt. Stanley in 1987 allowed 76 stolen bases in just 61 games behind home plate, also had 18 passed balls, and got the reputation as a wretched defensive catcher. He wasn't Bill Dickey, but he really wasn't that bad, either; in 1993 he led the American League in fielding percentage (.996), had only 6 passed balls, and allowed only 65 stolen bases in 122 games behind the plate, throwing out 31 percent of would-be base stealers.

The defensive reputation put pressure on him as a hitter, and he really didn't hit from 1988 to 1991 the way he was capable of hitting. The only season of his career in which his real ability came to the surface in all phases of his game was 1993.

18. Thurman Munson, 1977 (.308, 18 homers, 100 RBI)
Thurman, a high school shortstop, switched to catching so that he could help out a teammate, Jerome Pruett, who was a hot-shot prospect and became a fifth-round draft pick of the St. Louis Cardinals, but never played in the majors.

19. Bill Dickey, 1933 (.318, 14 homers, 97 RBI)
A "dickey" was a false-front shirt, worn with a tuxedo; maybe it still is, I don't know. I have no idea whether anyone still wears dickeys, or what they are called now. Why Bill Dickey was named after this appliance, no one knows, but it puts him on an All-Star team with Rick Schu, Pants Rowland, Don (Blazer) Blasingame, and George (High Pockets) Kelly.

20. Jorge Posada, 2002 (.268, 20 homers, 99 RBI)
Also 40 doubles. Posada in 2007 and Posada in 2002 are the only Yankee catchers to hit more than 35 doubles.

21. Thurman Munson, 1975 (.318, 12 homers, 102 RBI)

The essential difference between Yogi Berra and Thurman Munson is that Yogi had a sense of humor about being butt-ugly.

22. Elston Howard, 1964 (.313, 15 homers, 84 RBI)

I'm going to have to stop writing comments on every season, or this piece will be too long to publish.

23. Jorge Posada, 2006 (.277, 23 homers, 93 RBI)

24. Thurman Munson, 1976 (.302, 17 homers, 105 RBI, MVP)

25. Yogi Berra, 1948 (.305, 14 homers, 98 RBI)

26. Jorge Posada, 2004 (.272, 21 homers, 81 RBI)

27. Thurman Munson, 1973 (.301, 20 homers, 74 RBI)

28. Wally Schang, 1921 (.316, 6 homers, 55 RBI)

The Yankees had a young catcher in 1919 and 1920 named Muddy Ruel, whom they mistakenly traded away before he got to be good; they included him in a package deal with the Red Sox that brought them Waite Hoyt and Wally Schang. Schang was a very good player, with on-base percentages over .400 from 1919 to 1922 and in many other seasons, plus he threw out nine base runners in eight games in the 1921 World Series. But he was thirty-one years old when he joined the Yankees in 1921, and he was fighting time. He gave them three strong seasons, but within a couple of years, Ruel was a better player.

29. Bill Dickey, 1932 (.310, 15 homers, 84 RBI)

30. Jorge Posada, 2009 (.285, 22 homers, 81 RBI)

31. Bill Dickey, 1931 (.327, 6 homers, 78 RBI)

32. Jorge Posada, 2001 (.277, 22 homers, 95 RBI)

33. Mike Stanley, 1995 (.268, 18 homers, 83 RBI)

34. Bill Dickey, 1930 (.339, 5 homers, 65 RBI)

35. Elston Howard, 1962 (.279, 21 homers, 91 RBI)

36. Bill Dickey, 1929 (.324, 10 homers, 65 RBI)

37. Yogi Berra, 1949 (.277, 20 homers, 91 RBI)

38. Rick Cerone, 1980 (.277, 14 homers, 85 RBI)

The greatest fluke year by a Yankee catcher. Cerone was a .240 hitter who would hit 4 homers and drive in 30 runs a year, but he had this one really good season.

39. Bill Dickey, 1934 (.322, 12 homers, 72 RBI)

40. Yogi Berra, 1958 (.266, 22 homers, 90 RBI)

Studies show that no American can remember anything about the 1958 baseball season. Everybody over 60 remembers the 1961 season, when Maris and Mantle had the home run race, and lots of people remember the 1960 season or at least the 1960 World Series, when Bill Mazeroski hit a home run and Casey Stengel got fired. Lots of people remember 1955, when the Dodgers finally won, and 1956, when Mickey won the Triple Crown and Don Larsen threw a perfect game. A few people even remember some little snippets from 1959 (the Go-Go Sox, the beer on Fuzzy Smith's head) and 1957. But no one can remember anything about 1958.

41. Mike Stanley, 1994 (.300, 17 homers, 57 RBI)

42. Yogi Berra, 1959 (.284, 19 homers, 69 RBI)

Yogi and Phil Rizzuto were partners in a bowling alley near Clifton, New Jersey, that was so popular that you had to make reservations months in advance to bowl there. In 1959 burglars broke into the bowling alley and stole some money, but overlooked the four MVP Awards that were on display—Yogi's three, plus Rizzuto's from 1950. Asked why the burglars left the trophies, Yogi said, "They must have been Red Sox fans."

43. Bill Dickey, 1935 (.279, 14 homers, 81 RBI)

44. Thurman Munson, 1970 (.302, 6 homers, 53 RBI)

45. Johnny Blanchard, 1961 (.305, 21 homers, 54 RBI)

Blanchard, like almost all of the most famous pinch hitters in history, was never consistently effective as a pinch hitter; he actually did almost all of his hitting when he was in the lineup. Dusty Rhodes had a very famous year as a pinch hitter in 1954, but actually Rhodes hit only 3 pinch-hit home runs in his career—Blanchard hit 4 in 1961—and Rhodes's career average as a pinch hitter was .210. Gates Brown, whose real name was William James Brown, had a famous year as a pinch hitter for the 1968 Tigers, hitting .450 as a pinch hitter (18-for-40), but then he hit .205 and .244 as a pinch hitter the next two years.

Blanchard followed up his 21-homer season in 1961 (in 243 at-bats) by hitting 29 more home runs over the next two seasons, in a total of 464 at-bats. But whereas Blanchard was pretty good as a pinch hitter in 1961 (7-for-26, but four of them homers), he hit only .174 as a pinch hitter in 1960, .120 in 1962, and .071 in 1963. Blanchard was a really legitimate hitter, but nowhere near the equal of Elston Howard in terms of agility or throwing.

46. Jorge Posada, 2005 (.262, 19 homers, 71 RBI)

47. Yogi Berra, 1957 (.251, 24 homers, 82 RBI)

One of the challenges of putting Yogi in context is to reconcile his defensive reputation with his caught stealing percentages as they are now known. The American League for a few years in the 1920s actually counted and published stolen bases allowed and runners caught stealing by catchers, but then this data disappeared, not to reappear until the 1970s. When Yogi was playing, no one—literally, no one—had any data about the throwing records of catchers.

We shouldn't condemn the record-keepers for this; it is difficult for a modern person to understand exactly how tedious and time-consuming it was to keep detailed records before computers. In any case, the concept of catchers' records against base stealers reemerged in the 1970s, and in recent years, through a group called Retrosheet, there have been exhaustive efforts to re-create the play-by-play records of games from the past. These efforts have been fantastically successful, and we now have records of the games in which Yogi played that are not absolutely complete but remarkably close to that.

Yogi's reputation as a defensive catcher was never great. Yogi had what might be called an obvious catcher's body, but he got to the majors with little catching experience, and in 1947 his throwing was regarded as so substandard that it was almost universally believed by newsmen that the effort to make him a catcher had failed, and he would have to play out his career as an outfielder; even after the 1948 season, when Berra played 50 games in the outfield and 71 behind the plate, most reporters still thought of him as a makeshift catcher who would wind up in the outfield. This was after Bill Dickey had been called out of retirement to work as, in essence, Yogi's personal coach.

Later his defensive reputation improved, of course, but within ten years he was widely attacked as a low-energy, inactive catcher who just went through the motions behind the plate. Video that survives from the late 1950s does show him making loopy, high-arc throws to second base.

But the data now shows that Berra's stolen base allowed rates were very low, and that his caught stealing percentages were not only good, they were astonishingly good. In regular season play Berra is known to have thrown out 332 runners, while allowing only 329 stolen bases. In 1957 he threw out 37 of 66 would-be base stealers. This record from 1957 is complete; no games are missing. It was a different era and stolen base percentages were lower, of course, but Berra's throw-out percentages are higher, and his stolen base allowed rates lower, than any contemporary American League catcher with a substantial career (Sammy White, Sherm Lollar, Gus Triandos, Clint Courtney), better even than the defensive specialists like Jim Hegan, Del Rice, and Del Crandall. The only contemporary catcher who had better throw-out percentages than Berra was Roy Campanella.

We haven't yet recovered Berra's stolen base defensive data from the late 1940s; that will emerge within a couple of years, and there will be some minor gaps in it. But Charlie Silvera has been telling people for fifty years that Berra was very underrated as a defensive catcher, and this appears to be an argument that he eventually will win.

48. Elston Howard, 1959 (.273, 18 homers, 73 RBI)

49. Aaron Robinson, 1946 (.297, 16 homers, 64 RBI)

Named to the 1946 American League All-Star team; lost his job in mid–1947.

50. Jim Leyritz, 1993 (.309, 14 homers, 53 RBI)

51. Elston Howard, 1958 (.314, 11 homers, 66 RBI)

Yogi had run off quite a number of young catchers before 1958, some of them very good catchers, like Sherm Lollar and Gus Triandos. It was this season (1958) that got Howard over the hump, and eventually made him a regular. The Yankees saw a ton of left-handed pitching in those days, and Howard was very good against lefties, hitting .379 against them in 1958 (44-for-116), and .423 against them in 1961 (69-for-163)—whereas Triandos, although a right-handed power hitter, was exceptionally weak against left-handed pitching.

52. Jorge Posada, 1998 (.268, 17 homers, 63 RBI)

53. Matt Nokes, 1991 (.268, 24 homers, 77 RBI)

54. Wally Schang, 1922 (.319, 1 homer, 53 RBI)

55. Jim Leyritz, 1994 (.265, 17 homers, 58 RBI)
In the first half of the 1990s, Yankee catchers, collectively, were very nearly the best-hitting position on the team. In 1991 Yankee catchers hit .264 as a group, with 26 homers, 90 RBI; the power numbers were second best on the team, behind the left fielders. In 1992 Yankee catchers hit just .236, but led the team with 30 homers and drove in 87 runs (designated hitters led the team with 89). In 1993 Yankee catchers hit .288 with 31 homers, 103 RBI. In the strike-shortened 1994 season, which lasted just 113 games, Yankee catchers (primarily Leyritz and Stanley) hit .289 with 29 homers, 95 RBI. Yankee catchers in 1994 actually had a higher OPS than they did in 1961, when the Yankees had the famous catching combination of Elston Howard, Johnny Blanchard, and occasionally Yogi Berra, and the 1994 Yankees had the best record in the American League at the time the strike stopped the season. In 1995 Yankee catchers hit .280 with 22 homers, 103 RBI.

56. Jorge Posada, 2010 (.248, 18 homers, 57 RBI)

57. Bill Dickey, 1943 (.351, 4 homers, 33 RBI)

58. Yogi Berra, 1960 (.276, 15 homers, 62 RBI)

59. Bill Dickey, 1941 (.284, 7 homers, 71 RBI)

60. Thurman Munson, 1978 (.297, 6 homers, 71 RBI)

61. Wally Schang, 1924 (.292, 5 homers, 52 RBI)

62. Ron Hassey, 1985 (.296, 13 homers, 42 RBI)

63. Butch Wynegar, 1983 (.296, 6 homers, 42 RBI)
It's just a funny spelling of "Vinegar." Understanding this helps to explain a lot.

64. Pat Collins, 1926 (.286, 7 homers, 35 RBI)

65. Yogi Berra, 1947 (.280, 11 homers, 54 RBI)

66. Jorge Posada, 1999 (.245, 12 homers, 57 RBI)

67. Don Slaught, 1988 (.283, 9 homers, 43 RBI)

68. Joe Girardi, 1996 (.294, 2 homers, 45 RBI)

69. Elston Howard, 1955 (.290, 10 homers, 43 RBI)
Actually played only nine games at catcher in 1955, but I'm going to list him anyway, because otherwise I'd have to list John Ellis or John Flaherty or Roxy Walters.

70. Thurman Munson, 1970 (.261, 13 homers, 60 RBI)

71. Pat Collins, 1927 (.275, 7 homers, 36 RBI)

72. Jeff Sweeney, 1913 (.265, 2 homers, 40 RBI)

Take note of the name Jeff Sweeney. When you hear the name "Jeff Sweeney," wouldn't you tend to assume, without thinking about it, that he was a 1980s–1990s player rather than a player from 1913?

As it turns out, you should. Major league baseball had been around thirty-plus years before Jeff Sweeney, but Sweeney was only the second major league player ever named Jeff, and narrowly missed being the first. I should say "called" Jeff; neither of them was actually named Jeff. Big Jeff Pfeffer's real name was Francis Xavier Pfeffer; "Jeff" was a play on his last name. Sweeney's real name was Edward Francis Sweeney. There was another Jeff Pfeffer a few years later, whose real name was Edward Joseph Pfeffer, and then there was Jeff Tesreau, whose real name was Charles Monroe Tesreau. Probably this little explosion of ersatz Jeffs was triggered by the *Mutt and Jeff* comic strip, generally regarded as the first daily comic strip, which began syndication the same year that Sweeney made his major league debut (1908), and was enormously popular at the time.

The first "Jeff" in the majors who was actually named "Jeff" or something like that was Jefferson Lamar McClesky, but he played only two games in the majors, as the scouts thought he had too much name. There wasn't another one for twenty years after him, and then there was one Jeff in the 1930s and one in the 1940s. There was no major league player in the 1950s who was named or called "Jeff." When Jeff Burroughs reached the majors in 1970, he was just the tenth "Jeff" in major league history, and, by the end of the 1970s, there were still only fourteen.

Then, in the 1980s, forty players named "Jeff" reached the major leagues (forty that I have identified; I could have missed a couple). There were thirty-nine more in the 1990s, and about the same number have debuted since 2000.

A similar name is "Kevin"; believe it or not, the first "Kevin" to play in the majors was Mets' catcher Kevin Collins in 1965, and there was not another until 1974. By 1979 there had been five, and then in the 1980s there was an outbreak of Kevins that, in some counties, was reportedly worse than the plague of Jeffs. Hang in there, Torrealba; based on history I think we can now confidently predict that, by 2040, there will be sixty-two major league players named "Yorvit."

73. Yogi Berra, 1961 (.271, 22 homers, 61 RBI)

74. Buddy Rosar, 1940 (.298, 4 homers, 37 RBI)

A very effective half-time player in 1940 and 1941, splitting the job with Bill Dickey, Rosar lost his job in 1942 when he jumped the team without permission, to be with his wife, who was having a difficult pregnancy and was about to deliver.

75. Thurman Munson, 1971 (.251, 10 homers, 42 RBI)

76. Ivan Rodriguez, 2008 (.276, 7 homers, 35 RBI)

77. Jim Leyritz, 1995 (.269, 7 homers, 37 RBI)

Acquitted of vehicular homicide in 2010 because a jury thought that, in order to be guilty of vehicular homicide, a driver actually had to have done something that contributed in some way to the accident.

78. Les Nunamaker, 1916 (.296, 0 homers, 28 RBI)

79. Ron Hassey, 1986 (.298, 6 homers, 29 RBI)

80. Jake Gibbs, 1970 (.301, 8 homers, 26 RBI)

81. Matt Nokes, 1992 (.224, 22 homers, 59 RBI)

82. Thurman Munson, 1972 (.280, 7 homers, 46 RBI)

83. Buddy Rosar, 1941 (.287, 1 homer, 36 RBI)

84. Thurman Munson, 1979 (.288, 3 homers, 39 RBI)

85. Aaron Robinson, 1947 (.270, 5 homers, 36 RBI)

His wife was one of two 1946 Yankees referenced in the famous Simon and Garfunkel song.

86. Frank Fernandez, 1969 (.223, 12 homers, 29 RBI)

Fernandez had a career batting average of .199, but had tremendous power, and actually had more walks in his career (165) than hits (145). As a Yankee, he had 80 hits, 102 walks. He is the only player in Yankee history with more than 15 hits and more walks than hits.

87. Johnny Blanchard, 1963 (.225, 16 homers, 45 RBI)

88. Yogi Berra, 1963 (.293, 8 homers, 28 RBI)

89. Bill Dickey, 1940 (.247, 9 homers, 54 RBI)

90. Aaron Robinson, 1945 (.281, 8 homers, 24 RBI)

91. Bill Dickey, 1942 (.295, 2 homers, 37 RBI)

92. Johnny Blanchard (.232, 13 homers, 39 RBI)

Suppose that you take this list of 100 seasons, and you score them as 100 points for the #1 season, 99 points for #2, 98 points for #3, etc. If you do that, you get this list of the ten greatest catchers in Yankee history:

1. Yogi Berra	1,084
2. Bill Dickey	959
3. Jorge Posada	830
4. Thurman Munson	505
5. Elston Howard	466
6. Mike Stanley	217

7. Wally Schang	162
8. Jim Leyritz	128
9 tie. Aaron Robinson	79
9 tie. Johnny Blanchard	79

So Johnny Blanchard actually ranks as one of the ten greatest catchers in Yankee history, even though he was never a regular, and never batted more than 246 times in a season for the Yankees.

93. Bob Geren, 1989 (.288, 9 homers, 27 RBI)

94. Jim Leyritz, 1996 (.264, 7 homers, 40 RBI)

95. Butch Wynegar, 1984 (.267, 6 homers, 45 RBI)

96. Mike Stanley, 1992 (.249, 8 homers, 27 RBI)

97. Fred Hofmann, 1923 (.290, 3 homers, 26 RBI)

98. Jorge Posada, 1997 (.250, 6 homers, 25 RBI)

99. Wally Schang, 1923 (.276, 2 homers, 29 RBI)

100. Matt Nokes, 1993 (.249, 10 homers, 35 RBI)

Years from now, some researcher will debunk my analysis, and will claim that I really didn't put all that much thought into exactly how the seasons from 51 through 100 should be ranked. I throw myself on the mercy of the court.

twenty-one

The Dog Days

DAN BARRY

Somewhere amid the endless Long Island sprawl of aspiration, a father sits in his living-room chamber, sipping from his beer chalice as he considers the various financial threats to his split-level castle. Meanwhile, upstairs, his oldest child ponders more urgent matters as he lies on his bedroom floor, oblivious to the boyhood squalor that envelops him: the dirt-stiffened blue jeans, the grayish balls of formerly white socks, the ripped Hawkman comic books, the scattering of carefully collected wheat-ear pennies, some already worth twice their face value. Even the close air, redolent of a bologna sandwich misplaced and long forgotten, goes unnoticed.

Scrawny, bucktoothed, conditioned by bullies to greet each day with an anticipatory wince, the boy is poring over piles of small, rectangular documents spread out before him, searching for answers to why he has been denied his rightful place among the wreathed champions. He is confused beyond the confusion that is part of being eleven years old. You see, thanks to an inheritance from his brooding father downstairs, he roots with every ounce of his sixty-five-pound body for a perennial baseball underdog: the New York Yankees.

As I write this, I hear the hue and cry of outrage from across the continent, the angry dissent loudest in certain long-suffering precincts: the rain-wet hills of Seattle, the landmark-cluttered District of Columbia, the north side of Chicago, the lakefront of Cleveland. Even Boston, forced by two recent World Series victories to shed the lovable-loser status so meticulously cultivated over several generations, takes wicked umbrage. The New York Yankees? As underdogs? No — way! (Insert regional epithet of choice.)

Ah, but the indisputable documentation was laid out upon that bedroom floor back in the summer of 1969, and the boy has it still. That is, I have it still, stored in a Rockport shoebox whose location will remain classified: hundreds of old baseball cards, courageously saved from the sporadic cleaning frenzies that disrupted our home's natural disorder. Most of the cards are worth less than the face value of those wheat-ear pennies; some even bear the singe of fire damage (strange how I don't even remember burning out the eyes of California Angels outfielder Rick Reichardt with a magnifying glass). I keep them all as evidence, along with well-thumbed Yankee yearbooks that feature the mostly forgotten pre-Steinbrenner, Mike Burke, and a few crumbling newspaper clippings from January 1969, when Mickey Mantle, my broken idol, announced that he just could not play anymore, and I sensed, even then, that the Mick would never quite adapt to a work world without grass.

The Yankee cards among my tired collection are like mug-shot exhibits, prepared for presentation to the Court of the Beleaguered. From Jake Gibbs, catcher without bat, to Walt Williams, outfielder without neck, they confirm my childhood status as underdog. Here is Bill Robinson, one would-be phenom, batting .196; here is Steve Whitaker, another, batting little better. Here is first baseman Joe Pepitone, sporting his game-day toupee. Here is second baseman Horace Clarke, who so disliked body contact that he often failed to make the relay to first on potential double plays. Here are Roger Repoz and Ruben Amaro, Andy Kosco and Charley Smith, Fred Talbot and Hal Reniff, Frank Tepedino and Gene Michael and Joe Verbanic and Thad Tillotson and Johnny Callison and Danny Cater and Curt Blefary and Jerry Kenney and Jimmy Lyttle and Celerino Sanchez, poor Celerino Sanchez, and so many others you do not remember, probably by choice.

As hollow as it might sound, though, these were my heroes. I ached and rooted for every one of them as they failed daily on baseball's Broadway stage, Yankee Stadium, facing two opponents every time they stepped onto the field: the American League team of the moment and the Yankees teams of the past. My father's Yankees.

Who knows when a child first becomes baseball-aware? I fell under the game's spell at the age of seven, in the upside-down years of 1965. My mother came from rural Ireland, where sport meant soccer, rugby, hurling, and blood; she found baseball to be pastoral—almost like turf-cutting, only with uniforms. Still, she became conversant in the exploits of our central, post-Mantle heroes—Bobby Murcer, Mel Stottlemyre, Roy White, and Steve Hamilton—because she was a wife and mother, resolved to maintain the domestic peace that she occasionally managed to achieve. My father, though, was a New Yorker to his marrow, no matter how many times Gotham turned its concrete back to him. Raised in the belly of the Depression, he moved to or was evicted from one borough after another, never enrolled in one school long enough to develop friendships, never finding urban roots. He finished high school at night, found his higher education in the army during the Korean War, and returned to work on Wall Street—literally, on the street—as a cold-call salesman.

But he flashed his New York Yankees allegiance like a diamond-studded tie clasp; it granted a measure of elegance to his sweat-stained shirts, his sole-worn shoes, his striving. A child of flawed, alcoholic parents, whose babysitting options included leashing him to a post, he now rooted for baseball's best by day and vicariously socialized with them by night, sharing highballs at Toots Shor's or the Copa with that Rat Pack of baseball—Billy Martin, Whitey Ford, and Mickey Mantle. Winners, all.

By the time I was seven, then, I knew that Mickey Mantle was born on October 20, 1931, ten days after my father. That my father saw Don Larsen throw his perfect game in the 1956 World Series. That Ruth called a home run in the 1932 World Series; that Gehrig was the luckiest man on the face of this earth, but not really; that DiMaggio once hit in 56 consecutive games; that Berra was the best and Maris was the best and Mantle was the best, always, even with his damaged legs.

And son, the Yankees lost the 1964 World Series in seven games. They'll be back, though, son, because they're the top dogs, not the underdogs. The best, the best, the absolute best.

But just as I came of baseball age, in the spring of 1965, my precious inheritance broke apart like a tin toy from some discount store on Montauk Highway: the vaunted and suddenly lousy New York Yankees.

The statistics, including those contained on the backs of those baseball cards, tell the damning tale. In 1965, when I was seven, the Yankees finished under .500 for the first time since 1925—years before my father's birth. In 1966, when I was eight, they came to a thud in last place for the first time since 1912—so deep in the past that they were known then as the Highlanders, fielding a team with names like Hippo Vaughn, Cozy Dolan, and Klondike Smith. And in 1967, when I was—you guessed it— nine, they again lost far more often than they won to complete a hat-trick of failure not known to the organization since the administration of Woodrow Wilson.

In fact, the New York Yankees of my formative years were

mired in failure and mediocrity, with occasional competitive flashes, for eleven consecutive seasons. This fallow period was so startling, so un-Yankee-like, that you had to reach back to prehistoric times to see its like; that is, to those dark years before the purchase of Babe Ruth in 1919—two decades that are generally dismissed in the ballclub's hagiographic narrative as a kind of protracted spring training.

It is true that the Yankees would soon endure an even longer drought: the Mattingly Era, you might call it, when the impressive career of lion-hearted Don Mattingly, the Sisyphus of the Bronx, coincided with thirteen years of futility, from 1982 to 1994, that did not end until the team at least made the playoffs in 1995. But the earlier decade of failure, *my* decade, was still fresh in the collective Yankee memory; in many ways, it prepared the team's fans for their descent into sustained humiliation.

As with the collapse of other empires before it, the fall of the Yankees has been subjected to intense academic scrutiny— though, in the end, the reasons are effectively the same: age, self-satisfaction, the failure to anticipate. In 1965, the Yankees acquired a good-glove, no-hit catcher named Doc Edwards, who regarded his new teammates with boyish awe, but instantly recognized that these bandaged men beside him were no longer the famously dominant Yankees of years past.

"They were not the Mickey Mantle and the Whitey Ford and the Roger Maris that we knew," Edwards recalled. "They had reached a point in their lives where they were all hurt. You just don't take that many thoroughbreds and replace them with ponies—and, in my case, a draft horse—and win races. You just don't do it."

You just don't. But I didn't understand this. Weren't many of the surnames in the box scores the same as when the team owned October? Didn't the mere donning of pinstripes imbue a ball-player with Ruthian power and DiMaggio grace? I did not know, for example, that Mantle was paying the physical price for years of alcohol abuse, or that Ford and the catcher Elston Howard, at the age of thirty-six, were baseball Methuselahs.

Because of curious timing, then, and inherited allegiances, I became an underdog. And I am so grateful.

Otherwise, I would not have so keenly appreciated the need to find balance when the world turns upside down, as when a giddy nun wheeled a television into a sixth-grade classroom at Saints Cyril and Methodius School so that we could watch an event even more spiritually rewarding than the papal visit of 1965: the 1969 World Series, about to be won by New York's *other* team. The once-hapless Mets were up, the once-invincible Yankees were down, and the sons and daughters of those abandoned a decade earlier by the Brooklyn Dodgers and the New York Giants wept and rejoiced. Razzed then as a Yankee loser, I learned how to be a good sport; how to see the wonders of baseball beyond the sometimes confining bars of Yankee pinstripes.

Nor would I have fully comprehended the restorative powers inherent in loss, or the deep resonance in the clichéd vow to wait till next year. While other families bonded over victory, my family bonded over failure—a pervasive sense of inadequacy made more acute by the knowledge of the greatness that once had been. Let those in New England remember where they were when their beloved Red Sox clinched the 1967 pennant; I have never forgotten a Sunday earlier that season, in June, when the Yankees won the first game of a double-header at home against the Detroit Tigers, and were now trying for the sweep.

Imagine! Winning both ends of a double-header to come that much closer to .500, where official mediocrity resides! And then? Think of the possibilities!

My younger brother and I darted in and out of the house in boyish blurs, watching an inning on television, then playing an inning on the front lawn, watching an inning in black and white, playing an inning in color, pestering our father all the while about what we had missed. Yankees pitcher Fritz Peterson gave up six runs early in the game, but the team scrapped back—until, with one out in the ninth inning, Jake Gibbs stepped out of character to hit a pinch-hit home run and tie the game. Our Bobby Thomson moment: a shot heard 'round the living room!

Now our team's modest fortunes rested with the Yankee relief pitcher Dooley Womack, whose name never struck us as silly; he was just—Dooley Womack. He held his own through the tenth, eleventh, and twelfth innings, as the late-afternoon shadows encroached deeper upon the Stadium grass, as our telepathically delivered pleas failed once again to alter the standard performances of the likes of Bill Robinson (groundout) and Steve Whitaker (double-play groundout).

Then, in the top of the thirteenth, the Tigers loaded the bases, and stepping up to the plate with two out was their second baseman, Dick McAuliffe, to adopt that wide-open, gloriously eccentric batting stance we all mimicked when playing Wiffleball. Dick McAuliffe. Not what you would call a threat. Certainly not an Al Kaline or a Norm Cash. Just a Dick McAuliffe.

Well, batting left-handed, Just Dick McAuliffe drove a Dooley Womack pitch into the right-field bleachers for a grand-slam home run.

Nearly forty-five years later, I still remember the hurt contained in the loss of that inconsequential game: the deflating moment of McAuliffe's contact; the final score of 11–7, numbers that in other contexts are considered lucky; the sense of a small, sudden death in our living room; and the growing realization that my boyhood team simply was not good enough, and never would be. And I am grateful.

The seasonal failure of the Yankees made the game of baseball somehow sweeter. It became a kind of binding agent for a suburban family in need of one: a shared distraction; an ever-ready conversation changer. When my father lost his job, or temper; when our home's domestic quarrels became loud enough for the entire neighborhood to enjoy (Mets fans, all of them); when the three dogs slipped under the fence and ran away again, there was always this:

Dad, did you see that the Yankees are gonna get Rocky Colavito? Rocky Colavito?!?

Dad, watch me do a high-kicking windup, just like Lindy McDaniel!

Dad, guess what? Bobby Murcer is an All-Star!

Dad, it says here that Mickey is going to play in the Old-Timers' game. Can we watch that together? Can we?

◆

By the time Chris Chambliss ended the decade of Yankee failure with a walk-off home run that sent the team to the 1976 World Series, I was an eighteen-year-old college freshman—a man, technically—who erupted from my Rathskeller seat with an eleven-year-old's abandon the instant the ball cleared the wall.

But in the years to come, as the Yankees returned to collecting World Series championships the way I once collected wheat-ear pennies, my Yankee blood struggled with my underdog nature for dominance. I had been conditioned by bullies and baseball to wince, not gloat. I found myself rooting at times for small-market teams, like the Minnesota Twins, and Rust Belt teams, like the Tigers, as a way, quite frankly, of honoring my father: lifelong Yankee fan, lifelong underdog.

The family is long gone from that Long Island castle. The Irish mother is gone, too, and so is the Yankee father. But every now and then I open an old shoebox to lay out my inheritance before me, to recall again the few wins and the many losses, and to remember again what matters.

twenty-two

A Bad Case of the Yankees

ROGER DIRECTOR

My mother had never looked so shocked. She took one more glance at the thermometer.

"A hundred and five!" she gasped.

"Is that bad?"

"Oh my God, I better call Dr. Zarkey."

"Is a hundred and five bad, Ma?"

My mother didn't hear the question. She was already out of earshot, charging up the hall, swinging open the bathroom door, and cranking up the cold water in the bath. Next she appeared in a blur, her arms full of trays from the kitchen freezer, bombing ice cubes into the cold water.

"Get in the bathtub while I call Dr. Zarkey!—"

"But the water's freezing—"

"—Maybe he can meet us at the hospital. Did you hear me, young man? Get in the bathtub right this second!"

Immersed in the tub, I could hear my mother on the phone in a frantic yet formal tone.

"—Yes, doctor, a hundred and five . . . fifteen minutes ago . . ."

I began shaking uncontrollably. The medicine cabinet door was still open. Just as I had left it when I got out the thermometer after telling my mother I didn't feel well. But so much can change in a few short minutes—especially if you take the thermometer into your bedroom and hold it against the bare bulb of your reading lamp.

My mother appeared with a glass of water. My hands and feet were getting numb.

"Dr. Zarkey said to see if these bring your fever down," she said, handing me two St. Joseph's aspirin tablets. My chattering teeth bit them to pieces.

"Stay put in there for fifteen more minutes," she said.

Jeez! How blue would I have to turn before I could plausibly suggest getting out of the ice water? After all, there was nothing wrong with me. All I had was a bad case of the Yankees.

My favorite team was deadlocked with the Brooklyn Dodgers in the World Series, two games apiece, and I needed to watch Game 5, so I undertook the only logical course of action: get sick, miss school. I had to endure an ice bath to pull it off, but thanks to that thermometer and my reading lamp (the product of my father's cherished wish that I immerse myself in the world's great works of literature), I got to watch the fifth game of the Series.

The Yankees' manager, Casey Stengel, was starting Don Larsen. Larsen was a middling pitcher, a backup starter. The Dodgers had already smacked him to pieces like a bar of Bonomo's Turkish Taffy in Game 2, when he didn't last two innings and couldn't hold a six-run lead. Plus which: Larsen had no windup. The man had donkey ears and maybe a donkey brain, too. He just took the ball and threw it. You have to rear back. You have to kick your leg. You have to windmill. You have to rev. You can't throw the ball with all your might if you don't wind up! I knew that! Anybody knew that!

But not Don Larsen. Larsen looked as if the whole, epic business couldn't have meant less to him. Well, it meant something to me. I nearly gave my mother a heart attack so I could take in

Game 5 on TV. If Don Larsen couldn't even be bothered to go into a windup, he better pitch a little more effectively than he had in his prior outing.

As things turned out, of course, he did.

◆

I should be dead. Every October, it seemed, I'd get some bug that would make me sick. So sick I was unable to go to school. The coloring classes and the missed penmanship exercises—all of those enriching experiences were, sadly, irretrievably lost to me every autumn. It was one affliction after another, each more sudden and medically inexplicable than the previous year's.

Thus, uncannily, the following October, almost a year to the day after Larsen's perfect game, my legs, abruptly, with no hint of prior symptoms, were paralyzed. I was in the kitchen getting breakfast, standing and pouring myself a bowl of Wheaties. Then I collapsed on the floor.

"My God! Oh my God!"

Shrieking with horror, my mother ran toward me from the counter where she was preparing a bologna sandwich for my school lunch.

"What happened? What's wrong? Are you okay? Did you hurt yourself?"

"It's something with my legs, Mom."

"Oh my God. It's polio. I hope this isn't polio. Can you move your legs?"

"I'm not sure."

It was possibly—well, definitely—cruel of me to leave as much uncertainty in my voice as I did. But, then again, the Yankees were playing the seventh game of the 1957 Series against the Milwaukee Braves that afternoon, and I couldn't run the risk of assuring her I was okay.

I had begun feeling unwell right after the Yankees won Game 6 the day before. Over the next hours, a terrible throbbing began working its way from my devious mind to my knees as I found the listing in the dictionary of the torturous condition that threatened to leave Mickey Mantle a cripple.

"I don't think it's polio, Mom." I pulled myself to my feet and stood on shaky legs.

"Well, what is it?"

"I think it might be Osgood–Schlatter disease."

"What? Os . . . what? I never heard of that."

"They showed us a film strip in science about it last week."

"I never heard of that."

"You probably should call Dr. Zarkey, Mom."

"All right. I'll call Dr. Zarkey. What is the name of this, again?"

I wrote it down for her.

Then I hobbled back to bed. Well . . . fake-hobbled. All that truly ailed me that day was the knowledge that Milwaukee's starting pitcher was Lew Burdette. I hated Burdette. Burdette would hawk up a swamp's worth of pond scum to coat the ball before every key pitch, which he delivered from as far in front of the rubber as he could cheat while the umpire was transfixed by the pitcher's fingers as they fluttered past his mouth. If I could have produced as much phlegm at the snap of a finger as Burdette did, I would never have had to spend a single day in school.

The loogey-lunged Burdette had already bamboozled the Yanks in Game 2 and Game 5 of that '57 Series, and he did it again in the seventh game—an agonizing loss. But in '58, we fought back from a two-games-to-none deficit to force another winner-take-all finale against Milwaukee. Again, on the mound, starting for the Braves in Game 7, was our nemesis: Burdette. It made me sick to be so healthy—but not sick enough to stay home from school.

On Wednesday, October 8, admittedly clutching at straws, I told my mother the good news, which was that she didn't have to make me a bologna sandwich for lunch the next day.

"Why don't I have to make you lunch?"

"There's no school."

"No school?"

"It's a holiday."

"What holiday?"

I explained that it was a religious holiday that commemorated the time when a few embattled Israelites decided to take a stand and went out into the fields and gathered up all the chaff and tied it together with the sheaves of the most recent harvest after the full moon, and then bundled those into cubits that they used to smite their enemies. It was a very holy day. Extremely holy.

But my mother didn't buy it. This was discouraging, since I had no diseases to fall back on. I was in real danger of not being able to watch the Yankees take revenge on Burdette, the Nobel Prize winner in spitballs! It burned me up. How could a guy cheat by using spit and get away with it? It was confounding. But also inspiring.

In my bedroom the next morning, before heading into the kitchen for breakfast, I tore open a half-dozen packets of cherry Lik-M-Aid and poured them down my throat. Lik-M-Aid was a candy consisting of granular, fruit-flavored sugar whose artificial color was as vivid and indelible as iodine. And before I'd taken my first spoonful of Wheaties, I began expectorating—like a young Lew Burdette.

"Ma!"

"Oh my God! What's wrong with you?"

My mother rushed to my side.

"It just started." *Cough. Spit.* "I don't know what it is." *Hack. Huwawwkk.*

It was a tubercular display. Within seconds, my mother was shining a flashlight into my mouth.

"Your throat and tonsils are all red and bloody. Does it hurt?"

"My throat is really sore," I said. *Huwawkkk.*

"You're spitting up blood. I'm calling Dr. Zarkey."

◆

Over the ensuing years, illness and I parted ways (beating Burdette in that seventh game in '58 was a perfect start on the road back to health). I was growing into sturdy manhood. Come 1960, I was in the pink.

And so was my favorite new Yankee, Roger Maris. He batted lefty, like me, and I patterned myself after him, building my muscles so that one day I might wear my sleeves extra-short, like his, showing off a pair of menacing biceps and becoming the league's MVP. He led the Yankees to the pennant and then to the World Series, where we were clearly the better team, clobbering the Pittsburgh Pirates, outscoring them 44 to 17 . . . through the first six games. Unfortunately, in spite of our obvious offensive superiority, we still had to play a seventh game in Pittsburgh.

But there was no doubt who would win this one. No doubt meant there was no need to resort to lightbulb-induced fever, Osgood-Schlatter disease, bloody expectorations, or any other ploys. On the morning of October 13, I was the picture of health as I left for school.

Back home just before three thirty, I got a few cookies (all right—a box of Mallomars), poured myself a glass of milk, and turned on the TV, certain the Yankees would be pouring champagne.

A few hours later, there was a knock on the bathroom door.

"Are you okay in there?" my mother asked. She sounded alarmed by the noises she heard.

"I'm not sure."

"Are you sick?"

I struggled to reply. But it was hard to get the words out. My voice was thick with phlegm. My joints were weak. Snot dripped from my nose. My eyes were so red and puffy they were nearly closed.

I had been blindsided by a bug whose virulence I couldn't possibly have imagined: the dreaded Mazeroski syndrome.

"I could call Dr. Zarkey," my mother said.

twenty-three

Captain America

TOM VERDUCCI

Groundballs seemed to snicker as they passed him, remaining cruelly beyond Derek Jeter's reach, whether he lunged, stabbed, or dove for them. It was early spring of 2011, one of those bright, restorative afternoons in the Bronx, when the heavy curtains of winter are pulled back to reveal anew the blueness of the sky and the greenness of the grass. But the fresh baseball year showered none of its vitality upon the Yankees' thirty-six-year-old shortstop.

In the press box above the Yankee Stadium field, the great baseball writer Roger Angell watched knowingly, having so many times taken the measure of the familiar arc of a baseball life. Angell was born in 1920, during the days when a grand jury was convened to investigate the Black Sox Scandal of the previous World Series and six years after the birth of Joe DiMaggio, who in the wake of Babe Ruth's showmanship and excess would redefine the prototype of the great American baseball hero.

"I waited for DiMaggio to get to the Yankees, followed him

in the minors," Angell said. "I followed him beginning to end. That's how it is with a ballplayer. We see an entire life play out."

Baseball is the life within a life, the birth, growth, and thriving maturity, followed sooner or later, inevitably, by morbidity. No such baseball life ever played to a bigger audience under more candlepower and with less mystery than that of Derek Sanderson Jeter, playing the premier position for the premier franchise in the age of information.

It was nothing like this for DiMaggio. On December 11, 1951, the Yankee Clipper put on a cream-colored double-breasted suit and rode an elevator in the Squibb Tower on Fifty-Seventh Street in Manhattan to attend his own funeral as a ballplayer. There, in a Yankees' suite on the thirty-third floor, he announced to the press what he knew before the previous season began: he was done. His baseball life was over. One month earlier, he had turned thirty-seven, the age Jeter would reach in 2011.

DiMaggio's body was giving out. His right knee would buckle when he ran. His shoulders ached, sapping the snap from his swing, making it impossible for him to hit from the front of the batter's box anymore. He could still play decently—he hit .263 in 1951—but he was compromised and didn't like it.

"I no longer have it," he said.

Between the end of the 1951 World Series, in which DiMaggio hit .261 and the Yankees defeated the Giants in six games, and his retirement announcement a couple months later, *Life* magazine printed a scouting report on the Yankees that had been prepared by Dodgers scout Andy High. The scout had turned over his report to the Giants after the home run by Bobby Thomson beat Brooklyn in a one-game playoff and sent the Giants to the World Series. The section on DiMaggio was scathing:

> He can't stop quickly and throw hard. You can take the extra base on him . . . He can't run and won't bunt . . . His reflexes are very slow, and he can't pull a good fastball at all.

It was a brutal assessment of the great DiMaggio. In the same issue of *Life,* however, was an advertisement for a toaster that said something else profound about the era of DiMaggio's decline. The appliance was trumpeted as the "world's finest automatic toaster." It was, in 1951, at the cutting edge of modernity. "Now," the ad boasted, "make perfect toast from either side of the table."

Imagine. This is what passed for a technological leap at the end of DiMaggio's baseball days: handles on both ends of a toaster, so that you could plunge the bread into the heating coils from either side of the breakfast table.

The year 1951, with the advent of the double-sided toaster, was kind to an aging baseball hero. The decline of DiMaggio, just like his greatness, had passed largely unseen. The fading DiMaggio that the Dodgers scout saw every day was unfamiliar to his fans. To a baseball fan, the Yankee centerfielder existed mostly in newsreels, still pictures, newspaper stories, and box scores. DiMaggio never played on a team that drew more than 2.3 million fans. The first seven of the ten pennant-winning teams on which he played drew an average of between seven thousand and twelve thousand fans per game, leaving more seats empty than occupied in cavernous Yankee Stadium when Joltin' Joe was at his best. He played only 176 night games in his career. (DiMaggio claimed at his retirement press conference that night baseball took two years off his career.) He played in only nine ballparks, and played only 242 games out of the Eastern time zone—none of them west of Chicago and St. Louis.

The first live coast-to-coast television coverage of the World Series was his final World Series, in 1951. DiMaggio's last year also was the first year a baseball game was televised in color and the first year Yankees games were televised on WPIX, a local channel. When baseball was televised in DiMaggio's day, the broadcast typically used between one and three stationary cameras on the mezzanine level. There were no replays and no zoom. DiMaggio was a flickering black-and-white speck in a tiny rectangle, and was that visible only if you were able to position the rabbit-ear antennas just so.

Most of what people knew about DiMaggio was, in fact, either created or embellished by their own imagination, the willingness to fill in the massive blanks between the actual bits of information—the headlines and adulatory press coverage, the black-and-white newsreels, the game footage shot from afar. And because DiMaggio said nothing to make them think otherwise, the public happily filled those spaces with characteristics becoming to a hero. Following DiMaggio was like gazing upon the moon back then: at once familiar and mysterious, even romanticized.

But nobody writes songs or science fiction about the moon anymore. It is too well known. It's been mapped and measured and studied on a molecular level—exactly like a ballplayer today. The mystery and romance are all but gone.

Jeter may seem like DiMaggio, what with his career in pinstripes, his championships, his Madison Avenue appeal and a circumspect life in which he is never seen with his tie undone or a wrinkle upon his tailored clothing. But in truth, Jeter is nothing like DiMaggio, because his world is so different. Jeter is, rather, the most enduring star of the postmodern age. He has prospered through an era when ballplayers routinely lost their mystery and often their dignity, and that may be his greatest achievement of all.

Jeter played his first major league game in 1995, the year after the Web browser was introduced. He made his first All-Star Game in 1998, the year Google was founded. He hit a career-high .349 in 1999, the year the commercial camera phone was introduced. He reached 2,000 career hits in 2006, the first season after the debut of TMZ.

He has played in an era of expansion, expanded playoffs, the introduction of MLB Advanced Media and MLB Network, steroids and sabermetrics (in which every ground ball that eludes him is logged and inputted and analyzed by mathematical formulas). Yet through all this increased exposure and scrutiny, the only dirt that has stuck to Jeter has been the clay mixture from major league infields.

"You think about this day and age, with the Internet and everything," said Oakland general manager Billy Beane, "and everything he does has such a grace and a way about it. He's a good winner. It's hard not to admire him—hard not to like him. The Yankees' brand of this era is the Jeter Era. It's hard not to give credit to Pettitte, Posada, and Rivera, too. They helped stamp this era. But Jeter is similar to what DiMaggio was in his time."

In terms of public perception, that may be true, but as Gay Talese once wrote about Jeter, "You can't compare him to Joe DiMaggio, for DiMaggio didn't have bad manners—he had no manners. Where have you gone, man with manners? Here you are, Derek Jeter."

How could Jeter maintain his grace in such a graceless era? The answer begins with his upbringing. His father, Charles, was a substance-abuse counselor who grew up poor in Alabama, a black child raised by his mom. Jeter's mother, Dorothy, was one of fourteen children, her father a white church-handyman in New Jersey. Every August, Charles and Dot, as she is known to family, made Derek sign a contract in which he agreed to abide by eighteen behavioral clauses, such as a vow to avoid drugs and alcohol and arguing, and to respect girls. So when steroids began to take hold everywhere in baseball, including the Yankee clubhouse, just as Jeter was becoming a star—but one without the slugging ability of others in his shortstop fraternity, such as Alex Rodriguez, Nomar Garciaparra, and Miguel Tejada—Charles and Dot's kid said he wasn't so much as tempted to keep up with the juicers.

"I'm not trying to sound like anything, but my dad was a drug and alcohol abuse [counselor]," he said, "so I was pretty well educated about it. Regardless of what drug it is, alcohol or whatever, my sister and I were always taught about the risks of doing those kinds of things. My whole thing was that I would never want to disappoint my family. The temptation just wasn't there, you know what I mean? It never crossed my mind."

Jeter grew up dreaming of playing shortstop for the Yankees, and that came to pass only because of the great good fortune bestowed on him by the five teams that passed him up in the 1992 draft: the Astros (who took Phil Nevin), the Indians (Paul Shuey), the Expos (B. J. Wallace), the Orioles (Jeffrey Hammonds), and the Reds (Chad Mottola).

Truth is, Jeter was devoid of polish and smooth athleticism, and never looked the part of the can't-miss natural. There was a noticeable unorthodoxy, even awkwardness about his game. His swing was more salty than sugary, a jerky inside-out hack that seemed to underscore effort, not disguise it. When he ran, there was no glide to his stride, but rather the appearance of a series of mechanical hinges creating movement, like the way a marionette moves.

He was not a naturally gifted fielder, but had to work at making himself a Gold Glove shortstop. When Jeter first arrived at a Yankees instructional camp, for instance, one of his coaches, Brian Butterfield, had to teach him how to catch and throw the ball. Jeter would "give" with his glove hand every time he caught the ball; Butterfield taught him how to "take" with his hands, to go *get* the ball when receiving a throw. Jeter also threw like an outfielder, swinging the ball down and away from his body after taking it out of the glove. Butterfield cut his arm swing in half, instructing him when he was playing catch never to take the ball below his glove on his arm swing.

"We really broke everything down to the basics," Butterfield said.

In one area, though, it was immediately apparent that Jeter had a natural ease and ability: leadership.

"Right away," Butterfield said, "it was obvious that the players gravitated toward him. He was very well-liked. He had a great disposition, a good sense of humor, and a smile on his face. When it got time for working, that grin would melt into a serious look."

Jeter never had to work at leadership the way he did his hitting and fielding. He was bred to welcome responsibility. Said his mother, "When he was little he always wanted to be the last person up to bat, always wanted to catch the last pop-up. In basketball, he always wanted to shoot the last basket. In soccer, he always wanted the last goal. He always wanted to be the one responsible. That's his inner confidence."

The Yankees were in position to draft Jeter with the sixth overall pick only because they lost 91 games in 1991. (They lost 86 in 1992.) Until Jeter reached the majors in 1995, the Yankees did not make the playoffs for thirteen consecutive seasons, the longest drought in franchise history since 1920, the year Ruth was acquired. With Jeter, the Yankees assembled a modern dynasty, both on the field and on their balance sheet. They were one of the economic engines of the entire sport and of the media conglomerates that covered it.

As all of professional sports became a huge entertainment commodity, not just a diversion—or, to borrow the quaint word from DiMaggio's days, a "pastime,"—the zoom high-definition cameras and the always-on wired world of cell-phone videos along with the paparazzi and Twitterati chewed up and spit out the dignity of many of Jeter's contemporaries. In another era, many of those fallen sports stars might have remained admirable and pleasantly mysterious sporting icons: Bonds, Clemens, Favre, Vick, Rodriguez, Roethlisberger, James, Bryant, McGwire, Woods . . . so many became all too well-known. Jeter never fell. Charles and Dot's kid never changed.

Jeter has remained above the fray despite being highly accessible. He is a rare Yankee who before games is often at his locker, not hidden from the media in the off-limits labyrinth of lounges, food rooms, weight rooms, and training rooms in the well-appointed palace that is the new Yankee Stadium. He makes himself available after virtually every game.

The knock on Jeter from the media is that the valor of his accessibility is offset by the dullness of his quotes. Such a reputation can be partly explained again by his upbringing. In the Jeter household, the word "can't" was treated as an expletive.

"We weren't allowed to use that word," he said. "'Can't do this, can't do that . . .' My mom would say, '*What?*' She's always positive. I always think that in every negative you can find a positive, can at least learn from it. Even 0-for-32, you can still help the team doing something else. I don't like people always talking about the negative, negative, negative, because I think once you get caught in that mind-set it's hard to get out of it."

Negative lines of questioning are therefore abhorrent to Jeter, which means he won't bite when reporters fish in those waters. He also is not much given to public introspection, even in good times, because, as he said, "I just never liked people who talked about themselves all the time, gloat, talk about what they've accomplished."

So the media is left with an accessible superstar, but one who won't traffic in the self-serving pap or the gossip that more and more passes for reportage as sports have evolved from competition to entertainment. Jeter also won't allow his true feelings to be known, and positioning himself that way, he can come across as too safe, too judicious, all in the name of being completely inoffensive or, as a cynic would suggest, protecting the brand that is Derek Jeter.

There are two stories about Jeter that illustrate this self-imposed safety zone within which he operates. The first one comes from the visiting clubhouse of Bank One Ballpark in Arizona after Game 6 of the 2001 World Series. Given a chance to clinch their fourth straight championship, the Yankees were blown out by the Diamondbacks so badly that manager Joe Torre pulled Jeter,

Posada, and first baseman Tino Martinez by the fifth inning with his team trailing 15–0.

Jeter returned to the clubhouse to change out of his spikes and into more comfortable turf shoes. In the training room he saw pitcher Jay Witasik, a journeyman reliever for the Yankees who had just given up nine runs, a record-tying eight of them earned, while getting just four outs. Witasik was a bit too jovial about his horrendous performance. "Well, at least I had fun," he announced.

"*What?!*" Jeter shouted, and then he proceeded to go off on Witasik.

"Derek couldn't believe what he was saying and just jumped all over him," Posada said. "He was really, really hot. That was the angriest I've ever seen him."

Jeter could not believe anyone would accept losing so easily. "I don't understand it, will never understand it, don't want to understand it," he said, shaking his head when asked about the incident. "I can't relate to that."

Although the story of his jumping on a teammate makes the unflappable Jeter more human by cracking open the door to the furnace beneath his cold exterior, it is a story Jeter would never tell himself. It cuts against the grain of his humility, not to mention his belief in the sanctity of the clubhouse.

The other story he would never tell is set in 2004, when he's in the midst of a terrible slump. With two outs and a runner on second base, Jeter tried to bunt for a base hit—he fouled off the ill-advised attempt—rather than trying to drive in the man on second. It was bad baseball, and manager Joe Torre confronted him after the inning. "What was *that*?" he demanded.

Jeter laughed at himself and replied, "Mr. T., I need a hit."

Loathe to admit he was going so badly that he resorted to bad baseball in search of a hit, Jeter would not volunteer that story, either. With Jeter, there are certain absolutes, and no room for concession. He has no tolerance for negativity, as he said, but also does not curse, does not change the model of his bat, does not talk about his private life. And he does not use the word "slump," not even when he is 0-for-32, as he was in 2004 (a drought that ended with a huge home run in Yankee Stadium).

The former Yankees pitcher David Cone likes to tell his own story about Jeter, about the consistency of his character even when he was a rookie in 1996. Cone, Darryl Strawberry, and Tim Raines were among the veterans who ran the Yankee clubhouse that year, the guys who established the unwritten code of player conduct, what it meant to be a professional and a Yankee. They were especially quick to dispense lessons in baseball culture to rookies who might stray outside the boundaries of protocol. They watched Jeter closely when the Yankees made him their Opening Day shortstop in 1996.

"We had a veteran team that would have given him a rookie hazing if we thought he needed it," Cone recalled. "We couldn't find an opening anywhere. We were looking . . . the first six weeks, the first couple of months . . . looking for any reason to say, 'Hey, kid, you can't do that.' *Anything.* On the field, on the bus, at hotels, in his wardrobe . . . but there was nothing.

"When you talk about great makeup, a great background, he had it. The way he carried himself, his demeanor, was so impressive. He was kind of quiet, kept to himself, and didn't say anything wrong or dumb like most rookies do, which allows you to hammer them. Never happened."

It didn't happen after that rookie year, either. Jeter came ready-made for responsibility. "I would be the same person regardless of what I was doing and where I was playing," he said. "I think everyone has to understand they are responsible for their actions. I'm not trying to act a certain way to make people happy; I'm just who I am. But again, it's something that I learned at a young age."

There always was a preternatural cool about him, an aura that announced he was made for the big moments, that he would wind up on the winning side. Right before the first pitch of Game 7 of the 2001 World Series, Jeter and Arizona pitcher Curt Schilling looked each other in the eye and each gave a slight, knowing smile. The moment they shared was an acknowledgment by both that after six grueling games, they were perfectly happy to have the baseball season come down to one game.

"I remember it," Jeter said. "It was fun. Schilling was as big a big-game pitcher as there was. So Game 7 of the World Series and you're facing the best? That's fun."

Thirty-nine million people watched that game. Jeter and the Yankees lost, 3–2. "You're playing *a game,* whether it's Little League or Game 7 of the Word Series. It's impossible to do well unless you're having a good time. People talk about pressure. Yeah, there's pressure. But I just look at it as fun. If I stop having fun, then I'm not going to play."

As all the seasons and postseasons passed, Jeter, like a great Hollywood actor, became a fixture in the culture, a prime-time regular in October. Through 2010 he had played in 147 postseason games, more than any player in history, and the equivalent of almost an entire championship season on the biggest stage. People came to talk about Jeter moments the way they talk about De Niro films. Everyone had a favorite: the Flip, the Mr. November home run, the Subway Series leadoff homer, the two-strike double off Pedro Martinez to ignite the 2003 ALCS Game 7 comeback . . . as media platforms expanded and multiplied, no one was more visible than Jeter. The spotlight enhanced him. Even in 2010, a down year, when Jeter batted .270, more Jeter jerseys were sold than those bearing the name of any other player in baseball.

A few more nefarious groundballs might have eluded him as he has aged, but Jeter has stayed remarkably unchanged through his baseball life, a man true to himself and to his parents. In an era of unnatural power, it was Jeter who became the face of baseball without ever hitting 25 home runs or winning a Most Valuable Player Award, a testament to how he carried himself as much as to his statistics—the 3,000 hits, all those postseason records—or his championships. In such a knowing age, with mystery and romance leeched out of baseball life, it is the exceptional star who endures, even thrives, with integrity intact.

twenty-four

Yankee Mortals

STEVE RUSHIN

Seventeen miles north of the Bronx lay twin cities of the dead, the Kensico and Gate of Heaven Cemeteries, whose celebrated residents are a *Who's Who of Who's Through* in twentieth-century American entertainment.

This is life's after-party, where showbiz types, having strut and fret their hour onstage, while away eternity in the exclusive company of one another: Fred Allen by Anne Bancroft by Tommy Dorsey by Florence Ziegfeld of Follies fame. Jimmy Cagney is here. So is Soupy Sales. This is where Rachmaninoff stopped composing and started decomposing.

In this eternal Toots Shor's, the swells still clamor to be near the athletes—baseball men, mostly, some of whom are best remembered now for their serendipitous connection to the Yankees. Giants catcher Sal Yvars (1924–2008) made the final out of the 1951 World Series, a game cemented in history as Joe DiMaggio's last. Umpire John McSherry (1944–1996) was behind the plate for Game 6 of the 1977 World Series, when Reggie Jackson hit three home runs on three consecutive pitches.

But the biggest stars in this firmament are the Yankees, whose biggest star remains in *requiem aeternum* inside the Gate of Heaven. Babe Ruth was first buried on August 19, 1948, and is buried anew every day beneath an ever-refreshing array of mementoes— baseballs, hot dogs, Yankee caps, and bottle caps. In silencing their cell phones to pass a moment of silence for a man born in 1895, the pilgrims at Ruth's graveside form an era-melding tableau not unlike the one on Babe's headstone, in which a robed-and-sandaled Jesus walks side by side with a boy dressed for baseball.

Whatever Jesus said about the difficulty of a rich man entering heaven does not apply at the Gates of Heaven. In addition to Ruth you'll find the man who sold him—former Red Sox owner Harry Frazee—as well as the man who bought him, Jacob Ruppert. Indeed, the Colonel is interred in the grandest crypt of them all, a Greek-columned mausoleum that is the Acropolis of this necropolis, befitting the owner of the 1927 New York Yankees.

Down a little slope from Ruth lies Billy Martin, beneath several pairs of his signature sunglasses and the occasional cowboy hat. At Martin's funeral mass in St. Patrick's Cathedral, Bishop Edwin Broderick said: "The cathedral is the last place you'd expect to find Billy. But it so happens this *is* the last place we find him."

On the contrary, *this* is the last place we find Martin, and Lou and Eleanor Gehrig, and countless other souls whose names are known only to their descendants. Here is Billie Burke, who played Glinda the Good Witch, who tells the Wicked Witch in *The Wizard of Oz* "You have no power here."

That might be true of many here, but not of these Yankees, who still exert a strange hold on their fans. Gate of Heaven and Kensico have a western analogue, the Holy Cross Catholic Cemetery in San Mateo, California, where the great DiMaggio is buried near Frank Crosetti, by some measures the greatest Yankee of them all, thirty-seven consecutive seasons in uniform as shortstop and third-base coach still the longest in team history.

Crosetti scored in a record twenty-three World Series, in-

cluding 1956, when Don Larsen threw his perfect game. Umpire
Babe Pinelli was behind the plate that day and is beneath a plate
now, at Holy Cross, still connected—as he was then and ever shall
be—to the magnificent, midcentury, Mickey Mantle–era New
York Yankees.

The simple headstones of these famous men are testament not
to their extraordinary feats but to their ordinariness, evidence
that each of us is mortal—even the immortal.

◆

Generations of children growing up in New York believed that
the Yankee immortals were buried in Monument Park at Yankee
Stadium, accounting, in part, for the hushed tone on tours and
the veneration of the bronze plaques, to which a sun-blotting addition was made in 2010 when owner George M. Steinbrenner
died, necessitating an Ozymandian memorial.

But even growing up in Minnesota, I was acutely aware of
Yankee mortality, in all its combinations. One of my earliest notions of death came from televised sports movies, first *Pride of the
Yankees,* in which Gary Cooper as Lou Gehrig brushes aside his
"bad break" to declare himself the luckiest man on the face of the
earth. Later, and more alarming still, came the sight of William
Bendix as Babe Ruth promising to slug a homer for a dying boy
in the hospital.

The spectacle of my father weeping through *Brian's Song* every
fall in the seventies was the only evidence of Dad's working tear
ducts. I knew, even before reading "To an Athlete Dying Young,"
that there was something especially tragic about the early demise
of a ballplayer.

I was twelve years old, on a family vacation to Washington,
DC, on August 2, 1979, when news came over TV that Thurman Munson was killed in the crash of his Cessna Citation. There
were six of us in adjoining rooms of the Holiday Inn in Arlington,
Virginia. I can still remember—or think I can—the white noise

of the air-conditioner, the chlorinated smell of the carpet, the TV on its stand. I worried, too, about having to board an airplane to fly home that week. At twelve, Munson's death scared me in the way that only the death of the pope, a year earlier, had done.

He was, after all, "Captain of the New York Yankees," as his gravestone states. That monument, at Sunset Hills Memory Gardens in Canton, Ohio, is engraved with a portrait of the catcher in pinstripes, in his athletic prime.

It's a full-body portrait, but his funeral gave a fuller picture of Munson, when Neil Diamond songs were played and his favorite book was revealed as *Jonathan Livingston Seagull*. Funerals and graves are little snapshots of who we are, as well as who we think ourselves to be, and who our survivors want us to have been. The grave marker of manager Joe McCarthy, all-time winningest Yankee manager, reads, simply: HUSBAND.

The Munson memories were inescapable in 2006, when again I turned on the TV to see that Yankee pitcher Cory Lidle had died in a plane crash. Four summers later, news of Steinbrenner's death arrived on the radio, at Skaket Beach in Orleans, Massachusetts, where a man on a nearby blanket, in a near-parody of a Boston accent, profanely defamed the Boss. I could hardly believe, or forget, the sunbather's vitriol. Steinbrenner, Munson, Ruth—they remain indelible, all these midsummer Yankee partings.

Dying of throat cancer, Ruth famously said: "The termites have got me." The phrase echoed—in its offhand way—Gehrig's reference to his own "bad break," the disease that would bear his name and claim another Yankee Hall of Famer.

Termites and all, Ruth's death was Ruthian, with a hundred thousand mourners paying their respects at Yankee Stadium, where he lay in state for two days. At the state funeral, another seventy-five thousand stood in the rain on Fifth Avenue, and watched the cortege pull away from St. Patrick's, bound for the Gate of Heaven.

What's common to these Yankee funerals is not just their Yankeeness, though death is the inevitable end of one's "Yankeeography," as the Yankee biopics are called on Yankee state television, the YES Network. Mark Teixeira was probably speaking of his desire to retire as a Yankee when he said: "I'm going to be buried in pinstripes." Or maybe not—the last line of Jane Leavy's biography of Mickey Mantle is: "He was buried in pinstripes." And why wouldn't he be? The Yankee top hat logo is on Bill Dickey's headstone. Elston Howard's has a small number 32 and an interlocking NY.

But what is more common to the passing of Yankee mortals than even their Yankeeness is the mordant, manly humor that leaks out on these occasions. They don't let death rob them of their sense of humor.

Pallbearer Joe Dugan, at Ruth's funeral that long-ago August, said: "I'd give $100 for an ice-cold beer." To which teammate Waite Hoyt replied: "So would the Babe."

Mantle joked that he would be turned away at the Pearly Gates, only to be called back by St. Peter, who would tell him: "God wants to know if you'd sign these six dozen baseballs."

Casey Stengel, who once said, "Most people my age are dead at the present time," finally passed in 1975, at which time Jim Murray wrote: "Well, God is certainly getting an earful tonight." He was right: Stengel is still talking, in perpetuity, on his epitaph at Forest Lawn, where a memorial plaque says: THERE COMES A TIME IN EVERY MAN'S LIFE AND I'VE HAD PLENTY OF THEM. Above the words is a bronze relief of Casey, squinting, in Yankee cap and pinstripes.

Stengel died on September 29, at the end of Billy Martin's first season as Yankee manager. When Billy flew to Oakland for the funeral, he slept in Casey's bed the night before the service. It is these connections that bind the Yankees in eternal memory. When Martin, in his turn, was buried at Gate of Heaven on December 30, 1989, a worker found a note on Ruth's grave: "Dear Babe—Take care of Billy."

Nine months after he was diagnosed with ALS, I interviewed Catfish Hunter at his home in Hertford, North Carolina. When

I pulled my rental car into his driveway, he was waiting there to greet me. I extended my hand to shake his but Cat's arms hung limp at his side, stilled by Lou Gehrig's disease.

We went inside. He led me up a kind of stairway to heaven, a staircase with seventy-eight balusters, each baluster a Louisville Slugger, game-used by a Hall of Famer. At the top of the stairs was an attic filled with baseball memorabilia. "I got the last picture of Thurman in uniform," Catfish said up there. "It was the day before he got killed. He fouled a ball off his foot. I was jumpin' up and down in the dugout, screamin' like a dawg, imitatin' him, and a photographer took a picture: it's Thurman lookin' at me like, *You stupid son of a bitch*."

The story ran on September 6, 1999. Catfish died three days later and was buried in Cedarwood Cemetery, near his home. His headstone is in the shape of a baseball, engraved with his signature and the logos of the A's and Yankees. You can find pictures of it on the Internet, where fans still post memorial messages.

Of course, not all the Yankees immortals are still receiving visitors. But only because not all of them were buried. Phil Rizzuto was cremated, obviating the need for a funeral procession. In death, as in life, Scooter beat the traffic.

⫷Yankees⫸
by the
⫷Numbers⫸

HITTING

PITCHING

HONORS, AWARDS, AND TITLES

SABREMETRICS

BASERUNNING AND FIELDING

MANAGERS, OWNERS, AND STADIUMS

Mariano Rivera notched 291 of his record-breaking 603 career saves (through 2011) in Yankee Stadium; 312 were on the road. WALTER IOOSS JR./SPORTS

Hitting*

3   Yankees who hit home runs in their first major league at-bat: John Miller (September 11, 1966), Marcus Thames (June 10, 2002), and Andy Phillips (September 26, 2004). Thames's titanic blow came versus future Yankee Randy Johnson of the Diamondbacks on the first big-league pitch he saw. Phillips matched the first-pitch feat against Terry Adams of the Red Sox, the same team that Miller touched up for his clout.

61   Consecutive games in which nineteen-year-old Joe DiMaggio hit safely for the Pacific Coast League San Francisco Seals in 1933. Eight years later he would hit in 56 straight games for the Yankees, the longest streak in major league history.

33   Consecutive games in which Hal Chase hit safely in 1907, the second-longest streak in franchise history.

42   Career hitting streaks of ten games or more by Derek Jeter, the most in franchise history.

---

* All statistics through 2011.

373 Home runs hit from the left side of the plate by Mickey Mantle, enough when he retired to place him third among Yankees (behind Ruth and Gehrig) and sixteenth overall in career homers. But when his 163 right-handed home runs are added in, his total of 536 big flies placed him third in big-league history and second to Ruth in Yankee annals.

11 Runs batted in by Tony Lazzeri on May 24, 1936, against the Philadelphia Athletics, the American League record. Lazzeri hit three home runs—two grand slams and a solo shot—along with a two-run triple in New York's 25–2 shellacking of the A's.

7 Sixth-inning RBIs by Alex Rodriguez on October 4, 2009, setting the AL mark for an inning. In the frame A-Rod hit a three-run homer then a grand slam off of Andy Sonnastine. Those seven RBIs on the final day of the season gave Rodriguez an even 100 for the season, allowing him to extend his streak of 100-RBI seasons to twelve. (He since passed Gehrig and Jimmie Foxx to set the major league record of fourteen.)

659 Career home runs by Babe Ruth (of his career total of 714) that were hit as a Yankee. Only Hank Aaron, who blasted 733 bombs as a Brave, hit more for one team. Willie Mays placed right behind the Bambino with 646 for the Giants.

9 Career pinch-hit home runs by Yogi Berra, the most in franchise history.

23 Grand slams hit by Lou Gehrig, a major league record. Alex Rodriguez is one shy of the mark, which has stood undisturbed since 1938.

2 Yankees who hit three home runs in a World Series game. Babe Ruth did it twice, with his hat tricks in the Game 4 of the 1926 and the 1928 Fall Classics, and Reggie Jackson did it on three consecutive pitches off three different Dodger pitchers (Burt Hooton, Elias Sosa, and Charlie Hough) in Game 6 of the 1977 Series.

.200 Career batting average for Bucky Dent against Red Sox pitcher Mike Torrez as he stepped to the plate for his third at-bat in the 1978 one-game AL East playoff. Dent had been just 4-for-20 with two RBIs against the veteran right-hander but launched an improbable three-run home run over Fenway Park's Green Monster—just his fifth of the season—to give the Yankees the lead and ultimately the AL East crown.

12 Major league career record for walk-off home runs, shared by Mickey Mantle, Babe Ruth, Jimmie Foxx, Stan Musial, Frank Robinson, and Jim Thome.

4 Yankees who have hit game-ending World Series home runs: Tommy Hendrich, Game 1, 1949; Mickey Mantle, Game 3, 1964; Chad Curtis, Game 3, 1999; and Derek Jeter, Game 4, 2001.

2 Batters who have hit World Series game-ending home runs against the Yankees: Eddie Mathews, Braves, Game 4, 1957, and the only Game 7 Series ending shot by Pittsburgh's Bill Mazeroski in 1960.

Batting Average (Career)

Babe Ruth	.349
Lou Gehrig	.340
Earle Combs	.325
Joe DiMaggio	.325
Derek Jeter	.313

Batting Average (Season)

Babe Ruth, 1923	.393
Joe DiMaggio, 1939	.381

Lou Gehrig, 1930	.379
Babe Ruth, 1924	.378
Babe Ruth, 1921	.378

Hits (Career)

Derek Jeter	3,088
Lou Gehrig	2,721
Babe Ruth	2,518
Mickey Mantle	2,415
Bernie Williams	2,336

Hits (Season)

Don Mattingly, 1986	238
Earle Combs, 1927	231
Lou Gehrig, 1930	220
Derek Jeter, 1999	219
Lou Gehrig, 1927	218

Runs Scored (Career)

Babe Ruth	1,959
Lou Gehrig	1,888
Derek Jeter	1,769
Mickey Mantle	1,676
Joe DiMaggio	1,390

Runs Scored (Season)

Babe Ruth, 1921	177
Lou Gehrig, 1936	167
Babe Ruth, 1928	163
Lou Gehrig, 1931	163
Babe Ruth, 1920	158
Babe Ruth, 1927	158

Runs Batted In (Career)

Lou Gehrig	1,995

Babe Ruth	1,971
Joe DiMaggio	1,537
Mickey Mantle	1,509
Yogi Berra	1,430

Runs Batted In (Season)

Lou Gehrig, 1931	184
Lou Gehrig, 1927	175
Lou Gehrig, 1930	174
Babe Ruth, 1921	171
Joe DiMaggio, 1937	167

Home Runs (Career)

Babe Ruth	659
Mickey Mantle	536
Lou Gehrig	493
Joe DiMaggio	361
Yogi Berra	358

Home Runs (Season)

Roger Maris, 1961	61
Babe Ruth, 1927	60
Babe Ruth, 1921	59
Mickey Mantle, 1961	54
Alex Rodriguez, 2007	54
Babe Ruth, 1920	54
Babe Ruth, 1928	54

Singles (Career)

Derek Jeter	2,291
Bernie Williams	1,545
Lou Gehrig	1,531
Don Mattingly	1,469
Mickey Mantle	1,463

Singles (Season)

Steve Sax, 1989	171
Willie Keeler, 1906	167
Earle Combs, 1927	166
Derek Jeter, 2009	166
Willie Keeler, 1904	161

Doubles (Career)

Lou Gehrig	534
Derek Jeter	492
Bernie Williams	449
Don Mattingly	442
Babe Ruth	424

Doubles (Season)

Don Mattingly, 1986	53
Lou Gehrig, 1927	52
Alfonso Soriano, 2002	51
Robinson Cano, 2009	48
Don Mattingly, 1985	48

Triples (Career)

Lou Gehrig	163
Earle Combs	154
Joe DiMaggio	131
Wally Pipp	121
Tony Lazzeri	115

Triples (Season)

Earle Combs, 1927	23
Earle Combs, 1930	22
Birdie Cree, 1911	22
George Stirnweiss, 1945	22
Earle Combs, 1928	21

Strikeouts (Career)

Mickey Mantle	1,710
Derek Jeter	1,653
Jorge Posada	1,453
Bernie Williams	1,212
Babe Ruth	1,122

Strikeouts (Season)

Alfonso Soriano, 2002	157
Danny Tartabull, 1993	156
Jorge Posada, 2000	151
Jesse Barfield, 1990	150
Roberto Kelly, 1990	148

Walks (Career)

Babe Ruth	1,852
Mickey Mantle	1,733
Lou Gehrig	1,508
Bernie Williams	1,069
Willie Randolph	1,005

Walks (Season)

Babe Ruth, 1923	170
Babe Ruth, 1920	150
Mickey Mantle, 1957	146
Babe Ruth, 1921	145
Babe Ruth, 1926	144

On-base Percentage (Career)

Babe Ruth	.484
Lou Gehrig	.447
Mickey Mantle	.421
Charlie Keller	.410
Jason Giambi	.404

On-base Percentage (Season)

Babe Ruth, 1923	.545
Babe Ruth, 1920	.532
Babe Ruth, 1926	.516
Babe Ruth, 1924	.513
Babe Ruth, 1921	.512

Slugging Percentage (Career)

Babe Ruth	.711
Lou Gehrig	.632
Joe DiMaggio	.579
Mickey Mantle	.557
Alex Rodriguez	.550

Slugging Percentage (Season)

Babe Ruth, 1920	.847
Babe Ruth, 1921	.846
Babe Ruth, 1927	.772
Lou Gehrig, 1927	.765
Babe Ruth, 1923	.764

Hit by Pitch (Career)

Derek Jeter	158
Frank Crosetti	114
Jason Giambi	109
Alex Rodriguez	85
Kid Elberfeld	81

Hit by Pitch (Season)

Don Baylor, 1985	24
Don Baylor, 1984	23
Jason Giambi, 2008	22
Jason Giambi, 2003	21
Chuck Knoblauch, 1999	21
Alex Rodriguez, 2007	21

Sacrifices (Career)

Wally Pipp	226
Willie Keeler	211
Phil Rizzuto	193
Roger Peckinpaugh	190
Hal Chase	145

Sacrifices (Season)

Willie Keeler, 1905	42
Willie Keeler, 1906	35
Willie Keeler, 1909	33
Roger Peckinpaugh, 1915	33
Roger Peckinpaugh, 1921	33
Wally Pipp, 1921	33

Pitching

61.2 Percentage of the New York Highlanders innings pitched by either Jack Chesbro or Jack Powell in 1904 (845 of the team's 1,380⅔ innings for the season). Happy Jack won 41 games and completed 48 of his 51 starts—both modern major league records—while tossing 454⅔ innings, the second most in modern history. Powell chipped in a mere 390⅓ innings, winning 23 games and completing 38.

2.57 Highlanders staff ERA in 1904, the lowest in team history.

123 Complete games in 1904, the most in team history—but last in the major leagues that season.

.600 Career Yankee winning percentage of Ed Whitson, who was 15–10 in 1985 and part of 1986. Despite the winning record, he was among the most reviled Yankees in history, booed so vociferously by the home crowd that he was relegated to pitching only on the road in 1986. His 5.38 ERA is the worst among all Yankees pitchers with at least 25 decisions.

1.44 Home runs allowed per 9 innings by Mariano Rivera in his 10 career starts as a Yankee (50 innings, 8 home runs).

0.44 Home runs allowed per 9 innings by Rivera in 978 relief appearances (57 in 1,161 ⅓ innings), the best in the majors for any pitcher who threw at least 500 innings since Rivera's debut.

0.39 Home runs allowed per 9 innings by Sparky Lyle, the only Yankee to throw 500-plus innings after World War II with a better overall rate than Rivera's 0.48.

18 California Angels struck out by Ron Guidry on the night of June 17, 1978, one of just 24 instances in baseball history of 18 or more Ks by one pitcher in a 9-inning contest.

110 Rank in modern baseball history of Ron Guidry's Yankee record 248 strikeout 1978 season. That magical year Louisiana Lightning threw his slider to a 25–3 record and 1.74 ERA, finishing second in AL MVP voting.

20 Wins in 1978 for Ed Figueroa, the first (and so far only) Puerto Rican–born 20-game winner in baseball history.

4 Unearned runs allowed in 1 ⅔ innings by Don Larsen in Game 2 of the 1956 World Series. He fared much better in Game 5, throwing the only perfect game in Series history.

30 Wins by Herb Pennock in 38 decisions for the Yankees against his old Red Sox teammates, the most ever for a Yankee pitcher over Boston.

83.4 Percentage of the 1923 Yankees victories (82 of 98) that were credited to five former Red Sox hurlers during the first Yankees championship season.

5.52 Babe Ruth's ERA in five career outings on the mound for the Yankees. Despite allowing 19 earned runs in 31 innings over four starts and a relief appearance, Ruth's record was a spotless 5–0.

8 Yankees who have led the AL in ERA. The last time it happened was in 1980, when lefty Rudy May had a 2.46 ERA.

86 Appearances by reliever Paul Quantrill in 2004, the most ever in a Yankee season. Quantrill was 7–3 with a 4.72 ERA and 1 save in 95.1 innings.

35 Different moundsmen who have produced the fifty-nine 20-win seasons for the Yankees. Leading the way with four such seasons each are Lefty Gomez, Red Ruffing, and Bob Shawkey.

3 Yankee pitchers who walked at least 1,000 batters during their careers. All three (Lefty Gomez, Whitey Ford, and Red Ruffing) are enshrined in Cooperstown.

3 Former Yankee pitchers who at some point in their careers were the major league saves leaders: Johnny Murphy (leader from 1946 through 1961), Jeff Reardon (1992), Lee Smith (1993–2005). Of Murphy's 107 career saves, 104 came as a Yankee, but just 3 of Smith's 478 career saves and two of Reardon's 367 came for the Bronx Bombers.

3 Yankees who set the single-season saves mark: Joe Page (27 saves in 1949), Luis Arroyo (29 in 1961), and Dave Righetti (46 in 1986).

39   Mike Mussina's age when he won 20 games in 2008 to break the record for baseball's oldest first-time 20-game winner, surpassing Jamie Moyer of Seattle, who did it at 38.

8   Yankees who have lost 20 games in a season. Joe Lake holds the dubious distinction of losing the franchise-high 22 when he went 9–22 as a rookie in 1908.

819   Combined losses for the only seven Yankees hurlers to lose 100 or more games: Mel Stottlemyre, Bob Shawkey, Red Ruffing, Andy Pettitte, Whitey Ford, Fritz Peterson, and Lefty Gomez.

1,300   Combined wins for the aforementioned seven. That's a winning percentage of .613.

146   World Series innings pitched by Whitey Ford. He and Christy Mathewson (101.2) are the only pitchers to reach triple digits. Ford also holds the records for most wins (10), losses (8), and strikeouts (94), but his record 22 World Series appearances was surpassed in 2009 by Mariano Rivera, who now holds the mark with 24.

4   Consecutive complete-game shutouts thrown from May 11 to May 16, 1932, by the Yankee quartet of Johnny Allen, George Pipgras, Red Ruffing, and Lefty Gomez.

3.75   Millions of dollars over five years committed to Catfish Hunter on December 31, 1974, when he became the first free agent signed by the Yankees. Curiously, owner George Steinbrenner, a notorious spendthrift in the free-agent market, was serving an MLB-imposed suspension at the time and was not officially involved in negotiations.

63 Wins by Hunter during those five mostly injury-plagued seasons in pinstripes.

709 Combined career victories for Roger Clemens, Mike Mussina, and David Wells at the time they all pitched in a Game 7 victory over the Red Sox in the 2003 ALCS.

0 Major league appearances for left-handed pitcher Brien Taylor, the first overall pick in the June amateur draft in 1991. Ron Blomberg, New York's only other first overall pick, made history as baseball's first designated hitter.

16 Consecutive wins by Roger Clemens in 2001, the most in team history.

11 Consecutive losses for George Mogridge in 1916, the most in team history.

Wins (Career)

Whitey Ford	236
Red Ruffing	231
Andy Pettitte	203
Lefty Gomez	189
Ron Guidry	170

Wins (Season)

Jack Chesbro, 1904	41
Carl Mays, 1921	27
Al Orth, 1906	27
Joe Bush, 1922	26
Russ Ford, 1910	26
Lefty Gomez, 1934	26
Carl Mays, 1920	26
Joe McGinnity, 1901	26

Winning Percentage (Career)

Johnny Allen	.725
CC Sabathia	.720
Spud Chandler	.717
Jim Coates	.712
David Wells	.708

Winning Percentage (Season, minimum 15 decisions)

Ron Guidry, 1978	25–3	.893
Ron Davis, 1979	14–2	.875
Roger Clemens, 2001	20–3	.870
Whitey Ford, 1961	25–4	.862
Ralph Terry, 1961	16–3	.842

Starts (Career)

Whitey Ford	438
Andy Pettitte	396
Red Ruffing	391
Mel Stottlemyre	356
Ron Guidry	323

Saves (Career)

Mariano Rivera	603
Dave Righetti	224
Rich Gossage	151
Sparky Lyle	141
Johnny Murphy	104

Saves (Season)

Mariano Rivera, 2004	53
Mariano Rivera, 2001	50
Dave Righetti, 1986	46
Mariano Rivera, 1999	45
Mariano Rivera, 2009	44
Mariano Rivera, 2011	44

Strikeouts (Career)

Whitey Ford	1,956
Andy Pettitte	1,823
Ron Guidry	1,778
Red Ruffing	1,526
Lefty Gomez	1,468

Strikeouts (Season)

Ron Guidry, 1978	248
Jack Chesbro, 1904	239
David Cone, 1997	222
Melido Perez, 1992	218
Al Downing, 1964	217

Walks (Career)

Lefty Gomez	1,090
White Ford	1,086
Red Ruffing	1,066
Bob Shawkey	855
Andy Pettitte	820

Walks (Season)

Tommy Byrne, 1949	179
Bob Turley, 1955	177
Tommy Byrne, 1950	160
Vic Raschi, 1949	138
Allie Reynolds, 1950	138

Strikeout-to-Walk Ratio (Career)

Mike Mussina	4.02
Ron Guidry	2.81
Fritz Peterson	2.69
Andy Pettitte	2.22
Jack Chesbro	2.10

Strikeout-to-Walk Ratio (Season)

Jon Lieber, 2004	5.67
David Wells, 1998	5.62
Mike Mussina, 2001	5.10
David Wells, 2003	5.05
Mike Mussina, 2006	4.91

Strikeouts per 9 innings (Career ... minimum 100 innings)

David Robertson	12.0
Ryne Duren	11.21
John Wetteland	9.72
Jeff Nelson	9.67
Joba Chamberlain	9.24

Strikeouts per 9 innings (Career ... minimum 750 innings)

David Cone	8.67
Roger Clemens	8.27
Mariano Rivera	8.22
Al Downing	7.49
Dave Righetti	7.44

Strikeouts per 9 innings (Season)

David Cone, 1997	10.25
Roger Clemens, 2002	9.60
David Cone, 1998	9.06
Al Downing, 1963	8.76
Roger Clemens, 2001	8.70

Shutouts (Career)

Whitey Ford	45
Red Ruffing	40
Mel Stottlemyre	40
Lefty Gomez	28
Allie Reynolds	27

Shutouts (Season)

Ron Guidry, 1978	9
Russ Ford, 1910	8
Whitey Ford, 1964	8
Whitey Ford, 1958	7
Catfish Hunter, 1975	7
Allie Reynolds 1951	7
Mel Stottlemyre, 1971	7
Mel Stottlemyre, 1972	7

ERA (Career)

Mariano Rivera	2.05
Ray Fisher	2.60
Ray Caldwell	2.70
Ernie Bonham	2.73
George Modridge	2.74

ERA (Season)

Spud Chandler, 1943	1.64
Ron Guidry, 1978	1.74
Ray Caldwell, 1914	1.94
Whitey Ford, 1958	2.01
Nick Cullop, 1916	2.05

Home Runs Allowed (Career)

Whitey Ford	228
Ron Guidry	226
Andy Pettitte	211
Red Ruffing	200
Mel Stottlemyre	171

Home Runs Allowed (Season)

Ralph Terry, 1962	40
Orlando Hernandez, 2000	34
Javier Vazquez, 2004	33

Jim Bouton, 1964	32
Randy Johnson, 2005	32
Javier Vazquez, 2010	32

Yankees No-Hitters

George Mogridge 2–1 vs. Red Sox, April 24, 1917
Sam Jones 2–0 vs. Athletics, September 4, 1923
Monte Pearson 13–0 vs. Indians, August 27, 1938
Allie Reynolds 1–0 vs. Indians, July 12, 1951
Allie Reynolds 8–0 vs. Red Sox, September 28, 1951
Don Larsen 2–0 vs. Dodgers, October 8, 1956 (WS, PG)
Dave Righetti 4–0 vs. Red Sox, July 4, 1983
Jim Abbott 4–0 vs. Indians, September 4, 1993
Dwight Gooden 2–0 vs. Mariners, May 14, 1996
David Wells 4–0 vs. Twins, May 17, 1998 (PG)
David Cone 6–0 vs. Expos, July 18, 1999 (PG)

WS = World Series   *PG = Perfect Game*

No-Hitters Against the Yankees

Rube Foster, Red Sox 2–0, June 21, 1916
Ray Caldwell, Indians 3–0, September 10, 1919
Bob Feller, Indians 1–0, April 30, 1946
Virgil Trucks, Tigers 1–0, August 5, 1952
Hoyt Wilhelm, Orioles 1–0, September 20, 1958
Roy Oswalt, Pete Munro, Kirk Saarloos, Brad Lidge,
    Octavio Dotel, Astros 8–0, June 11, 2003

Yankee Killers

Hitters

C Carlton Fisk, Red Sox–White Sox 1971–93
190 games, 31 HR, 112 RBI, .270/.342/.458

1B Hank Greenberg, Tigers 1930–46
190 games, 53 HR, 179 RBI, .333/.408/.667

2B Charlie Gehringer, Tigers 1925–42
344 games, 33 HR, 196 RBI, .323/.411/.491

SS Alex Rodriguez, Mariners–Rangers 1994–2003
82 games, 28 HR, 74 RBI, .334/.368/.651

3B George Brett, Royals 1974–93
121 Games, 16 HR, 70 RBI, .310/.365/.501

LF Ted Williams, Red Sox 1939–60
327 games, 62 HR, 141 RBI, .345/.495/.608

CF Ken Griffey Jr., Mariners–Reds–White Sox 1989–2009
133 games, 36 HR, 102 RBI, .311/.392/.595

RF Manny Ramirez, Indians–Red Sox–Dodgers
1993–2010
203 games, 55 HR, 165 RBI, .322/.413/.617

DH David Ortiz, Twins–Red Sox
155 games, 31 HR, 117 RBI, .305/.392/.555

Pitchers
Starters

Lefty Grove, Athletics–Red Sox   1925–41
92 games, 34–26, 3.84 ERA, 4 Shutouts

Frank Lary, Tigers–White Sox   1954–65
56 games, 28–13, 3.32 ERA, 3 Shutouts

Roy Halladay, Blue Jays–Phillies   1999–2011
38 games, 18–7, 2.98 ERA, 3 Shutouts

Jim Palmer, Orioles   1965–83
55 games, 30–16, 2.84 ERA, 7 Shutouts

Luis Tiant, Indians–Twins–Red Sox   1964–78
53 games, 22–15, 2.84 ERA, 7 Shutouts

Dean Chance, Angels–Twins–Indians–Tigers 1962–71
41 games, 18–11, 2.34 ERA, 6 Shutouts

Relievers
Jeff Nelson, Mariners   1992–95, 2001–05
37 games, 5–1, 1.13 ERA, 1 Save

Dick Radatz, Red Sox–Indians–Tigers   1962–69
40 games, 6–1, 2.84 ERA, 13 Saves

Dan Quisenberry, Royals   1979–88
38 games, 4–2, 1.59 ERA, 16 Saves

Stu Miller, Orioles   1963–67
33 games, 4–5, 1.74 ERA, 11 Saves

Honors, Awards, and Titles

1,474   Players who have suited up for the Highlanders and Yankees since the start of the 1903 season.

38   Yankees players enshrined in the Baseball Hall of Fame in Cooperstown, New York, the most of any franchise.

2   Yankees who are enshrined in the Pro Football Hall of Fame: outfielder George Halas batted .091 in 12 games in 1919 before becoming the legendary coach of the Chicago Bears; outfielder Deion Sanders hit .178 in parts of the 1989 and 1990 seasons and became the only player to hit a major league home run and score an NFL touchdown in the same week when he homered on

September 5, 1989, against the Mariners and returned a 68-yard punt for the Atlanta Falcons against the Rams on September 10.

125 Wins during the 1998 regular season, playoffs, and World Series, the most by any team in baseball history. The 114 regular season victories set the American League record, but fell two wins short of the big league mark of 116 set by the 1906 Chicago Cubs.

2 Last place finishes since the team was officially renamed the Yankees in 1914. The 1966 team finished tenth in the American League, while the 1990 squad placed seventh in the AL East.

42.2 Percentage of seasons since the franchise moved to New York from Baltimore that the Yankees finished atop the league or division standings—46 first places in 109 seasons.

58 Times the Yankees defeated Early Wynn of the Senators, Indians, and White Sox from 1939 to 1963—the most losses by any opponent. However, Wynn also places second in wins over the Yankees, with 33. Only Lefty Grove had more, with 34 (for Philadelphia and Boston).

22 Innings played on June 24, 1962, a 9–7 win over the Tigers, the longest game in franchise history. The winning margin was provided by right fielder Jack Reed with the only home run of his major league career.

12 Major league teams (out of 27) that integrated before the Yankees during the post–World War II era. Catcher Elston Howard became the first African-American to don the pinstripes in an official game when he debuted on April 15, 1955, nearly six years after the Giants played Willie Mays and Monte Irvin, and one day shy of the eight-year anniversary of Jackie Robinson's first game with the Brooklyn Dodgers.

27 Yankees World Series titles, the most championships for any major North American sports team. The NHL's Montreal Canadiens come the closest to New York's dominance with 24 Stanley Cup titles. The NBA is topped by the Boston Celtics (17), while the NFL's best is the Green Bay Packers (13).

12 Yankee losses in 1990 to the Oakland A's, the only AL team in history to sweep a season series from New York.

19 Team record for consecutive victories (from June 29 to July 17, 1947), an AL standard unsurpassed until 2002, when the Oakland A's won 20 in a row.

1,307 Consecutive games played for the Red Sox and Yankees by Everett Scott, from June 20, 1916, to May 5, 1925, the most in major league history until Lou Gehrig, who played in 2,130 straight games from June 1, 1925, to April 30, 1939.

1,768 Combined consecutive games played for Japan's Yomiuri Giants and the New York Yankees by Hideki Matsui, including a record 518 from the start of his major league career.

58 Yankees who lost time due to military service: 18 during World War I, 26 during World War II, 6 in the Korean conflict, 8 in the Vietnam War.

.716 The Yankees' 1978 winning percentage after July 18, enabling them to erase a 14-game deficit to the Red Sox in the standings to win the AL East crown.

55 Major league players who have been part of at least five World Series Championship teams, only 4 of whom (Eddie Collins, Jack Barry, Dal Maxville, and Stuffy McInnis) failed to win at least one as a Yankee, and 39 of whom won titles only as Yankees.

10   Titles won by Yogi Berra, the most by anyone in baseball history and just one behind the record for major pro sports championships shared by Bill Russell of the Boston Celtics and Henri Richard of the Montreal Canadiens.

42   Players with at least 1,000 regular season games as a Yankee.

3   Thousand-game winners with New York who never played on a Yankees World Series team: Don Mattingly (1,785 games), Horace Clarke (1,230), Hal Chase (1,061). Unlike Clarke and Chase, Mattingly did manage to play in the postseason, a loss to the Mariners in the Wild Card round in 1995, his final season.

All-Yankee Teams

FIRST TEAM	SECOND TEAM	THIRD TEAM	FOURTH TEAM
C Yogi Berra	Bill Dickey	Jorge Posada	Elston Howard
1B Lou Gehrig	Don Mattingly	Tino Martinez	Wally Pipp
2B Tony Lazzeri	Joe Gordon	Willie Randolph	Bobby Richardson
SS Derek Jeter	Phil Rizzuto	Frank Crosetti	Tony Kubek
3B A. Rodriguez	Graig Nettles	Wade Boggs	Red Rolfe
LF Charlie Keller	Dave Winfield	Roy White	Lou Piniella
CF Joe DiMaggio	Mickey Mantle	Bernie Williams	Earle Combs
RF Babe Ruth	Paul O'Neill	Roger Maris	Reggie Jackson
SP Whitey Ford	Red Ruffing	Lefty Gomez	Ron Guidry
RP Mariano Rivera	Rich Gossage	Dave Righetti	Sparky Lyle

Games Played

Mickey Mantle	2,401
Derek Jeter	2,308
Lou Gehrig	2,164
Yogi Berra	2,116
Babe Ruth	2,084

Games Pitched

Mariano Rivera	986
Dave Righetti	522
Whitey Ford	498
Mike Stanton	456
Red Ruffing	426

Most Games Played, by Position

Pitcher	Mariano Rivera	1,042
Catcher	Jorge Posada	1,829
First Base	Lou Gehrig	2,137
Second Base	Willie Randolph	1,688
Third Base	Graig Nettles	1,509
Shortstop	Derek Jeter	2,426
Left Field	Roy White	1,521
Center Field	Bernie Williams	1,857
Right Field	Paul O'Neill	1,163
Designated Hitter	Don Baylor	372

Yankee Captains

Hal Chase	1912
Roger Peckinpaugh	1914–21
Babe Ruth	1922
Everett Scott	1922
Lou Gehrig	1935–41
Thurman Munson	1976–79
Graig Nettles	1982–84

Willie Randolph   1986–89
Ron Guidry   1986–89
Don Mattingly   1991–95
Derek Jeter   2003–

Retired Numbers

1   Billy Martin
3   Babe Ruth
4   Lou Gehrig
5   Joe DiMaggio
7   Mickey Mantle
8   Bill Dickey
8   Yogi Berra
9   Roger Maris
10   Phil Rizzuto
15   Thurman Munson
16   Whitey Ford
23   Don Mattingly
32   Elston Howard
37   Casey Stengel
44   Reggie Jackson
49   Ron Guidry
42★ Jackie Robinson
retired throughout MLB

Numbers Likely to Be Retired

2   Derek Jeter
6   Joe Torre
13   Alex Rodriguez
42   Mariano Rivera
46   Andy Pettitte
55   Bernie Williams

AL MVP

1936	Lou Gehrig
1939	Joe DiMaggio
1941	Joe DiMaggio
1942	Joe Gordon
1943	Spud Chandler
1947	Joe DiMaggio
1950	Phil Rizzuto
1951	Yogi Berra
1954	Yogi Berra
1955	Yogi Berra
1956	Mickey Mantle
1957	Mickey Mantle
1960	Roger Maris
1961	Roger Maris
1962	Mickey Mantle
1963	Elston Howard
1976	Thurman Munson
1985	Don Mattingly
2005	Alex Rodriguez
2007	Alex Rodriguez

Rookie of the Year

1951	Gil McDougald
1954	Bob Grim
1957	Tony Kubek
1962	Tom Tresh
1968	Stan Bahnsen
1970	Thurman Munson
1981	Dave Righetti
1996	Derek Jeter

Cy Young Award

1958	Bob Turley
1961	Whitey Ford

1977	Sparky Lyle
1978	Ron Guidry
2001	Roger Clemens

Triple Crown Winners

Hitting

1934	Lou Gehrig
1956	Mickey Mantle

Pitching

1934	Lefty Gomez
1937	Lefty Gomez

World Series MVP

1956	Don Larsen
1958	Bob Turley
1960	Bobby Richardson
1961	Whitey Ford
1977	Reggie Jackson
1978	Bucky Dent
1996	John Wetteland
1998	Scott Brosius
1999	Mariano Rivera
2000	Derek Jeter
2009	Hideki Matsui

Yankees in Hall of Fame

Frank "Home Run" Baker	Bill Dickey
Yogi Berra	Joe DiMaggio
Wade Boggs	Leo Durocher
Frank Chance	Whitey Ford
Jack Chesbro	Lou Gehrig
Earle Combs	Lefty Gomez
Stan Coveleski	Joe Gordon

Rich Gossage
Clark Griffith
Burleigh Grimes
Bucky Harris
Rickey Henderson
Waite Hoyt
Miller Huggins
Jim "Catfish" Hunter
Reggie Jackson
Willie Keeler
Tony Lazzeri
Bob Lemon
Mickey Mantle
Joe McCarthy
Bill McKechnie

Johnny Mize
Phil Niekro
Herb Pennock
Gaylord Perry
Branch Rickey
Phil Rizzuto
Red Ruffing
Babe Ruth
Joe Sewell
Enos Slaughter
Casey Stengel
Dazzy Vance
Paul Waner
Dave Winfield

Sabremetrics

**Yankees who led the majors in VORP
(value over replacement player)**

Alex Rodriguez, 2007	93.7
Derek Jeter, 1999	103.9
Don Mattingly, 1986	87.2
Mickey Mantle, 1961	99.1
Mickey Mantle, 1957	108.7
Mickey Mantle, 1956	112.6
Mickey Mantle, 1955	74.7

**Yankees among the top 25 in weighted on-base average
(career)**

PLAYER	WOBA	MLB RANK
Babe Ruth	.510	1
Lou Gehrig	.474	3

Joe DiMaggio	.439	12
Johnny Mize	.433	16
Mickey Mantle	.431	20
Charlie Keller	.428	24

**Yankee hitters among the top 50 WAR batting leaders
(wins above replacement)**

PLAYER	WAR	MLB RANK
Babe Ruth	172.0	1
Mickey Mantle	120.2	12
Lou Gehrig	118.4	13
Rickey Henderson	113.1	14
Alex Rodriguez	104.6	18
Wade Boggs	89.0	27
Joe DiMaggio	83.6	34
Reggie Jackson	74.6	49

197 Babe Ruth's career runs created normalized and adjusted for park and league (WRC+), the highest for any player in big league history. Lou Gehrig places fourth all-time (174), while Mickey Mantle is tied with Rogers Hornsby and Ty Cobb for fifth.

11 Times Ruth led the majors in OPS+, which normalizes on-base percentage plus slugging percentage against that season's league average.

9 Yankees, including Ruth, to lead the AL in OPS+: Ruth, Lou Gehrig, Joe DiMaggio, Charlie Keller, Snuffy Stirnweiss, Mickey Mantle, Bobby Murcer, Don Mattingly, and Alex Rodriguez.

**One-time Yankee pitchers among the top 50 WAR leaders
(wins above replacement)**

PLAYER	WAR	MLB RANK
Roger Clemens	128.4	2
Phil Niekro	96.8	T–8
Gaylord Perry	96.3	10
Randy Johnson	91.8	12
Mike Mussina	74.8	24
Rick Reuschel	66.3	30
Kevin Brown	64.8	34
Luis Tiant	60.1	T–42
Tommy John	59.0	43
David Cone	57.5	47
Dazzy Vance	56.4	50

Adjusted ERA+ (minimum 1,000 innings . . . 100 is average pitcher)

Mariano Rivera	206
Whitey Ford	133
Spud Chandler	132
Tiny Bonham	129
Dave Righetti	127

Baserunning and Fielding

19,525 Putouts by Lou Gehrig, the most for any player at any position in team history. Fittingly, the man who places second is the man Gehrig both surpassed for the record and usurped at first base for the Yankees, Wally Pipp.

107 Yankees games played in 2010 without an error committed, the most in franchise history. The club's 69 errors were the fewest in the team's 108 seasons, and its .988 fielding percentage was the best ever for the team and sixth best in baseball history.

.851 Franchise-best stolen base percentage for Rickey Henderson, who was successful on 326 of his 383 attempts. In three of his five Yankee seasons, baseball's all-time stolen base king set the single-season team record (breaking the old mark of 74 set by Fritz Maisel in 1914) with 80 steals in '85, then bettering it with 87 in '86 and then 93 in '88.

339 Stolen bases by Derek Jeter, the new franchise leader, who needed a dozen more seasons than Henderson to reach 326.

18 Consecutive games without an error for the 2009 Yankees from May 14 to June 2, breaking the major league record of 17 set by the 2006 Red Sox.

12 Combined Gold Gloves won by three Yankees pitchers: Bobby Shantz won the first four Gold Gloves awarded, 1957 through 1960; Ron Guidry was honored from 1982 through 1986; and Mike Mussina was named the AL's best fielding pitcher in 2001, 2003, and 2008.

10 Players with at least 10 steals for the 1910 Highlanders, who set the franchise mark with 249 stolen bases.

6 Team-leading stolen base total by Phil Rizzuto, who, along with Snuffy Stirnweiss were the only Yankees to steal at least five bases in 1948, when the entire team swiped just 24 bags.

18 Times a Yankee has stolen 4 bases in a single game. Rickey Henderson did it five times in pinstripes.

13 Stolen bases by Dave Collins, whose signing for the '82 season was supposed to signify a change in the Yankees from a power to a speed team. In the two preceding years, Collins swiped 105 bases for Cincinnati and in the two succeeding years he stole 91 for Toronto.

8   Seasons in which a Yankee has led the majors in stolen bases. Henderson (1985–86, 1988) and Ben Chapman (1931–33) did it three times each, while Snuffy Stirnweiss did it twice (1944–45).

2   Steals of home in one game (on August 15, 1912) by Guy Zinn, one of only eleven major leaguers ever to accomplish the feat.

15   Steals of home by Lou Gehrig, the Yankees' career leader.

8   Years in which Yogi Berra led all catchers in games behind the plate, a big-league record (since tied by Pirates, Athletics, and Royals backstop Jason Kendall).

Stolen Bases (Career)

Derek Jeter	339
Rickey Henderson	326
Willie Randolph	251
Hal Chase	248
Roy White	233

Stolen Bases (Season)

Rickey Henderson, 1988	93
Rickey Henderson, 1986	87
Rickey Henderson, 1985	80
Fritz Maisel, 1914	74
Ben Chapman, 1931	61

Stolen Base Percentage (Career)

Rickey Henderson	85.1
Alex Rodriguez	82.1
Fritz Maisel	81.2
Mickey Mantle	80.1
Derek Jeter	79.0

Stolen Base Percentage (Season)

Derek Jeter, 2002	91.4
Johnny Damon, 2007	90.0
Derek Jeter, 2001	90.0
Rickey Henderson, 1985	88.9
Paul O'Neill, 2001	88.0

Caught Stealing (Career)

Babe Ruth	117
Roy White	117
Bob Meusel	102
Lou Gehrig	101
Ben Chapman	93

Caught Stealing (Season)

Doc Cook, 1914	32
Roy Hartzell, 1914	25
Lee Magee, 1916	25
Ben Chapman, 1931	23
Babe Ruth, 1923	21

Most Outfield Assists (Career)

Babe Ruth	181
Joe DiMaggio	153
Bob Meusel	149
Mickey Mantle	117
Hank Bauer	101

Most Outfield Assists (Season)

Bob Meusel, 1921	28
Ben Chapman, 1935	25
Ben Chapman, 1933	24
Bob Meusel, 1922	24
Ray Demmitt, 1909	22
Joe DiMaggio, 1936	22

Highest Career Fielding Percentage by Position

P	Hank Borowy	.986
C	Elston Howard	.992
1B	Don Mattingly	.996
2B	Robinson Cano	.985
SS	Bucky Dent	.976
3B	Clete Boyer	.965
LF	Gene Woodling	.991
CF	Bernie Williams	.990
RF	Paul O'Neill	.988

Highest Fielding Percentage by Position (Season)

P	By many	1.000
C	Yogi Berra, 1958	1.000
1B	Don Mattingly, 1994	.998
2B	Robinson Cano, 2010	.996
SS	Derek Jeter, 2010	.989
3B	Wade Boggs, 1995	.981
LF	Rondell White, 2002	1.000
LF	Roy White, 1971	1.000
CF	Bernie Williams, 2002	1.000
RF	Paul O'Neill, 1996	1.000

Most Errors (Career)

Frank Crosetti	421
Roger Peckinpaugh	360
Tony Lazzeri	286
Kid Elberfeld	281
Phil Rizzuto	263

Most Errors (Season)

Neal Ball, 1908	81
John Knight, 1911	68
Kid Elberfeld, 1905	57

Roger Peckinpaugh, 1917   54
Kid Elberfeld, 1907   52
Mark Koenig, 1928   52

Passed Balls (Career)
Jorge Posada   142
Thurman Munson   93
Yogi Berra   76
Bill Dickey   76
Elston Howard   69

Passed Balls (Season)
Jeff Sweeney, 1913   19
Jorge Posada, 2001   18
Jorge Posada, 1999   17
Ron Hassey, 1985   15
Mike Stanley, 1995   15

Managers, Owners, and Stadiums

25   Managers of the Highlanders/Yankees (out of 32) who had career records of .500 or better. That includes twenty-three-year-old Roger Peckinpaugh, the team captain and shortstop who took the reins for 20 games in 1914 and went 10–10 while becoming the youngest man ever to manage in the big leagues.

2   Yankee managers with shorter tenures than Peckinpaugh's: Johnny Neun (the last 14 games of 1946, following Bill Dickey's abrupt departure) and Art Fletcher (11 games as the emergency replacement after Miller Huggins's sudden death in September 1929). Both Neun (.571) and Fletcher (.545) enjoyed winning records.

1,153 Regular-season managerial victories for Joe Torre in 17

National League seasons with the Mets, Braves, Cardinals, and Dodgers. (Postseason wins boost that total to 1,161.)

1,173 Regular-season managerial victories for Torre in twelve years at the Yankees helm. (Another 76 postseason wins lift his Yankee total to 1,237.)

5 Separate stints as Yankees manager by Billy Martin, the most ever by any man for any team. The Yankees won just two pennants and one World Series under Martin, but he ranks sixth in games, wins, and losses, and eighth in winning percentage in franchise history.

9 Members of the Baseball Hall of Fame who have managed the Yankees, including Clark Griffith, the first skipper and one of four Hall of Famers to play for and manage the team (the others being Yogi Berra, Frank Chance, and Bill Dickey).

19 Hundred-win Yankee seasons, the most by any team in baseball history. Eight different managers led the Bombers to triple-digit wins, including Joe McCarthy, who did it six times.

75 Percentage of the 1927 Murders Row infield that scout Paul Krichell was credited with signing, including two Hall of Famers (first baseman Lou Gehrig and second baseman Tony Lazzeri) along with shortstop Mark Koenig. Krichell would later discover two more Yankee legends, 1950 MVP Phil Rizzuto and the winningest pitcher in franchise history, Whitey Ford.

15 Months that George Steinbrenner was suspended from baseball, starting in November 1974, as a result of his illegal contributions to Richard Nixon's presidential campaign.

32 Months that Steinbrenner served of his "permanent ban" for paying Howie Spira, a known gambler, to help discredit Dave

Winfield. The Boss was reinstated on March 1, 1993.

413 Spectators on hand to see the Yankees beat the Red Sox 3–1 in the home finale on September 25, 1966—the smallest home crowd in team history.

12 Combined World Series games played at the Polo Grounds between the stadium's two tenants, the Yankees and the Giants, in 1921–22. The National Leaguers won 5–3 in 1921 and 4–0 in 1922 in the only Fall Classics played entirely in one ballpark.

142 Postseason games managed by Joe Torre—including 123 with the Yankees—more than any other manager in baseball history.

2,209 Games played by Torre without ever making a postseason appearance, the sixth most in major league history.

49 Seasons in which the Yankees have led the American League in attendance, including 1920 through 1922, when they called the Polo Grounds home.

0 Times the Yankees led the AL in attendance from 1982 through 2002.

4 Millions of fans who attended games at Yankee Stadium each year from 2005 to 2008, an average over 50,000 fans per game for four straight years.

Managers (By Winning Percentage)

	SEASONS	PCT.
Dick Howser	2	.632
Joe McCarthy	16	.627
Casey Stengel	12	.623
Bucky Harris	2	.620
Joe Torre	12	.605

Miller Huggins	12	.597
Joe Girardi	4	.593
Billy Martin	8	.591
Bob Lemon	4	.576
Johnny Neun	1	.571
Yogi Berra	3	.565
Bob Shawkey	1	.558
Gene Michael	2	.548
Art Fletcher	1	.545
Bill Dickey	1	.543
Ralph Houk	11	.539
Buck Showalter	4	.539
Lou Piniella	3	.537
Bill Virdon	2	.534
Clark Griffith	6	.531
George Stallings	2	.528
Hal Chase	2	.518
Roger Peckinpaugh	1	.500
Bill Donovan	3	.479
Clyde King	1	.468
Dallas Green	1	.463
Johnny Keane	2	.445
Stump Merrill	2	.436
Frank Chance	2	.411
Bucky Dent	2	.404
Harry Wolverton	1	.329
Kid Elberfeld	1	.276

OWNERS	YEAR	AMOUNT PAID*
Frank Ferrell and Bill Devery	1903	$18,000
Col. Jacob Ruppert and Col. Tillinghast L'Hommedieu Huston	1915	$460,000
Col. Jacob Ruppert (bought out Huston)	1922	$1.5 million

Dan Topping, Del Webb,
   Larry MacPhail   1945 $2.8 million
Columbia Broadcasting System   1964 $11.2 million
George M. Steinbrenner III   1973 $8.7 million

In 2010 the franchise was valued at $1.6 billion by Forbes

BALLPARKS	YEARS
Hilltop Park	1903–11
Polo Grounds	1912–22
Yankee Stadium I	1923–73
Shea Stadium	1974–75
Yankee Stadium II	1976–2008
Yankee Stadium III	2009–

Coaches (Ranked by Seasons)

Frank Crosetti	23
Jim Turner	19
Jim Hegan	16
John Schulte	15
Elston Howard	11
Willie Randolph	11
Bill Dickey	10
Dick Howser	10
Charlie O'Leary	10
Mel Stottlemyre	10
Jeff Torborg	10
Don Zimmer	10

Yankee Hat Tricks (Played/Coached/Managed)

Yogi Berra	Dick Howser
Bill Dickey	Gene Michael
Joe Girardi	Lou Piniella
Ralph Houk	Bob Shawkey

Acknowledgments

Many hands helped in the struggle to complete this book, and the time has come, as an old colleague used to say, to declare victory and hold a parade. I realize that the festivities to salute our heroes don't usually occur these days until the fires set in cars and trash bins by marauding fans have been extinguished, but if I wait till the celebratory wilding for this modest volume begins (much less ends), it could be a long wait. So I'd like to go ahead and express my heartfelt gratitude.

First and foremost, the writers: I want to offer my sincere thanks to them, and by extension, to their spouses, partners, children, agents, editors, and other enablers, for all the sacrifices made so that this collection might exist. The aim of the project from the outset was to bring together the most compelling voices possible and hear what they'd have to say about the Yankees. This is a subject, it must be said, that has not been overlooked in the literature of baseball (the term "Yankee books" yields around 60 million Google hits) so these distinguished writers agreed—for short pay and on short deadlines—to bear the burden of pulling something fresh and original from ground that seemed not merely well worked but exhausted. I am grateful for their efforts and dazzled, as ever, by their talent.

The role of other players might not be so obvious but was hardly less crucial. This book began when Dave Hirshey asked if I'd join him for world-class burgers at a Manhattan restaurant called Beacon, and then discuss with him and Dan Halpern a possible collection of writerly essays on the Yankees. Now, I love to talk about the Yankees, especially with old pals, but the truth is, he had me at "Beacon." From that first meeting, Dave has been there every step of the way, pushing the project forward and watching our backs, sometimes reading my endless e-mail screeds well into the second paragraph. You just don't find that kind of dedication in an editor these days. Whoever said you shouldn't do business with friends obviously never had the good fortune to work with Hirshey.

Whenever there was a sudden emergency (and isn't there always?), Barry Harbaugh was there to pick up the phone, and his skill as an editor and a crisis mediator averted disaster before panic had a chance to take hold. In baseball, we call this great anticipation—and in publishing, too, come to think of it.

Before Matt Weiland took his talents to South Beach, he made his mark on this project, generously sharing ideas, writers, and more anthologist's wisdom than a guy his age has any right to possess.

Many old friends also had a hand in this book, some because of their affinity for the subject, some despite a deep antipathy to it. No one embodies the latter group better than Esther Newberg, whose elegant office overlooking Fifth Avenue is nothing less than a shrine to the Red Sox. Because Esther is forthright and fearless in expressing her opinions (I have personally sat with her at a Yankee–Red Sox game in the Bronx, dodging projectiles aimed at the Boston cap she insists on wearing), her devotion to the Sox is well known. Representing the editor of this book (and four or five of the contributors) could not have been easy for her, and I am grateful, even to the point where I swear never again to mention what happened to Boston in the final month of the 2011 season.

At the other end of this baseball axis is Steve Fine, whose office walls are also adorned with magnificent sports images, not one of which has anything to do with Boston. Steve knows everything about the Yankees and even more about sports photography, so I shamelessly imposed upon him to show me a hundred or so classic pictures of four or five Yankee legends in order to choose the six shots we'd need for this book. Fine does tasks like this in his sleep (or would if he ever slept) and would've done this one on his own time (except that he is always working), but I am no less grateful to him just because he makes it all look so easy.

I also want to thank some of my other old friends and colleagues at Sports Illustrated, where I was lucky enough to work for many years with people who are astonishingly good at what they do: Cristina Scalet performed her magic, as usual, with pictures. If god is truly in the details, we should all bow down to Cristina. Nate Gordon, whose brain, though fixated on the Red Sox, apparently came bundled with an unabridged catalogue of great baseball photographs. Matt Gagne, whose dogged pursuit of subjects who did not wish to be found could be a model to teach young reporters how it ought to be done. Alex Belth, whom I want on my Jeopardy team when the big bucks are on the line and the category is the Yankees. Chris Hunt, whose excellent taste in writing happily overlapped to a remarkable degree with my own. And Chris Stone and Joan Rosinsky, who, among other things, have made possible my periodic presence at Yankee Stadium, so I could conduct the vital journalistic business of firsthand observation and reporting from a superb vantage point behind first base.

Finally, my hat is off to the home team, Nick, Carolyn, Jackson, and MJ, who made all those trips to the ballpark and hours glued to the YES Network so much fun for all those seasons.

The Contributors

Dan Barry is a columnist for the *New York Times*. He is the author of *Pull Me Up,* a memoir, and *City Lights,* a collection of his "About New York" columns from the *Times*. His account of baseball's longest game, *Bottom of the 33rd,* was published in 2011.

Roy Blount Jr. is a celebrated humorist, poet, dramatist, and a frequent contributor to many magazines, including the *New Yorker, Vanity Fair, Esquire, GQ,* and *Rolling Stone*. His seventeenth book, *Alphabetter Juice,* was published in 2011.

Frank Deford is often identified simply as the world's greatest sportswriter, though his work encompasses fiction and nonfiction and appears in print and on broadcast media as well as the stage and screen. He is the author of sixteen books, and his commentaries have been a fixture on National Public Radio since 1980.

Pete Dexter is the author of seven novels, including the National Book Award–winning *Paris Trout* and, most recently, *Spooner*. A 2007 collection of his newspaper columns and magazine stories, *Paper Trails,* will be published in paperback this year.

Roger Director is a novelist, journalist, and television writer and producer. He is the author, most recently, of *I Dream in Blue,* a twisted comic journey into the heart and mind of an obsessive Giants football fan.

Richard Hoffer was an award-winning columnist for the *Los Angeles Times* and a senior writer for *Sports Illustrated.* He is the author of books about Mike Tyson (*A Savage Business*), casino gambling (*Jackpot Nation*), and the social undercurrents of the 1968 Olympics (*There's Something in the Air*).

Bill James, the godfather of sabermetrics and the most influential baseball writer of his time, is the author of more than two dozen books, including multiple editions of his epic *Bill James Historical Abstract.* His latest book, though, concerns his other obsession, *Popular Crime: Reflections of the Celebration of Violence.* Since 2003, he has also been a senior advisor on baseball operations for the Boston Red Sox.

Sally Jenkins, a longtime columnist for the *Washington Post* and a former senior writer at *Sports Illustrated,* is the bestselling author of nine books, including *It's Not About the Bike* (with Lance Armstrong) and, most recently, *The State of Jones* (with John Stauffer).

Jane Leavy is a journalist, novelist (*Squeeze Play*), and the author of two acclaimed, bestselling biographies: *Koufax: A Lefty's Legacy* and *The Last Boy: Mickey Mantle and the End of America's Childhood.*

Will Leitch, the founding editor of the sports Web site Deadspin, is a columnist and contributing editor at *New York* magazine. He is the author of four books, including a novel, *Catch,* and most recently, *Are We Winning?,* a memoir about baseball and fatherhood.

Bruce McCall, a writer, illustrator, and humorist, was one of the original contributors to the *National Lampoon* and has been a regular for more than thirty years in the *New Yorker,* where his paintings have graced the cover more than fifty times. The most recent of his five books is *Marveltown.*

Colum McCann is the author of two short story collections and five novels, including most recently *Let the Great World Spin,* winner of the National Book Award, the IMPAC Dublin Literary Award, and numerous other literary honors. He teaches creative writing at Hunter College.

Leigh Montville, a columnist for the *Boston Globe* and longtime senior writer at *Sports Illustrated,* is the author of seven books, including bestselling biographies of Babe Ruth, Ted Williams, and Dale Earnhardt. His biography of Evel Knievel was published in 2011.

J. R. Moehringer was a Pulitzer Prize–winning feature writer for the *Los Angeles Times* and is the author of the acclaimed memoirs *The Tender Bar* and the bestselling *Open* (with Andre Agassi). His first novel will be published this year.

William Nack, the author of the bestselling *Secretariat* and two other books, was a longtime columnist at *Newsday* and a senior writer at *Sports Illustrated.* He has won seven Eclipse Awards for his turf writing and the A. J. Liebling Award from the boxing writers of America.

Daniel Okrent, widely known as the founding father of fantasy baseball and the first public editor of the *New York Times,* is also a prominent book and magazine editor, and the author of six books, including the 2010 bestseller *Last Call: The Rise and Fall of Prohibition.*

Michael Paterniti is a National Magazine Award–winning journalist and the author of *Driving Mr. Albert: A Trip Across America with Einstein's Brain,* which has been translated into twenty languages. His new book, *The Telling Room,* will be published next year.

Charles P. Pierce, a longtime Boston columnist and a regular on NPR's *Wait, Wait, Don't Tell Me,* has been a frequent contributor to many magazines, including *GQ* and *Esquire.* His fourth book, the bestselling *Idiot America,* was published in 2010.

Nathaniel Rich, a former editor at the *Paris Review,* is the author of *The Mayor's Tongue,* a novel, and *San Francisco Noir.* His work has appeared in *Vanity Fair,* the *New York Review of Books, Slate,* and many other publications.

Steve Rushin is the author of four books, including *The Pint Man,* a novel. The long and short of his first twenty years at *Sports Illustrated* were a 24-page feature for *SI's* fortieth anniversary (the longest story ever to run in a single issue) and his "Air and Space" column, an *SI* staple for nine years.

James Surowiecki is the author of *The Wisdom of Crowds.* Before he became the financial columnist for the *New Yorker,* he wrote "The Bottom Line" column for *New York* magazine. His work has also appeared in *Wired, Foreign Affairs, Fortune,* and many other publications.

Rick Telander, a columnist for the *Chicago Sun-Times* and a longtime senior writer at *Sports Illustrated,* was one of the original "Sportswriters on Television" in 1985 and has appeared often on ESPN's long-running version of that show. He is the author of eight books, including the basketball classic *Heaven Is a Playground.*

Tom Verducci is the senior baseball writer for *Sports Illustrated* and SI.com, and a reporter for TBS's national baseball broadcasts. His most recent book, *The Yankee Years* (with Joe Torre), was a number one *New York Times* bestseller.

Steve Wulf, a senior writer for *ESPN the Magazine,* is so senior that his previous piece about a Yankee second baseman was for *Sports Illustrated* in the 1970s, when Horace Clarke held the job. He is the author (or coauthor) of five books.

The Editor:

Rob Fleder was executive editor of *Sports Illustrated* and the editor of SI Books during his twenty years at Time Inc. He was also an editor at *Esquire, Playboy,* and *The National Sport Daily.*